Advance Praise for
What Inclusive Instructors Do

"This book is a timely and extraordinarily comprehensive resource for supporting instructors who wish to engage with inclusive teaching. Every facet of what makes teaching inclusive is unpacked and brought to life with quotes and examples from real instructors across different disciplines and institutional contexts, and the reflection questions embedded within each section create a natural way for instructors to engage more deeply with the text and think about applications in their own teaching. No stone is left unturned in connecting the practices shared and the research on why and how those practices support inclusion, making this a most valuable resource for instructors at any stage in their teaching careers."—***Catherine Ross**, Executive Director, Center for Teaching and Learning, Columbia University*

"The authors have created an essential resource for college instructors by bridging the gap between theory and practice. Their practical, adaptable guidance is informed by a national faculty survey and integrated with evidence from the educational literature. The book addresses why inclusive teaching matters and goes beyond classroom practices to consider inclusive institutional culture. Instructors and administrators at all types of institutions will benefit from this timely approach to a critical topic."—***Jennifer Frederick**, Executive Director of the Poorvu Center for Teaching and Learning, Yale University*

"This book is an invaluable resource for anyone aiming to engage in the 'ongoing process' of what inclusive instructors do. The range of faculty voices that appear throughout the book provide inspiration and confirmation—this is something faculty do across the disciplines and in many teaching contexts. The concrete advice and reflective questions have helped us—and, we are confident, will help you—to be more inclusive and intentional in teaching."—***Buffie Longmire-Avital and Peter Felten**, Elon University*

WHAT INCLUSIVE INSTRUCTORS DO

WHAT INCLUSIVE INSTRUCTORS DO

Principles and Practices for Excellence in College Teaching

*Tracie Marcella Addy, Derek Dube,
Khadijah A. Mitchell, and Mallory SoRelle*

Foreword by Buffie Longmire-Avital and Peter Felten

1996–2021 25TH ANNIVERSARY

Sty/us

PUBLISHING, LLC.

STERLING, VIRGINIA

Sty/us

Published by Stylus Publishing, LLC.
22883 Quicksilver Drive
Sterling, Virginia 20166-2019

Library of Congress Cataloging-in-Publication Data
Names: Addy, Tracie Marcella, author.
Title: What inclusive instructors do : principles and practices for excellence in
  college teaching / Tracie Marcella Addy, Derek Dube, Khadijah A. Mitchell,
  and Mallory SoRelle.
Description: First edition. | Sterling, Virginia : Stylus Publishing, LLC., 2021.
  | Includes bibliographical references and index. | Summary: "This book
  uniquely offers the distilled wisdom of scores of instructors across ranks,
  disciplines and institution types, whose contributions are organized into
  a thematic framework that progressively introduces the reader to the key
  dispositions, principles and practices for creating the inclusive classroom
  environments (in person and online) that will help their students succeed"
  -- Provided by publisher.
Identifiers: LCCN 2021013023 (print) | LCCN 2021013024 (ebook) | ISBN
  9781642671926 (cloth) | ISBN 9781642671933 (paperback) | ISBN
  9781642671940 (pdf) | ISBN 9781642671957 (epub)
Subjects: LCSH: College teaching. | Inclusive education. | Classroom
  environment.
Classification: LCC LB2331 .A34 2021 (print) | LCC LB2331 (ebook) |
  DDC 378.1/25--dc23
LC record available at https://lccn.loc.gov/2021013023
LC ebook record available at https://lccn.loc.gov/2021013024

13-digit ISBN: 978-1-64267-192-6 (cloth)
13-digit ISBN: 978-1-64267-193-3 (paperback)
13-digit ISBN: 978-1-64267-194-0 (library networkable e-edition)
13-digit ISBN: 978-1-64267-195-7 (consumer e-edition)

Printed in the United States of America

All first editions printed on acid-free paper
that meets the American National Standards Institute
Z39-48 Standard.

Bulk Purchases
Quantity discounts are available for use in workshops and
for staff development.
Call 1-800-232-0223

First Edition, 2021

This book is dedicated to all instructors who endeavor to be inclusive in their teaching.

CONTENTS

I t was a simple request early one semester, but the content of that request was anything but simple. A student in my (Buffie Longmire-Avital's) senior psychology course asked to speak with me after class. She was the only student of color in the 15-student class of women.

When I developed this course, I thought it was going to be a beacon to students of color. The entire course focuses on marginalized and historically underrepresented populations in psychological research. Every article, theory, and chapter we read is authored by a racial and/or sexual minority. I wanted the course to serve as a validating salve to my historically underrepresented students' experiences navigating higher education, a resounding affirmation that our experience matters—the closest thing to a psychological Wakanda I could create. However, given the limited diversity of the major, each year most students in the class have been white, cisgender women. However, this was the first time only one student of color was enrolled.

My student took a deep breath before she began to speak to me. Her voice was soft and pointed toward the floor. She explained that she had much to say about the topics we were discussing. She recalled the last in-class activity, which had the students working in small groups to generate examples of Yosso's (2005) six forms of cultural capital. She stated, "I had so many examples to give, but I am not comfortable sharing yet." She went on to talk about how hard it has been for her to talk about race when she is the only student of color in the classroom. The point of this conversation was not to ask for help. She was a senior at a historically White institution in the south, she already learned how to navigate this type of environment in previous years. Instead, she was offering me transparency and context for understanding the level of engagement she was presenting in class. She wanted me to know that her lack of verbal engagement was not reflective of a student that didn't care but was a radical act of survival.

We decided that she would only contribute when she felt comfortable and ready. I reminded her that the discussion boards due prior to every class would give me a sense of who she is and what her voice sounds like. Finally, I pledged to serve as an anchor, that I would be her silent partner throughout this course. I would not call on her, but I would physically stand near her and that it was my responsibility to offer examples, in addition to correcting students who made uninformed statements.

This story—like this book—illustrates the power and the complexity of what inclusive instructors do. This work involves far more than developing diverse activities and course materials. Inclusive instructors must be the literal embodiment of inclusion. Inclusive instructors generate spaces through their scholarship, service, mentorship, teaching, activism, and their very selves. To be an inclusive instructor is to critique and challenge traditions, systems, and structures that were constructed to exclude and to marginalize.

How do we shift and repurpose structures and frameworks when occupying our current positions within the system of higher education? Simply, how do you destroy the Matrix when you are still in it?

There is no simple answer, but we must start somewhere. This book is an invaluable resource for anyone aiming to engage in the "ongoing process" of what inclusive instructors do (p. 244). The range of faculty voices that appear throughout the book provide inspiration and confirmation—this is something faculty do across the disciplines and in many teaching contexts. The concrete advice and reflective questions have helped us—and, we are confident, will help you – to be more inclusive and intentional in teaching.

We take four core lessons from this book. What do inclusive instructors do?

1. They *take responsibility* for making their teaching and their curriculum inclusive.
2. They continue to *learn* about both their students and teaching.
3. They *care* about and for each and every student they teach.
4. They *change* their teaching based on evidence about the practices that support and challenge all students to thrive.

Those may seem simple, but the work of inclusive instructors is seldom easy. We will make mistakes. We will need to persist in the face of difficulty, even heartbreak. Still, doing what inclusive instructors do makes a profound difference in the education and lives of students – and by extension, in our communities and world.

Take a deep breath. It's time to get to work.

Buffie Longmire-Avital and Peter Felten
Elon University

I magine the first day of class when the instructor walks into the classroom to prepare to start teaching. A sea of new faces looks intently upon them as they set down their belongings. These learners bring not only their notebooks and pens but also their social identities, prior knowledge of the material, personalities, motivations, physical and mental capabilities, mindset, life experiences, circumstances, and much more. Many of these attributes may not be visible to the instructor, but they will likely have a large impact on whether each student succeeds in the course. Instructors teaching online courses similarly will likely teach a diverse group of students.

We wrote this book for instructors who encounter this scenario at their institutions and for those who will be future instructors and endeavor to be inclusive in their teaching. The book is also highly relevant for educational developers and staff who partner with instructors on their inclusive teaching efforts. We see much promise in reflective workshops, book clubs, and learning communities on the topics of this book. Another motivation for writing the book was, frankly, that there just did not seem to be enough comprehensive information available regarding what instructors who implement such approaches do in their classrooms. In general, the classroom continues to be a closed-off setting, and we are hopeful that this book provides more of an entry into what inclusive instructors do.

Further, while the book addresses equity and inclusion in teaching and learning more broadly, the anti-Black racist events transpiring in the United States around the time of writing necessitated a practical resource for addressing equity and inclusion in college and university courses beyond mere lip service. The unfortunate occurrence of COVID-19, resulting in health complications and numerous deaths, as well as the abrupt shifts to remote learning, also unveiled a number of equity concerns and disparities in teaching and learning spaces. By utilizing the concepts and principles in this book readers will be able to take steps to transform their courses into spaces that are equitable and welcoming and to adopt practical strategies to address the various inclusion issues that can arise. In general, we hope that throughout the book readers will recognize that instructors have the power to design and implement an inclusive course and transform the learning environment.

Our own stories also frame our motivations for writing this book. Based on her personal experiences, Tracie, a cisgendered Black American female who is an educational developer and administrative leader in teaching and learning at her institution, is committed to supporting instructors in designing inclusive learning environments. Her parents taught culturally diverse student populations in secondary education in the inner city and passed on to her the importance of educating all students and an appreciation for diversity. Her own experiences with inclusion as a student, and as a professional who taught in higher education classrooms, with broad experiences at a variety of types of institutions from community colleges, private research universities, liberal arts institutions, and public state universities, and with students ranging from undergraduates to graduate students and postdoctoral fellows, continue to shape her own views. She coauthored this book to have a readily available resource that describes the research basis for and actual practices of inclusive teaching, emphasizing the voices of instructors from diverse disciplines who are on the front lines and carrying out such practices.

Derek has experience teaching in higher education for over 10 years at institutions ranging from large, public, doctorate-granting institutions to small, private, liberal arts colleges, in courses with topics ranging from biology (in which he earned his PhD) to golf, to what the works of David Bowie say about the human condition. In these teaching experiences he has worked with students with a wide variety of educational, personal, and cultural backgrounds and directly felt the value of each student's individual set of experiences and perspectives. As a cisgendered Caucasian male, Derek coauthored this book for both his "younger self" and for those who, like himself, but no matter their personal background, desire to create an inclusive and equitable classroom and want to learn from the experiences and best practices of those who have been doing this well for years. His grand hope is that this book will be one stepping stone to a truly inclusive and equitable higher education environment.

Khadijah's passion for diversity, equity, and inclusion in education stems from her teaching experiences in inner city K–12 public schools, selective liberal arts colleges, and private doctoral research universities. For over a decade she has taught undergraduate, graduate, and massive open online courses in biology departments and schools of medicine and nursing. Her desire to create warm and welcoming classroom spaces stems from her own higher education experiences as a first-generation college student, scholar of color, and cisgendered Black woman in STEM. Khadijah coauthored this book with the aspiration that it will become every instructor's go-to resource for inclusive teaching. Before she retires, she hopes to see intentional inclusion of every student become the new standard across all scholar communities.

Mallory's commitment to inclusive education stems from a broader personal and professional motivation to promote a more robust, inclusive, participatory democracy. She believes that inclusive education is a critical tool to equip students from diverse backgrounds with the skills they need to navigate and influence their civic and professional communities for the better once they leave the classroom. Mallory has been fortunate to teach diverse groups of undergraduate and graduate students across a number of higher education contexts, including a large research university, a liberal arts college, and a degree-granting prison education program. As a queer White woman in the social sciences, her goal for this book is to provide a helpful resource for instructors at all stages of their career and from all backgrounds to reflect critically on and refine their own capacity to build more equitable and inclusive learning environments.

In writing *What Inclusive Instructors Do* we took the approach of not relying solely on our personal experiences with inclusive teaching, but on those of hundreds of instructors across ranks, disciplines, and institution types who completed a survey in a national study (Appendix A). We asked these instructors to define what inclusive teaching meant to them in addition to the inclusive teaching approaches implemented in their courses. The voices of these instructors ring loudly as we draw on their responses, allowing them to be the experts and frame the conversation about what inclusive teachers do. In this book we also integrate and discuss current literature relevant to inclusive teaching to ensure a research-supported approach.

A major goal for our readers who actively teach courses is to reflect on their own courses in a meaningful way and to consider which inclusive teaching approaches make sense to start, adapt, or continue in their own courses. To this end, questions for reflection are embedded throughout the book and compiled in Appendix B. For our educational development readers, the book provides a comprehensive overview of what inclusive teaching can look like in an in-person or online classroom in addition to resources for facilitating professional development sessions. For those considering becoming involved or those already involved in efforts aimed to evaluate inclusive teaching for institutional accountability, this book provides sample guidelines.

The content of this book attends to the multiple facets of inclusive teaching. Part One (chapters 1 and 2) includes evidence for why inclusion is critical in higher education and general knowledge and principles by which inclusive instructors abide by when teaching their students. These chapters are essential starting points for framing the work of inclusive teaching. Without recognizing why inclusive teaching is critical, knowing the mindsets of instructors adopting such as approaches, we are left with mere strategies without a rationale for implementation. In Part Two, chapters 3 to 5 describe practices of inclusive teaching. In chapters 6 to 8 in Part Three of the book, instructors are provided with tools to help them foster an inclusive environment and institutions are provided ideas for building and sustaining a culture of inclusive teaching.

Teaching and learning is at the heart of our institutional missions, and we need to take ownership in educating a diverse group of learners. Thank you for your willingness to embark on this journey with us and explore what inclusive instructors do.

ACKNOWLEDGMENTS

We thank all of the inclusive instructors who participated in our study for contributing their voices to this book. We are also grateful for the many students, faculty, and staff who provided input on the "Who's in Class?" form included in the book.

PART ONE

EVIDENCE SUPPORTING INCLUSION AND MAJOR PRINCIPLES

THE WHAT AND WHY OF INCLUSIVE TEACHING

[Inclusive instruction is] [t]eaching that recognizes and affirms a student's social identity as an important influence on teaching and learning processes, and that works to create an environment in which students are able to learn from the course, their peers, and the teacher while still being their authentic selves. It works to disrupt traditional notions of who succeeds in the classroom and the systemic inequities inherent in traditional educational practices.

—Full-time academic professional, doctorate-granting university, Education

The first two chapters of this book contain information critical to understanding what inclusive instructors do. Knowing how they define inclusive teaching, why they consider inclusive instruction to be an essential aspect of effective teaching, the instructional frameworks that undergird their teaching efforts, and the mindsets they espouse when implementing such approaches provides insight into why they adopt particular teaching strategies. Typically this instructional information is not widely accessible given that it lives within the minds of instructors and within closed off classroom spaces. Throughout these chapters, however, we increase the visibility of inclusive instructors' ways of thinking using both their voices and the relevant literature.

How They Define Inclusive Teaching

Like many terms within educational spaces, *inclusive teaching* is one that is seemingly elusive. However, as we start to operationalize the term through the voices of instructors participating in a national survey study, although their definitions vary as illustrated in the quotes that follow, there are overarching themes that unify them (see Appendix A for study details). When reading the subsequent definitions consider what they have in common.

Inclusive teaching uses pedagogical strategies that allow students to engage meaningfully with course content and skills no matter what they bring to the classroom, regardless of different abilities, mental or physical illnesses, or economic or social circumstances.

—Assistant professor, doctorate-granting university, Art History

Inclusive teaching involves practices that help learners perceive and/or increase their perception that they "belong" and that their cultural and life experiences are valued in their present learning context. It involves examining the content and language of a course or program from a stance of inclusion. It also involves drawing upon the findings of research to adopt (e.g., stereotype threat) practices that are beneficial to the well-being and success of students who are traditionally underrepresented in a given learning context.

—Adjunct professor, doctorate-granting university, Education

As an instructor, it is my responsibility to ensure that all students, regardless of any number of characteristics (such as gender, race, sexual orientation, ability, religion, socioeconomic status, educational background, style of dress, extracurricular interests, family situation, health situation, level of introversion, etc.—the list could be endless), have the tools and resources necessary to meet the objectives of the class. Everyone should be an important, integral member of the class community, with ample speaking and participation opportunities. As members of a diverse community, everyone should feel like any perceived "differences" will contribute to [the] learning environment, not detract from it. All students should feel that they are appreciated as unique individuals and should not feel excluded or compelled to hide any aspect of themselves that might be perceived as a "difference."

—Full-time academic professional, doctorate-granting university, Biology

Two themes emerge from their definitions—that to the instructors inclusive teaching involves designing learning environments that are (a) equitable, where all students have the opportunity to reach their potential, and (b) welcoming, and foster a sense of belonging. Equity and belonging are interrelated given that equitable learning environments can promote a sense of belonging. In addition to defining inclusive teaching, also important is to operationalize the terms *diversity, equality, equity* and *inclusion* used throughout the book in the context of teaching and learning. We consider diversity to be how learners differ from one another with regard to their social identities, demographics, perspectives, prior experiences, attitudes, knowledge, skills, and other attributes. Equality in teaching and learning suggests that all students should have identical learning experiences regardless of their differences, which we take the stance does not align well with inclusive approaches to instruction. Equity acknowledges the differences between learners, their diversity, and the types of learning environments that help diverse students succeed. Inclusion refers to creating a welcoming environment and intentionally not excluding any learners. In general, inclusive teaching, as described by the study respondents, dismantles the historic notion that cultural and other differences among students make them in some way deficient as learners. Instead, inclusive teaching embraces and responds to such diversity to create effective teaching and learning environments (Guo & Jamal, 2007).

One intriguing aspect of inclusive teaching is how it can manifest within institutions that vary in their missions, strategic goals, cultures and student populations. Fundamentally, while inclusive instructors may embrace equity and a sense of belonging as core elements of inclusive teaching, their conceptualizations can be influenced to some degree by contextual factors specific to an institution department or program. As an example, historically Black colleges and universities (HBCUs) are pioneers for inclusion and empowerment, providing educational opportunities to members of the Black community. HBCUs can also offer increased opportunities for Black students to be in community with each other which can enhance sense of belonging. Students have reported strong connections with their instructors at HBCUs, although groups of students may experience inclusion in different ways (Booker & Campbell-Whatley, 2019). One participant in the national study who worked at an HBCU noted that "Faculty seem receptive once they know what [inclusive teaching] means, [and] many of them do these techniques without knowing they are engaging in inclusive pedagogy." This quote emphasizes that while some instructors may not use the language or term inclusive teaching, they are using the techniques.

Community colleges continue to be leaders in designing accessible and affordable educational environments for diverse learners. An inclusive instructor noted, "The community college I teach at offers an entire suite of late-starting classes for students who struggle through registration paperwork (due to language barriers, financial status, family status, etc.) and offers an intensive suite of language services for English Language Learning students." When conceptualizing inclusive teaching, this instructor described how they support students from a diversity of linguistic and cultural backgrounds to "craft opportunities for all students to demonstrate their individual strengths," highlighting how this instructor's definition was framed in their institutional context.

As the college populations further diversify, institutions can also experience shifts in their student demographics, which can impact how they design inclusive learning environments. One survey respondent indicated:

> Our institution has shifted to minority serving in the last decade, and the institution
> is struggling to keep up with the changes. While there's a lot of controversy, the
> overall shared value of supporting students has helped keep it from being even
> more controversial. The vast majority of our faculty value inclusive pedagogy
> even if they're not always sure how to implement it in the classroom.

Instructors at other institution types may also espouse definitions of inclusive teaching largely framed by their institutional characteristics and cultures. An instructor from a master's college or university noted that to them inclusive teaching involves "making sure that every student feels like they have a voice in the classroom. . . . Ensuring that POC [people of color] are given as many opportunities to participate as White students." In teaching environments such as predominantly White institutions, instructors may espouse similar definitions of inclusive teaching.

Inclusive instructors adopt specific classroom practices that create learning environments that are equitable for their diverse students and foster a sense of belonging.

—Survey respondent; rank, institution type, discipline not identified

Reflection Questions

- What is (are) your institutional culture(s) around equitable and inclusive teaching practices? How would you respond if asked what inclusive teaching meant to you?

Why Inclusive Teaching Is Critical to Them

Inclusive instructors recognize that creating equitable and welcoming environments is critical in higher education given that exclusionary practices persist. Obtaining a college degree has been mostly afforded to those who are privileged, as those in power, with resources, built institutions but did not necessarily design such educational environments to support the success of a diverse population. Access continues to be an issue as do systemic inequities, which can impact student persistence. Inclusive instructors are aware of these challenges facing today's students and of the barriers in the educational systems in which they learn. One instructor highlighted, "Inclusive teaching creates a space that respects diversity in its many forms and structures the learning so that everyone has access to effective, comfortable learning." A desire to address systemic inequities and create accessible learning environments can motivate inclusive instructors to implement equitable practices.

Inclusive instructors teach as populations of students continue to diversify. Between the years of 1995–1996 and 2015–2016, most non-White racial and ethnic groups experienced increased enrollment at the undergraduate level, with the most growth seen with Hispanic learners (Espinosa et al., 2019). Increasingly more first-generation students, the first in their families to seek a bachelor's degree, matriculate into colleges and universities (Center for First-Generation Student Success, 2019). Such higher enrollments suggest progress made with regard to the increasing student diversity in institutions of higher education, but systemic and structural barriers still remain for many students that impede their academic achievement and attainment of degrees once enrolled. Increased diversity gives inclusive instructors pause as they ensure courses are carefully designed, reducing the risk of greater achievement disparities between students.

Inclusive instructors are aware that while inclusive teaching is an essential aspect of effective pedagogy, it can be overlooked, ignored, or narrowly defined. They describe major barriers of colleagues who do not implement, including not being aware of the many differences that exist between students, which can impact their learning; not knowing how to implement inclusive teaching practices; fear of accidentally offending students or not wanting negative consequences on teaching evaluations because of risk-taking; not wanting to change teaching practices; not considering themselves responsible for equitable and inclusive teaching; and challenges with managing conflict in student–student interactions (Addy et al., in press). To the contrary, inclusive instructors endeavor to understand who their learners are and take ownership over designing inclusive learning environments.

The Diversity and Systemic Barriers Facing Learners Necessitates Inclusive Teaching

Inclusive teaching is teaching in a way that engages student identity and experience.

—Associate professor, doctorate-granting university, Biology

[Inclusive teaching is] [r]ecognizing that students approach the course from many standpoints connected to race, culture, gender identity, socioeconomic status, and familiarity with college culture and expectations, and then finding ways to include them.

—Lecturer, master's college or university, Literature/Writing Studies

Inclusive instructors are aware of the specific equity challenges facing their diverse student populations. They may teach first-generation students, who are increasingly enrolled in college and university classrooms. In the years 2015 to 2016, 56% of undergraduates were first-generation students, as defined by having parents who did not hold a bachelor's degree (Center for First-Generation Student Success, 2019). First-generation students may also come from families of low socioeconomic class, and therefore have intersecting social identities. The median parental income for first-generation students was $41,000 compared to $90,000 for continuing-generation students.

The percentages of first-generation students in different sectors show their prevalence in higher education: public, 4-year (47%); public, 2-year (64%); private nonprofit, 4-year (43%); private nonprofit, 2-year (69%); private for-profit, 4-year (72%); private for-profit, 2-year (70%). Of minority-serving institutions, percentages of first-generation students were American Indian/Alaska Native–serving (67%), Hispanic/Latinx/a/o-serving (65%), Black/African American–serving, non-HBCU (65%), HBCUs (60%), non-minority-serving (49%), and Asian/Native Hawaiian/Pacific Islander–serving (48%). Additionally, first-generation students are more likely to have dependents compared to continuing-generation students.

Knowledge of whether students are first-generation helps inclusive instructors better design learning environments that support their success. Much of the focus in the literature has been on first-generation students assimilating into the culture of higher education (Ives & Castillo-Montoyo, 2020). In this regard, avoiding assumptions of what students should know about the college experience is implicit in how inclusive instructors support first-generation students' achievement. First-generation students may not have family and friends to help them navigate their college experience and therefore face more challenges in their transition from their first to their second year of college (Pratt et al., 2017). Low GPA is a significant predictor of lack of persistence of first-generation students (Dika & D'Amico, 2015). Other factors can contribute to the attrition of first-generation students. For example, in a study of first-generation students at a large urban university, a predictor of success for those majoring in STEM disciplines was prior preparation in math, while for non-STEM first-generation students it was their social fit at the institution (Dika & D'Amico, 2015). First-generation students can also experience tension with establishing their identities in college when they fall outside of their family expectations and norms (Covarrubias et al., 2018). College transition or bridge experiences and mentorship programs are needed to support these learners as they increase in number in academic institutions. To the classroom, first-generation students can bring resilience, an eagerness to learn and appreciate the opportunity to matriculate into institutions of higher education.

Reflection Question

- What are the percentages of first-generation students at the institution(s) in which you teach? Regardless of whether this information is readily available, consider inviting your students in a brave way to share whether they are first-generation students.

The general conception of who the traditional college student is continues to evolve, as many adult learners return to school to switch careers or further their education. Adult learners are distinct from what those traditionally perceived as college students, between the ages of 18 and 21. Adult learners can enliven the classroom environment by bringing their life experiences and a determination to learn. They simultaneously may have obligations outside of school such as employment and family commitments that can impact their learning experience. Lacking awareness of the constraints of adult learners without providing strategies and structures to support their learning can impact their academic success. Similarly, veterans returning to school can be a large asset in the classroom and necessitate a reevaluation of who college students are and how we support learning in the adult learner population.

Reflection Questions

- Are adult learners enrolled at the institution(s) in which you teach? In your classes? Why are they in school? What life experiences and factors can impact their success?

Socioeconomic class is another factor implicated in the exclusion of many talented college students. With regard to access, even today college is not affordable to everyone, which is corroborated by public opinion. In a 2020 poll only about 60% of the public believed college is available to those who need it (Marken, 2020). In the same poll only 27% of adults believed that higher education is affordable (Marken, 2020). Many colleges and universities have become need blind to address this disparity, opening their doors to more students regardless of their financial means. Such students can be very appreciative of their college experience and provide valuable perspectives in their college classrooms. They may not have had opportunities and prior experiences to build foundational knowledge and skills, unlike some of their peers, which can impact their transition into college. Some may need to work many hours during college to support themselves and their families, which lessens the time they can commit to study and engage in cocurricular and other social activities. Instructor awareness of course affordability and understanding of which types of technologies students can bring to class can make a difference for students from lower socioeconomic classes. Further, using research-supported strategies in the science of learning are all the more essential to help students attain their educational goals, amid other obligations and constraints on their time.

Reflection Question

- What course-related factors are important for you to consider if students in your course have limited financial means or time to study?

Another aspect of inclusive instruction is carefully taking into account the specific needs of students with accommodations to support their learning in the course. Typically, most institutions have an office for accessibility services that provide services to students with accommodations. Generally, students with documented accommodations are provided with a letter they can give to their instructor to describe their learning needs. There are many students with documented accommodations in institutions of higher education and a number who are undocumented. In 2015–2016, 19% of undergraduate students reported having a disability (National Center for Education Statistics, n.d.). The students responding in this report had visual, hearing, orthopedic or mobility, speech or language, learning, mental, emotional, psychiatric, or other health conditions classified as disabilities. A major consideration in supporting students with accommodations is not changing the content of the course but rather making it more accessible for all learners. Examples of student accommodations include extended time on assessments, a distraction-reduced environment, the capacity to take breaks, having a reader or a scribe to take notes, and using a computer to type rather than handwriting.

Reflection Question

- What are some accommodations that your learners have needed in the past or with which you have personal experience?

As a result of systemic discrimination, including racism, sexism, and classism, many students have been excluded from pursuing and completing degrees in specific disciplines in higher education. These include students of color, first-generation students, adult learners, students from lower socioeconomic classes, LGBTQ+ students, students with disabilities and specific learning needs, as well as learners of other social identities. For example, in science, technology, engineering, and mathematics (STEM) disciplines, structural inequities and the underrepresentation of POC in these respective fields are thought to go hand in hand. Disciplines such as economics have faced underrepresentation challenges with regard to gender. Evidence suggests that students who see positive female role models in the field are more likely to choose economics as a major, which is promising for inclusive instructors in this discipline seeking to create inclusive experiences for their learners (Porter & Serra, 2020). Chapter 2 describes how inclusive instructors are aware of the marginalization of students from various demographic backgrounds, the impacts such marginalization can have on learning, and the steps they as instructors can take to provide equitable and welcoming experiences for these students in their courses.

Reflection Questions

- What are equity issues in your discipline? How are they being addressed?

International students are also integral community members at many institutions of higher education and can be excited to experience learning in a different culture to further their educational goals. Domestic students can learn from their international peers. International students can also face inclusion challenges distinct from domestic learners. Language mastery and differing cultural norms can impact how they experience the classroom (Sherry et al., 2009). Socially, finding ways to build community is important for international students who are away from home. Specifically in the classroom, challenges around grading the writing of international students for whom English is not their native language continues to be an area of importance for instructors. Further, such norms such as speaking in class, directly to the professor and in groups, may have different cultural implications. Learning a new culture can be an adjustment for our international students. There are more supports available for international students at colleges and universities, such as offices that focus on students who speak multiple languages, and in the classroom, such as strategies and behaviors that can promote their learning.

Reflection Questions

- What are the relative numbers of international students at your institution(s)? From which countries do they originate? Regardless of whether this information is readily available, consider inviting your students in a brave way to share whether they are international students and developing an understanding of cultural norms that may implicate their classroom success.

One area of increasing concern is the mental health of our students, especially in light of the impacts of COVID-19 and racial inequities facing Black Americans. In a 2011 survey the National Alliance for Mental Health (NAMI) surveyed college students who were diagnosed with a mental health condition in the 5 years prior. Their sample of 765 college students was diverse with regard to geographic origin arising from 48 states, race/ethnicity as well as gender (Gruttadaro & Crudo, 2012). The majority of respondents felt that the services their schools provided were good and considered mental health training for faculty and staff extremely important. Twenty two percent of the respondents heard about on-campus mental health services from their instructors, highlighting an important role that instructors can play in referring students to the appropriate supports. Alarmingly, 64% of the students who withdrew from their school did so because of mental health concerns, and half of that group never sought out on-campus resources. In a 2018 report from the American College Health Association summarizing survey data from 88,178 students at 140 schools, 25% of females and 11.7% of males had been diagnosed or treated by a professional for anxiety, while 20.1% of females and 11% of males had been diagnosed or treated for depression.

A study examining 10 years of data from 2007 to 2017 revealed increases in the number of college students treated for mental health disorders, as well as increases in depression and suicidality prevalence among undergraduates (Lipson et al., 2019). A promising finding from this study was that mental health stigmas decreased with time. Generally, efforts to reduce the stigma of mental health disorders and encourage help-seeking behaviors continue to improve, as do the services provided to these students on college campuses through counseling centers and accessibility services, but many of these resources are being overwhelmed, as a 2017 report indicates that on average students were waiting 7 business days to see a counselor (LeViness et al., 2017). While students should be encouraged to seek out the proper resources to support their mental health, there are direct implications for the classroom. Many instructors may have students with performance anxieties, such as those around testing, or may have tried to support the academic success of a depressed student, aware or unaware of the condition. There are actions that can hinder the success and belonging of students with mental health disorders and those that can support them. Similarly, a number of students have conditions for which accommodations are necessary to support their success, such as other mental disabilities or physical disabilities. Ensuring an environment inclusive of students with mental health disorders is important for student success. Trauma-informed pedagogies that acknowledge the challenges students face, foster trust, support relationship building, and empower students to help them thrive are critical to supporting students' mental health

(Imad, 2020). The impacts of COVID-19 also call for increased emphasis on student mental health.

Reflection Question

- Identify any services provided on your campus(es) to support students with mental health concerns. Consider working with counseling services to determine how to identify and support such students.

Religious affiliation is another prominent social identity espoused by our students. Colleges and universities may have students from a variety of faith backgrounds, enriching our understanding of each other's belief systems. In teaching and learning, a student's faith may be implicated in religious holidays they observe and traditions they practice that can impact their classroom participation and attendance. For example, major religious observances may fall during the semester and impact student attendance in their course. Students, in effect, can be at a crossroads where they must choose between their religious observances and their coursework. Additionally, students from some religious groups have historically experienced discrimination in college and university settings. Muslim students who veil and wear a hijab have been subject to negative social reinforcement and isolation in academic settings, with many misinformed about the veil as an important aspect of their religion (Cole & Ahmadi, 2003). These occurred during their interactions with fellow students, staff, and their instructors. Jewish students have also experienced discrimination on various levels (Kosmin & Keysar, 2015). In a 2014 survey of 1,157 Jewish students from 55 university and 4-year college campuses, 54% indicated that they were victims or witnessed acts of anti-Semitism on their campus during one academic year. Of those surveyed, 29% reported that they encountered such discrimination from an individual student, 10% in clubs/societies, 10% in other contexts, 6% in lecture or class, 4% in the student union, and 3% by their university administrative system. There are other considerations for inclusion regarding religion, including students who may need to engage in rituals such as prayer during the day or not perform work during certain hours of the day.

Reflection Questions

- What are the religious affiliations of students at your institution(s)? Which major observances or traditions may need to be considered when designing learning experiences?

Our learners exhibit diversity in many other ways with regards to their social identities and attributes, such as their personalities, temperaments, political viewpoints, and preferences. In this chapter we set the stage to bring up some important student inclusion concerns. In no way is this content meant to be a comprehensive listing. As you digest the content of this chapter, consider the following reflection questions.

Reflection Questions

- Who are your learners? What diversity assets do they bring to the classroom? What challenges can they face with inclusion?

Research Supports Inclusion as Critical for Effective Learning

We can define inclusive teaching, and describe why the diversity of our students necessitates excellence in inclusive teaching, but the golden question is, "Does it actually work?" In other words, what is the evidence that inclusion can help our students achieve the objectives of their college education? There are a number of confirmations in the literature of which we sample key studies, focusing on the two essential aspects of inclusion that we presented previously: social belonging and equitable learning experiences.

The Importance of Social Belonging

Strayhorn (2019) defines belonging for college students as "[a] student's perceived social support on campus, a feeling or sensation of connectedness, and the experience of mattering or feeling cared about, accepted, respected, valued by, and important to the campus community or others on campus such as faculty, staff, and peers" (p. 4). Social belonging is a very human need; many individuals seek to be a part of groups in which they feel as if they can identify with its members. College students can face a variety of educational challenges when they feel as if they don't belong (Strayhorn, 2012). Inclusive teaching practices support social belonging as articulated by respondents in our national study.

Inclusive teaching involves practices that help learners perceive and/or increase their perception that they "belong" and that their cultural and life experiences are valued in their present learning context. It involves examining the content and language of a course or program from a stance of inclusion. It also involves drawing upon the findings of research to adopt (e.g., stereotype threat) practices that are beneficial to the well-being and success of students who are traditionally underrepresented in a given learning context.

—Adjunct professor, doctorate-granting university, Education

*I think [inclusive teaching means] to make sure that students
do not feel left out or alone. That they belong.*

—Full professor, doctorate-granting university, Engineering and Technology

Social belonging can have a particularly profound impact on students from marginalized groups as they may feel a sense of being excluded from the campus or classroom community (Walton & Cohen, 2007). Studies in the field of social psychology addressing social belonging can greatly inform inclusive instruction. There is evidence that social belonging is associated with higher achievement, particularly for students from marginalized groups. A randomized control study involving a brief psychological intervention suggested a linkage between social belonging and academic achievement for students from a minoritized group (Walton & Cohen, 2011). In the investigation, a group of African American students was told during their freshman year that although they may experience adversity on campus, it would pass. A group of European American students was also given the same intervention, and a group of African American students and a group of European American students did not participate in the psychological intervention. The researchers tracked the GPAs and health outcomes of all four groups across their 4 years at the university and found that African American students who participated in the social belonging psychological intervention had significantly higher GPAs than African American students who did not, reducing the achievement gap by half. These students also had better health outcomes. From these findings the authors suggest that social belonging can act as a psychological lever for student achievement and health, particularly for students from marginalized groups.

In addition to better health outcomes, peer-level social capital has also been shown to predict satisfaction with university life (Bye et al., 2019). Similar findings were found in a study of women pursuing engineering majors (Walton et al., 2015). In addition to a social belonging intervention, female students underwent affirmation training to help them address the social issues that arose in their educational experiences. Women participating in the intervention and training ended up with higher grade point averages compared to control groups.

There are also very specific and subtle ways in which classroom environments can have an influence on social belonging to a particular discipline. In a study of women in mathematics, when female students perceived that mathematical ability was fixed and that women were not as good in mathematics as men, they no longer felt social belonging to mathematics (Good et al., 2012). Other situational cues, or aspects of the environment, have been found to implicate social belonging for groups historically marginalized. In an investigation where women viewed a video of a math, science, and engineering conference where there was an unequal distribution of men compared to women they reported less social belonging and desire to attend the conference (Murphy et al., 2007).

A study involving a national sample of first-year college students revealed some of the nuances of belonging for first-year students (Gopalan & Brady, 2019). Both first-generation and students from racial/ethnic groups historically marginalized reported lower belonging at 4-year schools. However, researchers discovered the opposite at 2-year schools. Other predictors of belonging at 4-year institutions were mental health, persistence, and engagement.

Reflection Question

- Based on these studies, what actions taken by instructors might help promote inclusion in the classroom setting with regard to social belonging?

The Necessity of Equitable Teaching Practices

Another key component of inclusive teaching is equity, creating a classroom environment where all students have an opportunity to succeed regardless of their backgrounds. Designing equitable learning experiences is essential for inclusive instructors. In their own words, instructors said the following:

> *Inclusive teaching means to me equity not equality. It means seek[ing] strategies that help all students.*
>
> —Lecturer, doctorate-granting university, Biology

> *Every student who walks into my classroom, regardless of background and identity, has an equal feeling.*
>
> —Associate professor, baccalaureate college, Biology

Historically, equity in education was largely attributed to providing access to students with disabilities, particularly in K–12 education. This pattern can easily be observed by a general search revealing the topics of articles published on inclusive teaching over the last 20 to 30 years. Such focus has led to more resources and attention devoted to students with disabilities, including in higher education. There are offices devoted to supporting students with disabilities. As we continue to learn of the needs of different learners in higher education, we expand the populations to which inclusive teaching applies, acknowledging inequities can occur even more broadly across student populations and encompassing a broader definition about what an equitable college experience looks like given the inequities that still persist among students of various social identities.

Equity starts with having access to attending an institution of higher education. In a 2019 Gallup poll consisting of more than 1,000 American adults, only 60% believed that a college education is available to those who need it (Marken, 2020). Of those 60%, just 46% in the age range of 18 to 29 thought that education beyond high school was available. Also of concern, only 27% believed that higher education was affordable. The public perception that many feel college is not accessible to all is an equity concern. Beyond access, inequities persist once students reach college. For example, racial-ethnic achievement gaps continue in higher education, and investigations seek to uncover why such gaps exist. In a longitudinal study of the Black–White achievement gap, Spenner et al. (2005) found that even when they controlled for family background, parental involvement, prior educational attainment, and entering cultural capital, in addition to other factors, only half of the achievement gap was accounted for. A later investigation (Martin et al., 2017) examining the Black–White and Latino–White achievement gap for GPA found that campus climate around inclusivity in addition to choice of major explained half of the achievement gap, while the other was explained by family characteristics and prior academic preparation. This study highlights the importance of inclusivity in various aspects of the campus, including the classroom.

Some studies have looked at prematriculation interventions that can support the achievement of first-generation students to reduce disparities. In one study, researchers performed a distance education intervention for first-generation students where they listened to stories of students indicating how they shared their social identity and how they achieved success in college (Stephens et al., 2014). This intervention closed the achievement gap between first-generation students and other learners by increasing their help-seeking behaviors. As an example, in response to the question "Can you provide an example of an obstacle that you faced when you came to [university name] and how you resolved it," a student indicated, "Because my parents didn't go through college, they weren't always able to provide me with the advice I needed. So it was sometimes hard to figure out which classes to take and what I wanted to do in the future. But there are other people who can provide that advice, and I learned that I need to rely on my adviser more than other students" (p. 945). Instructors can support the academic success of first-generation students whether or not they were first-generation students themselves by sharing how they navigated college or providing their learners access to other resources.

Achievement gaps continue to persist among students of low and high socioeconomic classes, and psychological interventions have reduced such gaps (Jury et al., 2017). The experiences of low socioeconomic status (SES) with regard to emotion, identity management, self-perception, and motivation regulation can be quite different than students of higher SES. A student's social class background has also been found to play a role in whether they feel a sense of belonging and also whether they can adjust to college, with a sense of belonging being a mediator of class background and academic and social adjustment (Ostrove & Long, 2007). Three strategies that decrease achievement gaps include self-affirmation exercises where students write down what they value prior to assessments, difference education where students listen to others of similar backgrounds describe how they coped during college, and goal reframing where exams are framed as tools for learning rather than for selection (Stephens et al., 2014). Inclusive instructors can carry out each of these actions in their courses. Self-affirmation exercises have been found to close racial achievement gaps (Cohen et al., 2006, 2009).

These are just a few of the vast array of inequities occurring among students with diverse social identities in college; this list could be expanded. The main takeaway is that such inequities call for more inclusive practices in our classrooms so that all students have the opportunity to succeed when in college.

As illustrated throughout this chapter, inclusive teaching is critical for advancing learning for all students. A number of calls have also been made to advance inclusive teaching efforts. In her article "Small World: Crafting an Inclusive Classroom (No Matter What you Teach)," Mary A. Armstrong (2011) states,

> While many courses do not (and many cannot) include content that directly addresses diversity, and many classes and institutions (regrettably) do not reflect a powerfully diverse student demographic, I contend that all classrooms can contribute to an inclusive climate. Classrooms are social environments, and all social environments are places where inclusivity happens—or fails to happen. In short, there is no getting off the hook: if you have students sitting in front of you, you are interacting with a social group. And if you are interacting "My courses have nothing to do with diversity" is probably a sentence we have all heard and it is often used as a free pass to discharge us from responsibility with a social group, you have a job to do regarding the practice of inclusivity. (pp. 53–54)

In "A Case for Inclusive Teaching," Kevin Gannon (2018) indicates:

> We can design all the summer-bridge and first-year programs we want, but if we neglect pedagogy, then we're building a really nice house only to furnish it with stuff we found on the curb. Likewise, if the student-life and the academic-affairs folks aren't talking about how they can complement each other's efforts, then how can the institution hope for comprehensive improvement? Piecemeal planning produces piecemeal outcomes.
>
> But student success—especially for African-American and Latino/a students—is a systemic question that demands systemic efforts to answer. It's never been more important for us to make that effort. If we mean what we say about the intrinsic value of higher education, then we must ensure not just access, but success. Inclusive teaching promotes the effective and meaningful learning that's the vital foundation for student success.
>
> Beyond even that benefit, though, by focusing on inclusive teaching, we benefit our own institutions by keeping more students on our campuses and enabling them to graduate. Given the climate in which most of us are operating, there's simply too much to lose by not committing to inclusive teaching. Conversely, we have everything to gain. (paras. 25–27)

Reflection Question

- What factors should an instructor keep in mind when designing an equitable course?

Frameworks Supporting Inclusive Excellence

Instructors in higher education may find it useful to learn various frameworks that align with inclusive excellence in teaching. We describe three here: multicultural education, culturally relevant education, and universal design for learning UDL.

Multicultural Education

> *[Inclusive teaching is] involving all differences of students (culture, gender, gender identity, age, etc.) in the classroom.*
>
> —Associate professor, baccalaureate college, Nursing

Guo and Jamal (2007) categorize three major models of cultural diversity in higher education, aimed at different levels: individual diversity development (self), multicultural education model (classroom teaching), and antiracist education model (institution and community). Given the focus of this book on inclusive teaching at the level of the classroom, we describe here the individual development of the instructor with regard to cultural diversity in addition to the classroom teaching levels.

How instructors grapple with their own understanding of diversity is at the fundamental level (Chávez et al., 2003). Such development can pass through a variety of levels, each having cognitive, affective, and behavioral aspects from "lack of awareness of the other, awareness of the other, questions perceptions of self and others, confronts own perceptions of the other, and makes complex choices about validating others" (adapted from Chávez et al., 2003, cited in Guo & Jamal, 2007, p. 35). In the realm of teaching in higher education, this process is indicative of when an instructor personally becomes aware of differences between their students and adopts a framework where they validate such differences through their actions.

Multiculturalism acknowledges differences between learners and looks at such differences as assets to be celebrated (Guo & Jamal, 2007). Embracing multiculturalism in the classroom can help set the stage for building an inclusive classroom community. Color-blindness, to the contrary, is based on the belief in the importance of treating all students the same regardless of their differences, whether visible or invisible. By not acknowledging the diversity of learners, color-blindness can fall short of fostering social belonging and equity. Multiculturalism removes the blinders. There is evidence that instructors espousing multiculturalism versus color-blindness approaches are more likely to implement inclusive teaching practices (Aragón et al., 2017).

Reflection Question

- Reflect on your beliefs about equity and inclusion. What motivates you to read this book to learn more about inclusive teaching practices?

Culturally Relevant and Culturally Responsive Education Frameworks

> [C]ulturally responsive pedagogies that take into account students' needs and goals and preparedness, involves creating thoughtful learning [experiences that] take place in a way that promotes equity, leading to student success for all.
>
> —Full professor, master's college, History

Inclusive instructors may also utilize culturally relevant and culturally responsive frameworks (Aronson & Laughter, 2016). What unites both of these frameworks is the emphasis on culture in the design of the instructional environment. Culturally relevant pedagogy involves helping all students succeed academically, understand their own culture and build cultural competence, and gain an understanding of social inequities (Ladson-Billings, 2006). Culturally responsive teaching has been described as having six dimensions: social and academic empowerment of students; a multidimensional approach to instruction; validation of differing student cultures; a holistic approach to educating the student, building on student strengths; and freedom from oppressive structures in education (Gay, 2010). Wlodkowski and Ginsberg (1995) propose a framework for culturally responsive teaching that acknowledges that designing learning opportunities that tie into students' cultures can increase their intrinsic motivation and engagement with the material. Their framework includes four aspects. The first is establishing inclusion where both students and teachers feel a sense of connection and belonging. The second is helping students develop positive attitudes through culturally relevant teaching given that the learning experience is relevant to their personal lives and allows them to make choices. A third aspect is enhancing meaning by having students engage in relevant, thoughtful learning activities, and the last is engendering competence, which enables students to be aware that they can actually learn the items they value. An example of a culturally relevant or culturally responsive approach could be in an interdisciplinary course that is focused on environmental sustainability and that involves a project where students perform research on their hometown communities into practices for preserving resources. The students interview members of their community, integrate their own perspectives, and propose possible solutions to creating a more sustainable community.

After becoming aware of the cultural identities that their students bring to the course, inclusive instructors can embrace principles of culturally relevant and culturally responsive teaching in order to design meaningful learning experiences for their students. There are a variety of resources that instructors can access to support their understanding and implementation of culturally relevant and culturally responsive teaching, including *Culturally Responsive Teaching: Theory, Research, and Practice* by Geneva Gay (2010) and *Diversity and Motivation: Culturally Responsive Teaching in College* by Margery Ginsberg and Raymond J. Wlodkowski (2009).

UDL

Inclusive teaching incorporate[s] but is not limited to Universal Design for Learning (UDL). It also includes culturally responsive teaching wherein the instructor works to be conscious of bias and self-critiques and reflects upon biases. It includes the classroom (virtual or on-line) space, the course content, and the methodology.

—Associate professor, master's college, Rhetoric and Composition

[Inclusive teaching is] [d]eliberately implementing inclusive teaching strategies [where]
I take steps to create a class structure and atmosphere in which all students not only
develop a sense of belonging but also are truly an integral part of the class, with
accommodations made proactively (rather than on request, aka universal design).
Students are valued for their differences in backgrounds, experiences, abilities, perspectives,
internal and external pressures, and can share these freely or may choose not to do so.
The goal is success for all students, not ranking students on a normal distribution.

—Lecturer, doctorate-granting university, Psychology

Another instructional framework that is inclusive of diverse learners is the UDL (CAST, n.d.a.; Tobin & Behling, 2018). Inclusive instructors can use this framework to design instruction from an equity-minded perspective in that the learning experience is created with the diversity of the student population in mind. UDL focuses on learning across affective, recognition, and strategic networks, providing multiple means of engagement, representation of information, and action and expression. To attend to students' affective networks, the "why" of learning, instructors design experiences that engage and motivate students in their learning (CAST, n.d.c.). They do this by recruiting interest and sustaining effort and persistence, as well as providing options for self-regulation. For example, an instructor can allow student groups to choose topics that interest them for a course project, provide regular feedback, and provide avenues where they can reflect on their learning. Recognition networks acknowledge that learners may perceive of and understand information in different ways, necessitating the importance of instruction that engages multiple senses, relies on language and different forms of media, and helps students construct their own knowledge. To provide various recognition networks, the "what of learning," an instructor may offer various ways for students to view or hear information and ways to process this information. For example, this may involve providing a visual diagram as well as a simulation explaining the same concept. Lastly, to attend to strategic networks, the "how" of learning, involves instruction that incorporates multiple methods to help students achieve their learning outcomes by ensuring access, providing various options for communication and practice, managing information, and monitoring progress.

There are a number of UDL resources online available through CAST (n.d.b.) that can help instructors who would like to apply UDL to their courses. Another resource for those more interested in learning more about UDL is Tobin and Behling's (2018) *Reach Everyone, Teach Everyone: Universal Design for Learning in Higher Education*. They advocate the "plus one" approach for implementing UDL, recommending that instructors design instruction and think of one additional element to add to support student learning.

Reflection Question

- How can each of these frameworks support an inclusive classroom experience for diverse learners?

Now that we have defined inclusive teaching and provided evidence for its importance in higher education the next chapter highlights what inclusive instructors know about creating learning environments that are equitable and welcoming.

Key Points

- Inclusive instructors foster classroom environments where diverse learners feel a sense of belonging and the teaching approaches utilized are equitable.
- Inclusive instructors value inclusive teaching given that both feeling a sense of belonging and equitable teaching practices can significantly reduce achievement gaps between students of diverse demographic backgrounds and also enhance general well-being. The literature affirms the importance of inclusive teaching.
- Various frameworks such as multicultural education, culturally relevant and culturally responsive pedagogy, and UDL can be particularly useful for inclusive instructors as they seek to be equitable in their teaching.

2

WHAT DO THEY KNOW ABOUT BEING INCLUSIVE?

As described in chapter 1, two essential aspects of inclusive teaching are the ability to make meaning of such approaches and to understand the significance of their impacts on the learning environment. In this chapter we highlight how inclusive instructors also have core knowledge and adopt particular mindsets that guide their implementation of various strategies and lead to effective teaching. The course scenarios described are either hypothetical or based on real examples.

Inclusive instructors know that being aware of the diverse attributes that their students bring to their courses is essential for creating environments where all students can meet learning goals. Inclusive instructors view the diversity of their learners as an asset and leverage the differences between students to create excellent learning opportunities that can benefit all members of their classroom community. They recognize that some students can be particularly vulnerable to the harms of stereotypes, and thus they are deliberate in affirming all students' identities. Inclusive instructors view themselves as responsible for fostering an inclusive learning environment, rather than considering it solely the responsibility of individuals or offices designated for equity and inclusion initiatives. They espouse a mindset of inclusion and have empathy for their learners. They know that empathy is critical to the intentional design of courses that are equitable and welcoming. They teach to the whole student rather than solely to their intellectual capacities. They enact instruction that is focused on learners. Inclusive instructors also recognize that they are also learners; they have limitations, but they seek to grow in their efforts. In this chapter we parse out these key aspects of what inclusive instructors know about being inclusive, applying various frameworks described in chapter 1.

They Recognize That Understanding Who Their Students Are Is Critical for Advancing Learning

Instructors who adopt inclusive teaching approaches seek to understand who their students are in their courses in order to maximize the learning that occurs. They do not make assumptions about their students, but rather base their understanding on information obtained on their learners at the institutional, program, classroom, and individual levels. In this sense, their understandings are evidence-based.

Who Are the Students at the Institution?

At the institutional level, an Office of Institutional Research (or similar unit) may have access to student demographic information and provide profile summaries. This may include information on factors such as gender, race/ethnicity, Pell-eligibility (qualification for Pell grants because of low-income status), and first-generation status. These data may be published on institutional websites and can be particularly useful for instructors new to teaching at an institution as well as those interested in understanding how student demographics change over time at the institution. For example, if the strategic plans of an institution include diversifying the student population by becoming need blind, if successful, the number of students from a more diverse range of socioeconomic classes will increase. Instructors may find that more students have outside employment, or may experience more financial challenges with purchasing course materials such as textbooks and electronic devices such as computers and laptops for assignment completion. Not being able to purchase required materials for a course can have detrimental impacts on student achievement. Inclusive instructors recognize that they should be aware that students in their classes can face such hardship, and consider how they can reduce the cost of materials, use alternatives and connect students to necessary resources. In general student demographic profiles can vary greatly between community colleges, HBCUs, minority-serving institutions, private and public master's, baccalaureate institutions, and doctorate-granting universities, as well as other institution types. Inclusive instructors recognize the need to be aware of the institution-specific demographics of enrolled students as they design their courses, an aspect that is essential for effective teaching that can be easily overlooked.

Reflection Questions

- Does your institution have an office devoted to institutional research? If so, seek out any demographic information this office can provide about the students at your college or university.

- On first glance, what if any relationships do you see between the institutional data and the students within your courses?

Who Are the Students in the Department or Program?

At the departmental or program level inclusive instructors may obtain key information from institutional datasets, or departments and programs may generate their own assessments that provide more information about the students in a particular major or minor. For example, Offices of Institutional Research may collect and synthesize basic demographic information on students in a particular major and examine other factors such as students' intent of major at prematriculation. Some departments or programs may also conduct exit surveys with their majors to assess their experiences in the program as well as provide insight into their future plans. Alumni offices may also be able to provide this information to departments if their assessments include a categorization of students by their major or minor. Such information is important to obtain for various reasons as it allows departments or programs to assess whether there are equity gaps, and, if so, propose strategic plans to reduce disparities that would promote greater education equity. This data also allows inclusive instructors to have an understanding of the profiles of students in the major.

Reflection Question

- Is there any information available on students in your department or program major or minor that could inform your teaching efforts?

Who Are the Students in My Course?

The classroom level is our primary unit of focus in this book. Inclusive instructors seek to understand which attributes their learners bring with them in their course so that they can leverage them to design an inclusive learning environment. This quote exemplifies the actions of an instructor who desires to better understand what their students bring to the classroom:

> [I go about this by] [g]enerating activities throughout the semester to find out more about my student audience: their career interests, their misconceptions about different topics, how their cultural, geographic and generational experiences inform their own interests, perceptions of future career goals, and self-evaluation.
>
> —Full professor, doctorate-granting university, Biology

By being aware of students' career interests, as described in the quote, an instructor can integrate activities that align with course learning goals and help equip students with skills and habits of mind that encourage their future success. Identifying students' misconceptions through formative exercises such as concept inventories or other assessments can allow instructors to design more effective interventions or learning activities that help students learn and thus form appropriate schema. Another key aspect of learning is motivation. Having an awareness of the cultural, geographical, and other experiences of their students can help instructors carefully design relevant assignments that motivate and encourage students to meet learning goals through culturally relevant pedagogies.

There are also a variety of other attributes that inclusive instructors may desire to learn about their students at the beginning of the course and various ways to obtain the information. For face-to-face courses instructors may choose to pass out index cards at the beginning of the semester and ask students to provide information such as their prior experiences with the course material, their feelings about the class, and other attributes that might influence their success in the course. In either online or on-ground courses, such information can be shared in an anonymous feedback form or other format, such as in the "Who's in Class?" form described in chapter 6. Instructors may choose to make personal connections with students by learning more about their students during office hours, attending cocurricular activities, and volunteering for student committees and events. This area is discussed in further detail in chapter 4.

Some institutions also use data-driven approaches to obtain demographic information on students enrolled in their courses. For example, the University of California, Davis, developed a tool called the Know Your Students app, which provides a dashboard of information on learners such as the number of those who are underrepresented, English-language learners, and low socioeconomic class in addition to grade distributions of students in related courses and in past terms (UC Davis, 2019). Instructors undergo a cycle of progress, with the stages of awareness, understanding, action, and reflection to improve inclusivity in their courses. The University of North Carolina at Chapel Hill (UNC) developed the "My Course Analytics" dashboard, which instructors can use to look at how course grades aggregate by such as gender, Pell eligibility, first-generation status, and other factors (UNC, 2020). Whether through a digital tool or via other means such as notecards, surveys, assignments, class discussions, office hours, or combinations thereof, inclusive instructors seek to learn more about their students' backgrounds so that they can advance learning. Such strategies can also be employed in online courses to build community among learners, where distance and a virtual environment can pose a unique challenge but need not be a barrier to understanding who learners are. For online learners issues of equity and inclusion may be even more apparent for reasons that may reflect why they choose to take a course in an online environment, which may include competing priorities for work and childcare, among others.

In *Teaching to Transgress: Education as the Practice of Freedom*, bell hooks (1994) writes that:

> As a classroom community, our capacity to generate excitement is deeply affected by our interest in one another, in hearing one another's voices, in recognizing one another's presence. Since the vast majority of students learn through conservative, traditional educational practices and concern them-selves only with the presence of the professor, any radical pedagogy must insist that everyone's presence is acknowledged. That insistence cannot be simply stated. It has to be demonstrated through pedagogical practices. To begin, the professor must genuinely *value* everyone's presence. There must be an ongoing recognition that everyone influences the classroom dynamic, that everyone contributes. These contributions are resources. Used constructively they enhance the capacity of any class to create an open learning community (p. 8).

Notably, inclusive instructors take interest in their learners and seek understanding of their backgrounds, interests, and motivations for learning in order to design excellent learning environments.

Course Scenarios

As a hypothetical example, a seasoned instructor who has taught online, asynchronous courses for many years is aware of the positive impacts of better understanding her learners. At the beginning of each course she builds community by sharing aspects of herself with her students. She creates a warm, welcoming video introducing herself and the course and provides explicit information about how she will communicate with the class as well as how they can communicate with one another. In the welcome video she discusses how she values learning more about the students. She also invites all learners in the class to share a photo or video clip of themselves and a fact or two to share with the class as part of an early, low-stakes course assignment. She uses this information on her learners to build a more inclusive course. For exam-ple, in one course she found that many of her students were working parents with young children. Rather than have a close-of-business or 5:00 p.m. dead-line for assignments, which would be the time when several of the working parents would be just finishing up the workday to take care of families, she allowed for later evening assignment submissions. This change was agreed on and favored by the entire class.

As another example, an instructor shared with his class of mostly freshmen that he was a first-generation college student, in addition to strategies for how he navigated through his university experience. This opened up doors of opportunity for the instructor to invite the students in the class to seek advice. The instructor already had insight that there could potentially be a few students who were first-generation in the course given the student demographics for the institution. During office hours a few students shared with him that they were also first-generation college students. Sharing his own social identity and path allowed him to also better understand who his learners are in the course, and he daily considered such diversity assets in his instruction to support the learning experience for all students.

Reflection Question

- How can you better understand the attributes and social identities your learners bring to your courses?

They Consider Student Diversity an Asset and not a Deficit

[Inclusive teaching] does not see students through a deficit model. It embraces equity in the classroom—acknowledging and working with the skills in the classroom and helping students amplify and extend what they bring.

—Full professor, baccalaureate college, History

In a national study we asked instructors to identify any major barriers for implementing inclusive teaching at their institutions (Addy et al., in press). Lack of awareness of the diverse attributes that students bring to their classroom and not knowing how to be more inclusive in instruction were described as major impediments. In other words, some instructors reported that their colleagues were not aware that there were differences between students, or they embraced a color-blindness mindset and viewed all learners as the same. Others reported that their colleagues did not believe it to be their responsibility to implement inclusive teaching approaches, but rather offices of diversity or others on campus involved in diversity, equity, and inclusion efforts. Such mindsets that do not to acknowledge the many positive attributes that diverse learners can bring to the classroom experience are detrimental for everyone. These mindsets also fail to acknowledge the collective effort needed by instructors as well as others at institutions of higher education to support an inclusive environment. As will be discussed in the epilogue, fostering an inclusive culture is a collaborative effort.

To the contrary, inclusive instructors view the differences between students as assets rather than deficits, aligning with multicultural education and other frameworks previously described (Guo & Jamal, 2007). As described by Smit (2012), there are clear problems with deficit models of thinking at colleges and universities:

> The dominant thinking in higher education attempts to understand student difficulty by framing students and their families of origin as *lacking* some of the academic and cultural resources necessary to succeed in what is presumed to be a fair and open society. This constitutes a deficit thinking model: it focuses on inadequacies of students and aims to "fix" this problem. In the process the impact of structural issues is often ignored or minimised. Employing a deficit mindset to frame student difficulties perpetuates stereotypes, alienates students from higher education and disregards the role of higher education in perpetuating the barriers to student success. (p. 369)

R. Filback and A. Green (2013) adapted work by previous scholars to describe "A Framework of Educator Mindsets and Consequences." The consequence of applying such ideas is the erroneous assumption that all students entering their institution should be able to conform to the norms of college, that some students of specific cultural backgrounds will not succeed, and that they should have lower expectations for some students with regard to achievement.

Instructors implementing inclusive teaching approaches consider the many skills, cultures, experiences, attitudes, perspectives, habits of mind, personalities, and other characteristics that students bring to the classroom as having the potential to augment the learning environment during the course. For example, a diversity of student perspectives can lead to rich discussions in a seminar course and expose students to viewpoints that they had not previously considered. Diverse teams of students working together may create an original project that neither of them could design independently. As stated by the late author and scholar Dr. Maya Angelou (2014), "In diversity there is beauty and there is strength."

Inclusive instructors are also aware of the many identities that their students hold and the interrelationships between them. The term *intersectionality* was originally conceived of by Kimberlé Crenshaw (1989) to describe how both gender and race are social identities of Black women which have implications for employment. This term now has been applied more broadly and can be defined as "a paradigm that addresses the multiple dimensions of identity and social systems as they intersect with one another and relate to inequality, such as racism, genderism, heterosexism, ageism, and classism, among other variables" (Task Force on Re-envisioning the Multicultural Guidelines for the 21st Century, 2017, p. 166). Awareness and acknowledgment of students' intersecting identities can have direct implications on learning environments. The American Psychological Association (APA) (2020) provides the example of a person who is a Jewish American that has a visible appearance of being in a majority group and experiences privilege as a result but also confronts religious discrimination. Instructors should also be aware of their own diverse attributes and how they may impact their teaching and the experiences of their learners.

Course Scenarios

An instructor teaches a freshman composition course with a diverse group of learners, including some for which English is not their first language. A main learning goal for the course is for students to advance their writing skills across different genres. The instructor views student language diversity as an opportunity to include a more culturally relevant array of course readings. Additionally, the instructor employs a variety of inclusive teaching practices to support the success of all students, such as providing an organized structure for writing assignments, having students create multiple drafts, providing regular feedback, and having students engage in peer review. The instructor also informs students of the resources offered by an office that provides academic support for students who are English-language learners. These actions are in contrast to a deficit model, where an instructor may instead hold lower expectations for English-language learners in their course.

In another scenario, the course learning outcomes involve students becoming familiar with a diversity of perspectives during group work. The instructor assigns students to diverse groups to complete a learning activity where students collaboratively solve a challenging problem. The course is interdisciplinary and the instructor mixes up groups of students from different majors. Students are to work collaboratively and harness the diversity of the perspectives of their teammates in order to come up with an original solution.

Reflection Questions
- What are problems with the deficit model in higher education?
- What are some assets your diverse learners bring to your course?

They Are Aware of and Mitigate the Harms of Stereotype Threat and Affirm Student Identities

[Inclusive teaching is] [t]eaching that recognizes and affirms [a] student's social identity as an important influence on teaching and learning processes, and that works to create an environment in which students are able to learn from the course, their peers, and the teacher while still being their authentic selves. It works to disrupt traditional notions of who succeeds in the classroom and the systemic inequities inherent in traditional educational practices.

—Academic professional, doctorate-granting university, Education

Students from social identities stigmatized as having lower intellectual capabilities can underperform in academic settings, particularly if academic success is important to them (Steele, 2010). This effect is known as stereotype threat and was initially identified by the social psychologist Claude Steele. Steele's work emerged from investigations of Black students at the University of Michigan who academically entered the institution with much promise based on excellent high school records but ended up underperforming in college. Steele's research group found that many of these students were affected by stereotype threat. That is, because of the stigma pressures experienced and internalized, they were unable to achieve to their potential. Another study showed that females who are also vulnerable to being perceived as having lower intelligence in mathematics also succumb to the effects of stereotype threat (Spencer et al., 1999). Similar investigations were carried out with White male and Asian students taking mathematics assessments (Aronson et al., 1999). The majority group, the White male students of equivalent academic capability, underperformed as compared to the Asian students because they internalized the stigma pressures of being inferior to Asians in mathematics.

As is evident by the groundbreaking studies of Steele and others, the impacts of stereotype threat can clearly be a large impediment to the academic success of diverse learners in college and university classrooms. Inclusive instructors who view diversity as an asset and seek to understand who their learners are in the classroom are also aware of the harms of stereotype threat. Inclusive instructors know that affirming students' social identities and values can have a dramatic positive impact on their learners, particularly those more likely to experience stereotype threat. A simple values affirmation exercise might include asking students to write down and reflect on what matters to them and why. Studies show that when students are given the opportunity to affirm their values in this way at key moments in a course or prior to an assessment, achievement gaps can decrease (Jordt et al., 2017; Miyake et al., 2010). As the instructor quoted at the start of this section notes, inclusive teachers create environments where students can be their "authentic selves." Students in their courses feel comfortable about their own social identities.

Inclusive instructors are also aware of the harms caused by microaggressions, more subtle forms of discrimination that can occur anywhere including in a course setting. They directly address microaggressions when they happen and use preventative strategies throughout the course to limit their occurrence. Inclusive instructors are also aware of and utilize models such as restorative justice when conflicts happen in the classroom that necessitate making amends and rebuilding trust.

Course Scenarios

An instructor teaching an introductory science, technology, engineering and mathematics (STEM) course is very aware of the underrepresentation of women and students of color in the discipline. He recognizes the talents in these learners in his course and how they are more vulnerable to stereotype threat. He investigates different approaches to supporting the achievement of his diverse learners and ultimately decides on having students complete values affirmation exercises prior to them completing a test. He read in the literature how doing this simple exercise can reduce achievement gaps between learners, likely by reducing the harmful impacts of stereotype threat by providing a space for students to affirm their identities. The activity involved asking all students to write down two or three of their values. The instructor noticed that compared to other semesters there was a reduction in the achievement gaps in test scores between male and female students as well as between minority and majority students.

At the beginning of most semesters an instructor runs an activity in which students bring in a physical or digital object that represents an aspect of their identity that they would like to share with the class. Each has a few minutes to share it with the class, and other students are welcome to ask questions. The instructor also shares an object. This activity is modified from having students create a culture box, which involves them gathering items that represent aspects of their cultures. Students typically enjoy sharing about themselves and learning more about their classmates during this activity. This experience also allows the instructor to affirm the identities of all students.

Reflection Question

- How can you affirm the social identities of all students, including those most susceptible to stereotype threat?

They Take Ownership Over Fostering an Inclusive Learning Environment and May Use Anti-Oppression Pedagogy

Inclusive teaching is a set of practices that emerge out of my intrapersonal awareness of my positionality and interpersonal awareness of who is in my course. It includes pedagogical choices, curricular choices, and communication choices that seek to empower all learners to meet their potential and to avoid practices that serve to marginalize students in my courses.

—Full professor, doctorate-granting university, Chemistry

It relates to the choices I make as an instructor and how those choices impact students (emotionally, physically, intellectually) and their ability to learn in my class.

—Lecturer, institution type unknown, Biology

Inclusive teaching means (1) creating space in class for various perspectives and personal experiences to be shared and (2) leveraging those unique perspectives and personal experiences to help the entire class learn.

—Lecturer, master's college, Chemistry

Provid[e] safe, brave spaces for students to flourish in the context of their individual and intersectional identities.

—Associate professor, master's comprehensive institution, Psychology

One theme that stands out in these quotes is that inclusive instructors make a choice to teach their diverse learners using equitable strategies that promote belonging. Inclusion is their responsibility to foster and influences the decisions they make about the design of their course—the content and the strategies employed are all critical in fostering a welcoming environment. They are aware that as instructors they can empower or marginalize learners in their courses and take their responsibilities seriously, seeking to do what's best for their students. Inclusive instructors are also proactive. They recognize that an inclusive environment is one that is to be thoughtfully and carefully designed and flexible to the needs of their learners. There will be a variety of practical strategies discussed in subsequent chapters illuminating this idea.

A second relevant theme revealed through the quotes is the need to create a brave space regardless of the type of classroom space whether virtual or face-to-face. In this space students feel as if they can share their own viewpoints comfortably without fear of shame or being looked down on. Inclusive instructors recognize that it is their responsibility to create an environment where all students feel welcome. They are aware that their learners can be the victims of microaggressions (Sue, 2010). "Racial microaggressions are brief and commonplace daily verbal, behavioral, or environmental indignities, whether intentional or unintentional, that communicate hostile, derogatory, or negative racial slights and insults toward people of color" (Sue et al., 2007, p. 271). This term was coined by Pierce (1970). There are many forms of microaggressions including microassaults, microinsults, and microinvalidations. "A microassault is an explicit racial derogation characterized primarily by a verbal or nonverbal attack meant to hurt the intended victim through name-calling, avoidant behavior, or purposeful discriminatory actions" (Sue et al., 2007, p. 274). Microinsults are "verbal and nonverbal communications that subtly convey rudeness and insensitivity and demean a person's racial heritage or identity." An example is when a White employer tells a prospective candidate of color "I believe the most qualified person should get the job regardless of race," or when an employee of color is asked "How did you get your job?" The underlying message from the perspective of the recipient may be twofold: (a) POC are not qualified, and (b) as a minority group member, you must have obtained the position through some affirmative action or quota program and not because of ability" (Sue et al., 2007, p. 274). Microinvalidations are "communications that subtly exclude, negate, or nullify the thoughts, feelings or experiential reality of a person of color." For instance, this can occur when "Asian Americans (born and raised in the United States) are complimented for speaking good English or are repeatedly asked where they were born, the effect is to negate their U.S. American heritage and to convey that they are perpetual foreigners" (Sue et al., 2007, p. 274). Any of these can occur in the classroom setting, and inclusive instructors are quite aware of when they occur and seek to address them.

Allowing microaggressions to go unaddressed in a course, whether online or face-to-face, can be damaging. While more research is needed, the literature suggests that those who experience discrimination, whether overt or subtle, are more subject to psychological distress and other negative outcomes on their physical health (Wong et al., 2014). These may include a higher prevalence of cardiovascular diseases, anxiety, low self-esteem and more. Microaggressions can be damaging for those experiencing them whether they are intentional or not.

Given that inclusive instructors believe diversity is an asset in the classroom, they address any microaggressions that occur in their courses (Nadal, 2014), whether they are based on race, gender, or other identities. There are various approaches that inclusive instructors can take to address microaggressions. Nadal (2014) suggests a process for determining how to address a microaggression: Should I respond? How should I respond? The decision to respond is contingent on weighing relevant risks. This reflective process enables understanding to be reached and a response made based on judgement. The RAVEN approach is another method for addressing microaggressions and involves redirecting the conversation, asking clarifying questions, clarifying *v*alues, *e*mphasizing thoughts and feelings, and discussing *n*ext steps (Wood & Harris, 2020). The ACTION framework is similar to these other approaches (Souza, 2018): *a*sking clarifying questions, *c*oming from curiosity rather than judgement, *t*elling the individual that what was observed was problematic, *i*mpact exploration or telling them the potential harms on others of the microaggression, *o*wning one's thoughts and feelings about the offense, and *n*ext steps. Inclusive instructors do not shy away from these difficult conversations and are proactive in promoting belonging in their classrooms by directly addressing microaggressions.

Course Scenarios

The SARS-CoV2 coronavirus that led to the COVID-19 crisis was found to have origins in Wuhan, China, before it spread globally. The public health crisis necessitated that colleges and universities abruptly switch to remote learning. During this time individuals of Asian descent experienced an alarming number of microaggressions. An instructor who normally taught face-to-face courses held a synchronous class session during which a student made a comment that seemed to be negatively portraying Asian students. The instructor was concerned that this could be a microaggression and could have harmful impacts on students of Asian descent in the class and negatively impact the classroom community. The instructor was proactive and felt it important to address the potential offense during the class by asking the student to clarify what they meant. Ultimately, he determined that the student's comment was actually not a microaggression and still used it as a teachable moment to facilitate a class discussion on discrimination during the COVID-19 crisis.

A Muslim student in a course spoke confidentially with her instructor about concerns that the time of the course overlapped with when they needed to perform a daily prayer ritual. The student was required to take the course for her major and it was the only one being offered. The instructor understood and let the student know that she was welcome to step out when she needed to and also arranged with the Registrar's Office to hold the class closer to the college prayer room so that the student did not miss much class. Over the course of the semester students seemed to understand when she had to step out to pray. One day, however, while students were conducting group work, a student in the class made a comment questioning why this student had to step out at the same time each day, considering it abnormal and that she could just wait until the end of class to leave. The instructor recognized this microaggression and used it as an opportunity to discuss the traditions of various religions and the importance of daily prayer rituals for many of those of Muslim faith. This affirmed the identity of the student and did not put her in the spot to speak on behalf of her religion.

Reflection Questions

- Have you ever witnessed or been the victim of a microaggression in a teaching and learning setting? As an instructor how can you be proactive in addressing these in your courses?

They Know That a Mindset of Inclusion and Empathy Supports Intentional Course Design

Be . . . intentional regarding engaging and challenging all students in the classroom.

—Visiting professor, institution type not identified, Education

It means teaching in a way that intentionally recognizes and supports ALL students including those marginalized by race, gender/gender identity, SES political views, religion, disability status, etc.

—Associate professor, doctorate-granting university, Biology

Not only do inclusive instructors take responsibility for inclusion and are proactive in their efforts, they also are intentional about how they design welcoming courses. Chapter 3 will highlight the intentionality in course design that inclusive instructors take to ensure that learning occurs for their diverse learners. They are intentional because they are empathetic and have compassion toward their students, regardless of whether they themselves have experienced similar circumstances. They think in the best interests of their students, imagining that they are in their shoes. They consider student voices and their own life experiences and how they frame their empathy toward their students.

Inclusive instructors are empathetic toward their students. There is evidence in the literature that professional development on culturally responsive teaching can support teachers' development of empathy (McAllister & Irvine, 2002). When teachers underwent such an experience they had better interactions with their diverse learners, were able to foster more positive inclusive classroom environments, and used more classroom practices that focused on their learners. Empathy is an attribute that has been considered as necessary for culturally responsive pedagogy to be effective (Rychly & Graves, 2012). In general the required culturally responsive teacher characteristics have been reported to be caring and empathetic, reflective about their attitudes and beliefs about other cultures, reflective about their own cultural frames of reference, and knowledgeable about other cultures.

Course Scenarios

After administering an anonymous class survey an instructor becomes aware that there are students in the course who do not have the financial means to purchase required course materials. The instructor recognizes that not having access to these course materials will be detrimental for the learning of these students and is empathetic to their circumstances. As a result she ensures students have copies of course materials available in the library on reserve so that all learners have access. The instructor also investigates open education resources that are available at minimal or no cost, which are substitutes for more expensive course materials and still allow students to meet learning goals.

A student who entered college with metastatic cancer periodically received chemotherapy treatments at the hospital that left her weak and unable to attend her laboratory course section and other classes. Regardless, she had a strong spirit and would quickly recover and was remarkably a top scorer in the course. The instructor knew that the health circumstances of this student called for flexibility to account for her serious health condition. The student was able to turn in assignments late when she had treatments and was excused to miss class so that she could undergo treatment or heal. The student completed the course with highest achievement. A few years later sadly she succumbed to the disease, and the instructor later found out from her parents that the course had been a bright light for their daughter.

Reflection Question

- How can instructor empathy for students help foster a more inclusive classroom environment?

They Teach the Whole Student

> *Inclusive teaching, to me, means having [a] holistic view of each student and also, that the instructor "holds" the needs of individual students and the larger group in mind, and uses this understanding to inform her pedagogy.*
>
> —Full professor, doctorate-granting university, Social Work

Inclusive instructors see their students as more than empty vessels whose minds are waiting to be filled with information. They view each as having unique traits, personalities, attitudes, and experiences that they bring to the classroom and consider such factors important to the learning environment. In *Teaching the Whole Student: Engaged Learning with Heart, Mind, and Spirit*, Schoem et al. (2017) discuss the importance of viewing students beyond their intellectual capacities. They posit that teaching holistically is a strategy that supports student persistence and ultimately retention in higher education. To these authors, teaching the whole student involves the heart, mind, and spirit and focuses on a learning community involving students and instructors, with a critical focus on student–teacher relationships. Such teaching is also engaging and enables students to be active participants in their learning.

In implementing a holistic approach to teaching, inclusive instructors are aware of students' intersecting identities and diverse attributes and view them as essential components to consider when cultivating the classroom learning community. Holistic pedagogy engages both inclusive instructors and their leaners. As bell hooks (1994) indicates, "Engaged pedagogy does not seek simply to empower students. Any classroom that employs a holistic model of learning will also be a place where teachers grow, and are empowered by the process" (p. 21).

Course Scenarios

In order to create an engaging environment for a diverse group of learners, an instructor partners with the Center for Civic Engagement on campus to design a community-based learning experience in their course where the students worked in groups on a project to support the mission of a local nonprofit organization focused on sustainability. This experiential learning opportunity helped students form interdisciplinary connections between the content of their course and environmental justice. The instructor received positive feedback from students of diverse backgrounds in the class on how working with the nonprofit impacted them beyond an intellectual level. Several students in the course later participated in internships with the organization as a result of this transformative learning experience.

An instructor recognizes the many items that compete for their students' attention such as text messages, social media, peer and family concerns, and other anxieties. She knows that such factors can heavily impact student achievement in a course and desires to incorporate more embodied learning experiences. She investigates contemplative pedagogy to determine if such practices can advance the learning of her students. She has students engage in reflective journaling upon entry to class and sees marked improvements in focus for all learners compared to previous semesters.

Reflection Question

- What does or might a holistic approach to learning look like to you when enacted in a course setting?

They Espouse a Learner-Centered Mindset

Inclusive teaching is learner-centered teaching that gives all students a voice and makes them feel like they belong and are respected as individuals and members of groups.

—Full professor, doctorate-granting university, Journalism, Media Studies, and Communication

Inclusive instructors embrace learner-centered approaches in their courses. Learner-centered instruction focuses on helping students acquire knowledge, skills, and attitudes to meet learning goals. In contrast, instructor-centered approaches focus on the transmission of information to learners and the instructor as the originator of knowledge. In *Learner-Centered Teaching: Five Key Changes to Practice,* Weimer (2013) describes how in student-centered instruction, the role of the instructor is to facilitate learning, students have some level of control over what they are learning, instructors help students apply content rather than simply ingest content, students are held responsible for their learning, and instructors view evaluation as a means to advance learning and encourage students to perform self-assessments. Active learning environments where students are engaged in the construction of knowledge have been shown to close achievement gaps between diverse learners (Freeman et al., 2014; Haak et al., 2011).

Inclusive instructors, while having appropriate expertise in their disciplines, do not view their role to impart knowledge to their students, but rather to serve as a guide and facilitate a learning community. They consider what course activities will best help students accomplish the learning goals. They invite students as collaborators in designing the learning experience.

A variety of examples of learner-centered approaches are discussed in the forthcoming chapters.

Course Scenarios

After teaching a course several times, an instructor has a good sense of which concepts students have the most difficulty understanding and applying. The instructor recognizes value in the learner-centered approach of students teaching one another. In order to help students grasp the difficult concepts he gives a brief overview on the topic and then sets the class up as a learning community where students work together in small groups to answer questions related to the topic to help each other learn. After implementing these small groups, the instructor notices marked improvements in the achievement of all learners, including students initially scoring low on the first major assessments.

An instructor would like to provide students with more choices in their learning to account for their diverse interests and skills and integrate UDL. For a course project he decides to allow students to choose the mode they would like to utilize to complete the project, such as creating a video clip, infographic, podcast, or website. The students perform remarkably on this project at the end of the semester, accurately integrating course concepts as well as creating very polished products. On the end-of-semester evaluations, the instructor received a lot of positive feedback on this project from students.

They Know That They Have Limitations and Espouse a Growth Mindset

Teach . . . without implicit or intentional bias based on stereotypical traits.

—Lecturer, master's college, Earth Sciences

In 2006 Carol Dweck published the book *Mindset: The New Psychology of Success*. Her book highlights differences between fixed and growth mindset, and the concepts are transferable to many contexts, including college courses. Those espousing fixed mindset view intellectual ability as static and avoid challenges, do not confront obstacles, do not see the value in their efforts, do not use negative feedback, and view the success of others as a threat. Because of these beliefs and behaviors they do not rise to their full potential. On the contrary, those with a growth mindset seek challenges, persist even in the most difficult of situations, value putting in good effort, learn from critique, and appreciate the success of others. Those with a growth mindset often have higher levels of achievement than those with a fixed mindset.

While typically applied to learners in the classroom, this two-mindset framework can also be considered by professors utilizing inclusive teaching approaches in their classrooms. Inclusive instructors recognize that as humans they are fallible and know that being inclusive is a continual process for which they can continue to grow. They have never fully arrived. They are aware that everyone harbors biases, including themselves. However, they seek to become aware of these biases and take steps to minimize any harmful impacts. There may be occasions where they are not satisfied with their inclusive efforts because of what they seemingly perceive of as errors of practices; however, because they value inclusive teaching and espouse a growth mindset, and believe that with intentional practice they can improve, they seek to become more equitable in their teaching efforts. Their actions may involve reflecting on assumptions that they espouse about their diverse learners to raise awareness of their own biases, inviting trusted individuals to help them reveal their own biases and being humble and open to hear feedback and taking intentional actions to mitigate any harmful impacts of such biases.

Inclusive instructors also understand that they too can mistakenly commit microaggressions. If they become aware they have done this, they will be admitting it and being willing to listen to the person who was harmed if confronted (Nadal, 2014). They seek to have a better understanding of what microaggressions are and those that are most prevalent in our society. They may choose to read the literature on bias and stereotype threat, such as various books cited in this chapter, be intentional about reflecting on their own biases, or, as described in the epilogue, participate in professional development experiences where such topics are expounded on.

Course Scenarios

In a previous course taught by an instructor a student committed a microaggression during the class characterizing student athletes as second-class citizens. There were many student athletes in the class who heard this statement. The instructor froze and did not address the microaggression. On end-of-semester course evaluations the instructor received a number of comments from students disappointed that this incident was not handled properly and negatively impacted the climate of the course. The instructor saw his own limitations and recognized he needed to seek advice.

At the beginning of a course an instructor made sure to invite all students to share their pronouns and seek to use them appropriately. At the end of the semester the instructor realized that she had been using the wrong pronouns for one student. Although the semester had ended she apologized to the student and was very careful to use the correct pronouns of her learners in future courses.

Reflection Question

- What are some next steps that you can take toward becoming more inclusive in your teaching?

Key Points

Inclusive instructors espouse a variety of mindset about teaching and learning that help them create equitable learning environments. They know inclusion necessitates the following:

- Recognizing and understanding the diverse attributes their students bring to the course
- Considering student diversity an asset and not a deficit
- Being aware of and mitigating the harms of stereotype threat and affirming student identities
- Taking ownership over fostering an inclusive learning environment
- Having a mindset of inclusion and empathy to support intentional course design
- Teaching the whole student
- Espousing a learner-centered mindset
- Accepting their own limitations and espousing a growth mindset

PART TWO

THE PRACTICE OF
INCLUSIVE TEACHING

HOW DO THEY DESIGN
AN INCLUSIVE COURSE?

Deliberately implementing inclusive teaching strategies means that I take steps to create a class structure and atmosphere in which all students not only develop a sense of belonging but also are truly an integral part of the class, with accommodations made proactively (rather than on request, aka universal design). Students are valued for their differences in backgrounds, experiences, abilities, perspectives, internal and external pressures, and can share these freely or may choose not to do so. The goal is success for all students, not ranking students on a normal distribution.

–Lecturer, doctorate-granting university, Psychology

Understanding the necessity for inclusive teaching, particularly in the dynamic environment of higher education, is a first step. Becoming comfortable with a working definition of inclusive teaching is the next. But what happens when instructors try to realize inclusive pedagogy in their own teaching? The following three chapters will discuss in greater detail how inclusive instructors put theory into practice. We begin our exploration in this chapter, as most courses begin, with syllabus design. Before the elements of inclusive teaching can be implemented in the classroom, instructors need to develop a strategy—a roadmap—for an inclusive course. And that roadmap typically takes shape in the form of a syllabus. This chapter explores how inclusive instructors think about, design, reformulate, and navigate challenges with creating inclusive syllabi.

Conceptualizing Syllabi for Inclusive Instruction

Before delving into how instructors think about the principles of inclusive syllabus design and the finer details of its execution, it is worthwhile to consider what syllabi are and why they play such an important role in establishing an inclusive classroom. Of particular relevance is questioning to what extent our syllabus design reflects or accommodates inclusive teaching practices.

Scholars of pedagogy in higher education have long noted the critical role that syllabi play in setting the stage for a successful course. Indeed, studies have found that collegiate instructors and administrators frequently cite the syllabus as the most important contributor to effective teaching (e.g., Cooper & Cuseo, 1989). Why do educators place so much emphasis on syllabus design for effective instruction? Syllabi represent one of the earliest opportunities for students and instructors to interact within the bounds of a particular course (Eberly et al., 2001; Grunert, 1997). As such, syllabi can be a critical tool to establish principles of inclusivity and to communicate them clearly to students. Whether implicitly or explicitly, syllabi convey (a) an instructor's goals for the course, and whether students have a role to play in setting those goals (Dean & Fornaciari, 2014b; Grunert, 1997); (b) information about who belongs and whose voices are privileged or valued; (c) an articulation of the rights and responsibilities students and instructors have and owe to one another in the context of the classroom community (Danielson, 1995; McKeachie, 2002); and (d) critical information about how students can succeed (Matejka & Kurke, 1994). Each of these, as we will see in the following pages, reflect important decisions that inclusive instructors make when designing their own courses.

While accounts of the syllabus typically agree about the document's significance to the overall efficacy of a particular course, they diverge in their assessments of how instructors should conceive of a syllabus. Scholars have employed a number of different frameworks to conceptualize the role of the syllabus, with implications for its substance, structure, and tone. In general, we can think of these approaches as falling into one of three broad categories: the syllabus as a contract, as a communication tool, or as an organizational plan. (See, for example, Eberly et al., 2001; Matejka & Kurke, 1994.) While most of the scholarship on the concept of the syllabus does not engage explicitly with inclusive pedagogy, each of these models still have obvious implications for inclusive course design—including both strengths and weaknesses.

Perhaps the most robust pedagogical tradition contends that the syllabus is a contractual device intended to lay out the explicit responsibilities of both students and instructors (Grunert, 1997; Lowther et al., 1989; McKeachie, 2002; Parkes et al., 2003; Veliyath & Adams, 2005). According to this approach, "The syllabus as a contract can serve as the document by which the classroom practices, expectations, and norms are discussed and codified" (Danielson, 1995, p. 8). Some scholars follow the idea of syllabus as contract to its logical extreme, presenting the syllabus as something akin to an actual legal compact. Indeed, there is a considerable literature that debates whether the inclusion of legal language at the end of a syllabus can, once signed by students, function as an actual legal document (see, for example, Matejka & Kurke, 1994). This approach is often described as creating a defensive syllabus (Dean & Fornaciari, 2014b). A defensive syllabus is one intended to protect instructors from both formal and informal challenges from students and administrators.

The idea of a syllabus as contract holds some appeal for inclusive pedagogy, particularly in its emphasis on the clear articulation of what both instructors and students owe to one another—an approach that will be discussed in greater detail later in this chapter. Conceptualizing the syllabus as a contract, however, also introduces a number of obstacles for the creation of an inclusive classroom. Perhaps most obviously, using the syllabus as a defensive tool to protect instructors from students can create an adversarial relationship that can inhibit belonging in the classroom. The contractual approach can also reinforce power disparities between instructors and students, further challenging the creation of a community of belonging (Baecker, 1998; Singham, 2005). The addition of rules can communicate that students must be told how to behave (Kohn, 1993), which can generate feelings of alienation among students (Singham, 2005). Depending on its execution, this model can also inhibit students' ability to inform the content and evolution of the course—a critical aspect of both student-centered and andragogical (adult-centered) learning (Davis & Schrader, 2009; Dean & Fornaciari, 2014a, 2014b; Knowles, 1984; Nelken, 2009).

A second approach focuses on the syllabus as a communication tool. According to this framework, syllabi are a symbolic document in as much as they are a practical one. The syllabus can signal the tone for a course and set expectations about the instructor's approach and personality in the classroom (Baecker, 1998; Grunert, 1887; Habanek, 2005; Harrington & Thomas, 2018; Matejka & Kurke, 1994; McKeachie, 2002; Smith, 1993). Attending to these tonal elements of the syllabus can, as we will discuss in greater detail later in the chapter, play a critical role in establishing a sense of belonging and equity in the classroom. But considering the syllabus solely as a communication device or symbolic document overlooks some of the critical substantive elements that an inclusive syllabus needs to provide.

A final framework—addressing the syllabus as an organizational document—fills in some of the structural gaps that the syllabus-as-communication approach might overlook. This approach pays careful attention to outlining the substantive goals for the course and the clear path to achieving those goals. Its strength is emphasizing the need for clear and complete information about how the course should unfold for students over the course of the semester (Matejka & Kurke, 1994). But the syllabus-as-plan model has far less to say about creating belonging or equity in devising that roadmap.

By combining the strengths of these different approaches—the contractual, communicative, and organizational—along with a discursive approach that allows for either the explicit or implicit involvement of students, we might begin to think of the syllabus as a living constitution. A living constitution is, by its nature, designed to construct a thriving community. It outlines membership in the community and what we can expect from and owe to ourselves and our fellow community members. These are all benefits of the contractual approach. A living constitution also serves as a symbolic tool to communicate the goals and ethos of the community, encapsulating the strength of a syllabus-as-communication tool. Furthermore, a living constitution sets out the goals and procedures along which the community functions—the critical aspect of an organizational approach to syllabi. Most importantly, however, a *living* constitution invites participation, allows for evolution (or amendment), and accommodates a community's changing needs. Of course, this way of thinking about a syllabus is not inherently inclusive; rather, it allows for its creator(s) to design and redesign it to reflect the substantive course goals and an inclusive pedagogical philosophy.

Reflection Questions

- What is your main goal when writing a syllabus? What do you expect it to accomplish?
- Does your approach to the syllabus mirror any of the models described?
- What changes would you need to make to your syllabus in order for it to reflect the strengths of the different approaches? What do you think is currently missing or underdeveloped from those models?

They Use Principles of Inclusive Course Design

Recall how the instructors from chapter 1 described what inclusive teaching means to them. They expressed the importance of demonstrating to students, irrespective of background, that they belong in the classroom—promoting *belonging*. They also focused on the necessity of allowing for meaningful engagement and success across a range of skill levels—promoting *equity*. In this chapter, we will discuss how our course designs, and the syllabi we create to communicate them, lay the foundation for an inclusive classroom by generating conditions for belonging and equity. In doing so, we will explore how instructors incorporate a variety of pedagogical strategies—including concepts of universal design, student-centered learning, a growth mindset, and multicultural and culturally relevant learning—to design inclusive syllabi.

The chapter will discuss strategies for inclusive syllabus design, drawing on the experiences of inclusive instructors from a variety of institutions and disciplines. It began with a brief overview of the evolving scholarly conceptions of the syllabus, considering how each of these approaches might influence inclusive course design. Next, the chapter explores how to create a syllabus that serves not only as a simple reference for course activities, but also as a living, discursive tool of inclusive pedagogy. Specifically, we will ask three main questions to help us think about designing an inclusive syllabus. First, does the syllabus demonstrate to students that everyone has a place in the field of study? Second, does the syllabus encourage everyone to play a role in the learning process? Third, does the syllabus promote the conditions for every student to succeed in the course? As the descriptions from inclusive instructors will demonstrate, questions 1 and 2 are especially critical for our efforts to establish a sense of belonging in the classroom. Questions 2 and 3 are similarly important for generating equity in our courses. The chapter concludes by addressing some of the challenges instructors might encounter in their efforts to establish and improve their inclusive practices when it comes to course and syllabus design.

Of course, how we answer each of these questions will vary from course to course. And as chapter 1 explains, in order to adequately address some of these queries, we would ideally like to know more about who our learners are. By asking these questions as we embark on designing (or redesigning) our courses, however, we can work to weave inclusive practices into the very fabric of our instruction.

Before we continue, take a few minutes to think about whether and how you may already be trying to build inclusive principles into your pedagogy at the course and syllabus design stage.

Reflection Questions

- Do you typically think about making your course inclusive—creating the conditions for educational equity and belonging—when you first begin to design your syllabi?
- If so, at what stage of course design do you consider inclusivity?
- What are you currently doing to try and design your syllabus to reflect inclusive teaching?

They Know the Importance of Making Space for All Students

Does your syllabus demonstrate to students that everyone has a place in your field of study? Why is this an important question to ask? How will it help us to foster an inclusive class environment? Recall from chapter 1 that fostering a sense of social belonging is a critical element of successfully engaging students in course material (Strayhorn, 2019). Pedagogically, we might find it challenging to create a sense of belonging in a course when some students cannot imagine themselves as part of the community of scholarship and practice. Furthermore, as academic and professional fields seek to diversify their own ranks, the importance of creating a more inclusive pipeline is critical (e.g., Calhoun, 2009).

Accomplishing these goals requires a course design that clearly demonstrates to the increasingly diverse cohort of students that they, as well as their peers, belong in a given scholarly and professional community. So, how do inclusive instructors convey to students that they belong in the field? Their strategies typically involve incorporating diverse and culturally relevant perspectives into the course material, as well as creating the conditions for inclusive participation in the classroom.

They Incorporate Diverse Perspectives

When inclusive instructors are asked to think about how their syllabi reflect inclusive teaching practices, our data show that the most common response is to focus on integrating diverse perspectives into the course material assigned on the syllabus.

> *[I use] practices and content that includes as many viewpoints as possible from non-Western authors/scholars/persons presented with a critical consideration of privilege and oppression. . . . [I create a] race/gender/sexuality/ethnic balanced syllabus.*
>
> —Teaching fellow, doctorate-granting university, English

> *[I am] very intentional about creating a syllabus that includes readings by and about marginalized communities.*
>
> —Associate professor, doctorate-granting university, Sociology

> *[I] include research from scientists that are not old, White men.*
>
> —Associate professor, baccalaureate college, Biology

This represents a common practice in discussions of inclusive syllabi. The tendency to do so is, perhaps, unsurprising given the lengthy and ongoing debate over the importance of and challenges with incorporating multicultural perspectives into collegiate reading lists (see Banks, 1993b; Nieto, 1999). This frequently politicized issue has played out most publicly in debates over the value of "Western civilization" curriculum. But the question of whose knowledge matters and what the consequences are for student engagement when curriculum is unrepresentative apply across disciplines.

Let's take a moment to think about the value of representing multiple, intersecting perspectives in the curriculum and how that practice can enhance inclusive teaching (while not serving as a stand-in for other inclusive practices). One of the primary motivations instructors might have in doing so is to increase a sense of belonging among students who have historically been underrepresented in the academy (e.g., Banks, 1993b). By this logic, including perspectives from scholars who represent diverse communities with respect to their race, ethnicity, nationality, gender identity, sexual orientation, class, disability, religion, political affiliation, and so on can help students who are historically underrepresented see that they have a place in the field. As chapter 1 explains, promoting social belonging in this way is a necessary step in demonstrating to students from marginalized backgrounds that they are welcome members of a scholarly community. Furthermore, this approach gives those students a familiar lens through which to see, understand, and critique the course material—an important promoter of equity in the classroom.

But the benefits of incorporating diverse material in a course's design is not limited to fostering belonging among historically marginalized students. In fact, studies show that exposing all students to a diversified curriculum has a number of positive effects on the learning process. This approach treats diversity as an asset—meaning that differences in perspective can facilitate learning among all community members (Guo & Jamal, 2007). Another major benefit of this approach is that it enhances the capacity for all students—including those who do not come from traditionally marginalized communities—to be attentive to and build positive attitudes toward diversity (Smith & Wolf-Wendel, 2005).

When we think about inclusive teaching more holistically, as an opportunity to demonstrate the value of all students not only to themselves but to their peers as well, it becomes clear that incorporating diverse voices shows those who are used to seeing and learning from people like themselves that other perspectives have value and, indeed, add critical insights into our collective understanding.

So, how much is enough diversity? And where can instructors locate more diverse scholarship? There is no rule of thumb when it comes to creating a reading list for a course that incorporates multiple scholarly perspectives. One strategy might be to ensure that half of all of the authors on your syllabus reflect underrepresented perspectives in the academy. Another strategy is to consider each reading and ask whether an equivalent source exists whose author reflects an underrepresented perspective.

Adopting these approaches may present a bigger hurdle in some types of courses relative to others. In introductory courses that rely primarily on a textbook, for example, the ability to incorporate a broader range of voices may be necessarily limited. One alternative in such cases may be to reconsider whether a textbook is the best strategy for your course. If the answer is yes, then supplementing textbook readings with additional articles, forms of public scholarship, case studies, or even in-class examples that reflect diverse scholars may be the best solution. Very real deficits in the diversity of scholarship in specific fields may also present obstacles. Increasingly, however, professional associations have begun to assemble tools to help their members create more diverse curricula. This should be a first port of call when seeking assistance. Other collective projects, like the Women Also Know Stuff databases in fields like political science, history, and law, can provide critical references to help diversify syllabi. Another resource is to crowdsource recommendations through social media platforms.

They Incorporate Resonant Course Material

Beyond trying to reflect who students are in the material assigned for a course, instructors also cited the importance of incorporating material that resonates with the cultural and lived experiences of students.

> *Syllabi [should] provide connections to non-academic life. . . . Intentionally choosing examples and articles that represent different approaches, people, and institutions.*

—Full professor, baccalaureate college, Biology

> *I include diverse scholars and diverse perspectives into my curriculum. I intentionally talk about the sociopolitical and historical conditions that lead to inequity. I make space for students to share their own experiences without calling out underrepresented students in the classroom.*

—Associate professor, master's college, Education

As chapter 1 explains, course designs that are culturally responsive to the students in the classroom can incentivize students to engage more fully with the material (Wlodkowski & Ginsberg, 1995). Higher education is also experiencing increasing pressure to make learning experiences relevant to potential professional pathways after graduation. Designing a syllabus that includes work that matters to students is necessary both for creating belonging in the classroom and laying a foundation for equitable success. Of course, this effort can be expanded through the examples we use in class, as later chapters will discuss. But addressing the question of cultural and professional relevance is key at the stage of course design as well. As the inclusive instructors mention, this might include assigning readings that reflect salient local community issues—current or historical—or that address common problems in relevant professional fields. Cultural resonance can also be demonstrated by assigning different types of media that students are likely to be familiar with (e.g., podcasts, TED talks).

Reflection Questions

- What perspectives does your syllabus already include? Whose voices do you think are currently missing from your syllabus?
- What would you need to do to include those missing voices?

They Promote Student Engagement

Does your syllabus encourage everyone to play a role in the learning process? As inclusive instructors were frequent to explain, this is a critical question to address, not only to help create a sense of belonging in the classroom, but also to establish equity in the scholarly community.

> [I] attend to different participation styles and comfort levels in classroom discussions, address the cultural differences among the students in the classroom, establish safety and respect for all in discussions, and use gender neutral pronouns in syllabus and assignment instructions.

—Assistant professor, doctorate-granting university, Counseling

> I allow students to self-identify, and I self-identify at the beginning of class. I have a statement in my syllabus regarding the importance of including multiple and varied voices in our discussions and reading material. I provide specific instructions for students if they find there are barriers to their learning.

—Associate professor, master's college, Rhetoric and Composition

A good course design and syllabus can give students both the permission and the tools to be full participants in the course. This concept is consistent with one of the key scholarly principles of andragogy: Adult learners benefit from playing an active role in guiding their own learning experience (Knowles, 1984a; Knowles et al., 2005). In particular, the syllabus can help to set expectations around classroom citizenship and invite student participation in the learning process.

They Set the Tone for an Inclusive Classroom

When it comes to setting an expectation of community belonging and equity, syllabi are critical tools for several reasons. First, they help set the tone for the course. A syllabus is frequently one of the first forms of communication students receive from an instructor (Eberly et al., 2001). As such, the language of a syllabus can set the tone for course communication. Indeed, scholars increasingly emphasize the importance of a syllabus as a signaling, or communication, tool (Dean & Fornaciari, 2014b). This suggests that we must be attentive to the language we use in our syllabi (and, indeed, all course artifacts), and inclusive instructors report a number of strategies for setting a welcoming tone in their syllabi.

> *Inclusive teaching means pedagogy that aims to make the classroom a safe and welcoming space for all students, both in its form and its content (e.g., in practices and in what appears on the syllabus).*
>
> —Visiting professor, baccalaureate college, Writing

> *[I include] a welcoming statement related to diversity in syllabus.*
>
> —Associate professor, doctorate-granting university, Biology

Language and tone are critical tools in establishing a sense of belonging in the classroom. One important strategy for using syllabus language to help set an inclusive tone is to incorporate wording that is genuinely community building (Dean & Fornaciari, 2014b). Using "we" language, and drafting syllabi to reflect a conversational, collaborative tone, can remove implicit hierarchy between students and instructors that can impede creating classroom spaces of belonging (Thompson, 2007).

Scholars have also demonstrated the importance of writing the syllabus in a warm or friendly tone in order to engage students. Experimental work finds that the difference between a friendly and an unfriendly tone in the syllabus has critical implications for how students view the course instructor (Harnish & Bridges, 2011). Most notably, students who received a syllabus written in a friendly tone were more likely to evaluate the instructor positively (Denton & Veloso, 2017) and more likely to report that they felt the course would not be too challenging for them (Harnish & Bridges, 2011). This second point in particular may be important for creating a sense of belonging among students who are otherwise predisposed to believe they cannot succeed with the material in a particular field.

Another way to set the tone for an inclusive classroom community is to incorporate a welcoming statement that articulates the benefits of diversity in the classroom. For example, a syllabus might include language like the following:

Differences in opinion, background, and skills provide an opportunity for intellectual growth. In this course, we are committed to creating a community that is inclusive of diversity in its many manifestations, including race, ethnicity, SES, gender, gender identity, sexual orientation, religion, disability, place of origin, and political affiliation. We all benefit from being aware of and welcoming these differences.

Beyond the language, inclusive instructors also note how visual cues can also set the tone for a course.

My syllabus contains pictures of and quotes from men and women from different races to illustrate content or inspire students to keep trying.

—Survey respondent, associate college, rank and discipline not identified

[I] creat[e]class artifacts (syllabus, etc.) . . . that explicitly include multiple demographics (images include both genders, multiple races and classes, etc.).

—Dean, baccalaureate institution, English

Does your syllabus incorporate images? If so, what do those images suggest about who is represented in the course? Images and quotations, as the examples demonstrate, can be an important source of information to students about belonging. Furthermore, different fonts or formats can convey tone in meaningful ways. As Dean and Fornaciari (2014b) explain, for example, the choice between a more traditional font like Times New Roman and a more modern typeface like Calibri might send different messages to students about the formality or tenor of the instructor and, subsequently, the course. The language and design of your syllabus is thus a key tool to consider for the message it conveys to students about their participatory role in the course.

They Set Expectations for Inclusive Classroom Citizenship

A second way the syllabus can promote a sense of belonging is to clarify expectations about whose voices are accepted in the classroom community.

I have a syllabus statement on equity and inclusion.

—Associate professor, master's college, Education

It may be the first impression students get about what they can expect from the instructor and whether they will play a role in guiding the course (Danielson, 1995). An inclusive syllabus, therefore, ought to help set the terms of what you expect from students, what they should expect from you, and what they can expect from one another. If we return to considering the syllabus as a constitution, clarifying expectations is consistent with setting out both rights and responsibilities for participants in the course.

This can take many different forms. Perhaps most common to instructors are portions of the syllabus that tell students what they are expected to produce and when. In essence, this information clarifies what responsibilities students have to the instructor. While this is critical information to include to help students successfully navigate the course, a syllabus that only incorporates student responsibilities to the instructor is far more likely to create a hierarchical structure instead of one that promotes inclusivity and belonging.

In order to do the latter, it is also important to let students know what rights they have in the course. Or, put another way, what responsibilities do you as an instructor have to your students? This may take the form of information about how students might appeal their grade, how students can secure accommodations to which they are entitled, how quickly the instructor will turn around graded assignments, and information about when and how you will make yourself available to students.

It is also important to incorporate information about what students might owe to one another (or what they can expect from their fellow classmates). When it comes to making space for student voices, a description of the expectations for participation in the classroom community falls into this category. Explicitly stating to students that multiple perspectives are not only welcome, but are also, in fact, critical to the learning experience is consistent with this goal. You might choose—as several inclusive instructors in our survey describe—to incorporate your own institution's diversity statement as part of this discussion. Similarly, the syllabus might explain how you will handle any violations of the standards set for inclusive participation (strategies that will be discussed in the following chapters). Another way to think about what students owe to one another in pursuit of an inclusive classroom might be a discussion about activities (e.g., use of technology outside the bounds of class activities) that might serve as a distraction for students.

In general, incorporating a full discussion of the rights and responsibilities that all members of the classroom community owe to one another can also open space for participants to discuss and set some of those goals as a collective. For example, choosing to create classroom guidelines or even learning outcomes and course goals with your students would be fully consistent with this approach to syllabus design (Dean & Fornaciari, 2014b). Indeed, negotiating the terms of the syllabus with students at the outset of the class can provide an excellent opportunity to build practices that reflect the needs and competencies of learners (Knowles, 1990; for a discussion of syllabus strategic bargaining, see, Kaplan & Renard 2015).

They Create Conditions for Inclusive Participation

Finally, when it comes to fostering belonging through syllabus design—giving everyone a chance to participate in the learning process—inclusive instructors note that it is critical to explain to students what participation means in the context of the class. What avenues do students have to engage, and how can they do so successfully?

> *[I] establish a classroom culture that promotes civil discourse; classroom discussion that provides for anonymous contributions re: charged topics.*

—Associate professor, doctorate-granting university, Biology

This is a good time to start thinking about the different strategies you will use to make space for student voices. Are students expected to participate in classroom conversation? Will they be asked to engage with one another outside of scheduled class time? If the course takes place online, what forms for participation are included? For example, will the course use synchronous methods for engagement among peers or with the instructor, or will all discussion take place asynchronously through discussion boards or other media? It is also critical to communicate to students what you mean when you say "participation." Are you interested in the quality of student participation? The quantity? Does every student need to contribute to a larger class discussion, or does participation include things like engaging in think-pair-share activities—a collaborative learning strategy wherein students are given time to formulate their own thoughts on a topic or question before sharing those thoughts with a partner or small group. What about asking questions?

It is critical at the point of course and syllabus design to establish our own expectations for student participation. Can we define what we are looking for from students? For example, syllabi might include language to delineate different forms of meaningful participation, like responding to questions from the instructor, participating in small group discussions, or even asking relevant questions. If our course includes a grade for participation, can we articulate how it will be calculated? Will students be assessed based on the quantity of their participation? What about the quality, and how would quality be measured? How might disruptive or disrespectful participation factor into a participation metric? As inclusive instructors sketch out the substantive meaning of participation for their course by considering these questions, it is important to think about what types of students might be left out of a particular conception of participation. How can we create opportunities, and convey them to students, that will help all students find a way to contribute their voice? Making decisions about the answers to these questions and then communicating them to students in a syllabus is necessary for generating the conditions for full participation in the classroom.

Of course, making space for participation will be an ongoing task throughout the course, and the next chapters will offer more suggestions about how to accomplish that goal. But setting the stage for inclusive participation begins with the course design, and a syllabus can convey meaningful information to students.

Reflection Questions

- Does your syllabus currently use inclusive, warm language? How could you change the tone and language of your syllabus to reflect these goals?
- Does your syllabus clearly articulate both rights and responsibilities for instructors and students?
- Does your syllabus convey a clear explanation for participation in the classroom? Does it meaningfully convey to students that all voices are not only welcome but critical for the learning process?

They Give Students the Tools for Success

The final theme that emerges from inclusive instructors' descriptions of their own course design relates to student success. Does your syllabus give every student the tools they need to succeed? Designing an inclusive course means being mindful of how differences in academic preparation, background, and skill set will shape students' abilities to successfully navigate the material and assessments. An equitable course will try to anticipate these differences and plan accordingly.

One of the best ways to ensure that your course gives students from diverse backgrounds the opportunity to thrive is by incorporating in your course design and syllabus information for students that explains what, how, and why you are asking them to do certain things in certain ways. This approach is consistent with the principles of universal design described in chapter 1. Recall that the UDL suggests that instructors address three distinct "networks" for students. Recognition networks help students navigate the "what" of learning, strategic networks are necessary to convey the "how" of learning, and affective networks attempt to communicate to students the "why" of learning.

With respect to the "what" of learning, inclusive instructors and scholars of pedagogy note that it is important for courses to be designed to incorporate multiple learning modalities as well as clearly articulating expectations for student performance. To address the "how" question, instructors note the necessity of providing accessible information and resources to help students from disparate educational and cultural backgrounds navigate the course requirements. Finally, inclusive instructors detail the need to provide a rationale in the syllabus for the various requirements, resources, and responsibilities detailed therein to reflect the "why" of learning.

They Embrace Multiple Modalities of Learning

One of the most commonly cited practices among inclusive instructors for helping students succeed is to engage students in a variety of different learning modalities.

I make attempts to provide a range of learning materials—discussion, texts, film, writing experiences—to accommodate different learning modalities. . . . I also do class activities, show films, and conduct writing activities and small group discussions. I am working actively to develop other methods of instruction that provide opportunities for different types of learners as well as for people of different backgrounds to meet and share in a safe space.

—Assistant professor, master's college, Anthropology

I create assignments of various types (e.g., written, scholarly, reflective, oral, exams with multiple kinds of questions). I write assignments to address varied student experiences and language proficiencies (e.g., not dependent on knowledge of a particular movie, avoiding idiomatic language.

—Assistant professor, doctorate-granting university, Counseling

Students earn points in my classes in multiple categories (low and high stakes) including studying with an adaptive learning platform called Cerego (which my students love!). I have students work individually on some assignments and I have them work in groups for other assignments.

—Postdoctoral associate, doctorate-granting university, Biology

The notion of providing opportunities for students with different "learning styles" has become a common refrain in discussions of inclusive teaching across age groups. Popularized beginning in the 1970s and 1980s, studies have shown that upward of 90% of instructors from global educational settings subscribe to the idea that students differ in their ability to learn from varied modalities of instruction (see Papadatou-Pastou et al., 2018). But recent scholarship suggests that the idea of student learning style differences is a neuromyth (Dekker et al., 2012).

Despite the debunking of the learning styles approach, there are still several reasons to believe that incorporating different modalities of learning into a course's design can improve inclusivity and enhance successful course engagement. Most notably, for example, principles of universal design suggest that increasing the forms for engagement in the classroom benefits all student learners (Meyer et al., 2014). As will be discussed in greater depth in chapter 5, universal design recommends promoting learning strategies that account for student differences in pattern recognition, perception, and development (Rose & Strangman, 2007).

In practice, this can mean building a syllabus that incorporates different types of media and multiple methods of student engagement and assessment. Relatedly, as inclusive instructors detail in their own practice, scholars suggest that courses embrace multiple, low-stakes opportunities for the evaluation of student performance.

> *[I create a] learner-centered syllabus . . . frequent formative assessment[, and] many low-stakes assignments.*
>
> —Associate professor, master's college, Social Work

> *[I] provide frequent low-stakes assessments leading up to major assignments so that learners have an opportunity, in mentorship with the faculty and perhaps also peer feedback, to identify and develop key proficiencies they may have initially overlooked.*
>
> —Adjunct professor, doctorate-granting university, Education

> *I include a number of means of assessment beyond exams, because exam performance can be influenced by things other than if the student studied.*
>
> —Associate professor, baccalaureate college, Biology

Combining these two strategies is consistent with a growth mindset approach to student learning, and both are consistent with the notion that an equitable and inclusive course design offers learners multiple opportunities to engage, to be assessed, and ultimately to succeed in a particular course.

They Set Expectations for Success

Designing a course with multiple learning modalities is not, on its own, sufficient to offer equitable avenues for success. An inclusive syllabus, as our instructors describe, also needs to clearly communicate what students need to do to navigate those learning modalities. Scholars have demonstrated, for example, that students are looking for clearly presented course schedules, deadlines, and assignment descriptions when it comes to the syllabus (Marcis & Carr, 2003). Does your syllabus tell students what they need to do and by what date? One critical piece of this is to be mindful of the assumptions we make about what students already know. So, for example, if we ask students to read something, what are we as instructors assuming that entails? Do we want them to take notes? If so, should they bring those notes to class? Do we expect them to look for something specific in the readings? Will all of our students have the training to intuit what we want? Probably not. As the next instructor explains, an inclusive syllabus can clarify many of these aspects for students.

> *I have rewritten my syllabus to be more inclusive including . . . a section on how to get help, a section on what office hours mean and in general have demystified many aspects of the syllabus.*

> —Associate professor, doctorate-granting university, Biology

That is why, in addition to telling students what we want, we need to give them sufficient information about how to complete the assigned tasks. One method is to convey, either through the syllabus or through in-class discussion (and ideally both) what it means to "do the readings" or to "write an essay." A course designed to allow all students to succeed shouldn't assume that students will all understand how to go about completing the work of the course. It is our job to explain what that entails.

They Provide Resources for Success

Another key feature of explaining to students how to complete the assigned task is to make sure the syllabus provides them with resources they may need—information on how to do the work. This is a commonly cited practice among inclusive instructors.

> *Mak[e] expectations and resource availability explicit in the syllabus.*

> —Lecturer, doctorate-granting university, Biology

> *[I] create . . . policies that provide access to university resources, managing course costs, being transparent about practices, etc.*

> —Assistant professor, master's college, English

When it comes to resources, there are a number of options for inclusion on the syllabus. First, what resources does your campus have available to assist students with completing their assignments? Do you have a writing center or a tutoring program that students might use? Do you have a dedicated librarian or library guide for students in your course? Are there other academic resources on campus that might help students develop study skills, work plans, or other effective means of workflow management that might be critical to succeeding in your course? Does your institution have specific resources available to assist English-language learners? The syllabus is an excellent place not only to include information about these resources, but also to do so in language that normalizes their use. Convey to students that research demonstrates these resources are beneficial to everyone. For example, the syllabus might open a section on resources with the following language:

Are there any other resources that might help me in this course?

[Name of institution] has several resources designed to support your academic pursuits throughout your time at [institution], and I encourage you to take advantage of them. These aren't just resources for students who are "struggling"—studies conducted at several universities find that students who take advantage of academic support services like these perform better both in and out of the classroom. Following are a list of several resources, along with information about how to access them, that may help you succeed in this course.

Another critical resource to provide in line with equity goals is any information students need about securing accommodations. Not only can this help direct students—particularly those who may be new to your institution—to the necessary help to succeed in the course, but it also conveys to students that you are mindful of and open to discussions about accommodations.

Finally, are there other external tools that students might benefit from, for example access to citation style guides or tutorials for data analysis or software that you want to bring to their attention. The course syllabus is an excellent place to highlight what these resources are and how students might access them.

They Provide a Rationale for Success

Once we have provided students with information on what they need to do to succeed in the course and how they might carry out those tasks, it is important to explain to students why you are asking them to do these things. This final strategy is perhaps easiest to overlook, but it can be the most important for inclusive instructors.

I advocate for transparency, in assignment design, in course policies, and even in my choices of in-class activities. I want students to know why we're doing what we're doing.

—Instructional staff, doctorate-granting university, Faculty Development

I go over what a growth mindset is and encourage students to have a growth mindset and to keep working hard. My expectations and policies are clearly stated in the syllabus, and each day at the beginning of class.

—Assistant professor, associate college, Biology

Do . . . your best to recognize how each and every student is experiencing your class. Be . . . aware of many perspectives/positions that students are coming from.

—Lecturer, doctorate-granting university, Engineering

Providing students with a rationale for everything from assignment design to deadline decisions to seemingly routine policies like office hours can be a critical tool for leveling the academic playing field and creating an equitable classroom. First, explaining to students why we have set particular expectations gives them better insight into what they are really supposed to be accomplishing. It illuminates for students how their instructors are thinking about and evaluating different aspects of the course. Second, providing a rationale for course policies and resources gives students information about how and when to make use of those. It can allow students to better advocate for their own needs if they understand where the instructor is coming from. These are both essential outcomes for students who may be coming into the classroom without the benefit of social networks or previous educational experiences that illuminate the "hidden curriculum" that is often necessary to succeed in higher education (Sambell & McDowell, 1998).

From Principles to Practice

So, what does all of this look like in practice? One of the critical tradeoffs instructors must consider when balancing the need to provide clear articulations of their expectations and rationales with the needs of student learners has to do with syllabus length and complexity. On the one hand, studies suggest that more structured approaches tend to help all student learners. As Sathy and Hogan (2019) explain in a recent articulation of inclusive syllabi for the *Chronicle of Higher Education,* "In our experience, all students appreciate and thrive from additional structure, and some benefit disproportionately" (para. 15). This is consistent with a significant body of research suggesting that "more is better" when it comes to syllabus design (e.g., Davis, 1993; Habanek, 2005). Indeed, scholars have found that students feel more secure when syllabi offer clear and explicit guidance for a given course (McKeachie, 2002).

On the other hand, culturally responsive approaches to teaching suggest that oppressive structures in education can harm inclusive pedagogy (Gay, 2010). And a growing body of research—particularly andragogically-driven approaches to adult learning, suggest that pared-down syllabi may be preferable for the needs of today's students (Dean & Fornaciari, 2014b). The desire for shorter syllabi may increase as students rely on mobile devices with data and formatting limits to access their course material (Dean & Fornaciari, 2014b).

So how can we strike a balance between the demand for clear, detailed information and the problems that lengthy syllabi may create for today's student learners? One option is to provide the most critical information to students in smaller, more digestible forms. So, for example, while the syllabus might preview an assignment, a separate document can be created to detail each assignment and its rationale. Instructors might also use creative formatting to highlight the major provisions of a syllabus, or they might provide a quick reference guide in addition to the more detailed descriptions. Finally, a Web-based approach to syllabi might allow instructors to make use of links to lead students to the more detailed descriptions and rationales for the course while allowing them to interface with a shorter main document. Of course, this final strategy may depend on whether the student population consists predominantly of students who are comfortable with digital technology and have access to the necessary technology to rely on a Web-based course syllabus.

There are a number of elements that can be included in a syllabus to help promote student success along the dimensions discussed. While a simple Google search, or a visit to your institution's center for teaching and learning, can provide instructors with a number of checklists from which to draw ideas about what information ought to be included in a course syllabus, following is a list of some common—and frequently university-mandated—items for inclusion:

- contact information and pronouns for instructor
- course title, time, and meeting location
- time, location, and description of office hours
- course goals and learning objectives
- information about course readings, including schedule, location of materials, and description of when and how material should be read
- information about course assignments and assessment, including schedule, procedures for submitting late work, information about grade appeals, and description of grading policy and turnaround time
- explanation of instructional methods and tools
- attendance and participation policies, including description of inclusive participation and methods of participation
- technology use policies
- course and university resources and accommodation procedures
- class schedule

Accessibility for Successful Inclusive Pedagogy

Whatever the approach, being attentive to issues of access is critical. Inclusive instructors frequently cite the need to create accessible documents and policies—and that begins at the stage of syllabus design.

> *I have a clear teaching philosophy and approach to inclusion and accessibility stated in my syllabus and I make myself available after class and during office hours with the explicit invitation of feedback about the learning environment and issues of access and accommodation.*

—Assistant professor, master's college, Anthropology

> *[I am] careful with language. [I don't use a] no-tech policy that would affect some students' ability to take good notes. [I include a] statement in the syllabus that we do our best to make everything accessible, but to please talk to us if they need something (and attempts to make ourselves super easy to talk to).*

—Lecturer, doctorate-granting university, Engineering

> *I make accommodations to the best of my ability. I have information on mental health support and food insecurity in my syllabus. I do not require doctor's notes for class absences, because not every [student] can go to a medical professional.*

—Associate professor, baccalaureate college, Biology

Accessibility takes many forms, but some are more relevant at the course design stage. First, as the comments convey, the syllabus itself (along with other course artifacts) should be accessible to all learners. There are a growing number of both domestic and international standards that address accessibility in education. Chief among them is the recognition that documents, like a syllabus or course readings, must be navigable for all students in a timely manner. That means that documents must accommodate students who use a screen reader, and visual or audio material should include closed captioning, transcripts, and descriptions of images. Institutions increasingly have personnel and resources available to help instructors make their course materials accessible.

Inclusive instructors also describe how the substance of course policies can present obstacles for accessibility. For example, policies that limit technology use may hinder some students more than others, or they may single out those students who are allowed technology-based accommodations. Attendance policies, and the process of securing exemptions from them, may also place disparate burdens on students with certain types of mental or physical health conditions or students who observe religious holidays. It is also important to consider how the timing of assessments aligns with major holidays from across different faiths.

Finally, an accessible course also needs to take into account resource disparities among students. One type of resource disparity to consider is financial. While financial aid may help students from a range of socioeconomic backgrounds afford tuition and room and board, those funds rarely cover the cost of course materials. As a result, it is important for inclusive instructors to consider whether the cost of course materials may disadvantage certain students. Designing a course that relies as much as possible on open educational resources (OERs) is an important step in resolving this issue of accessibility. The use of OERs is increasingly common with the growth of open-access textbooks and educational content with a creative commons license. University libraries are an excellent resource for instructors to get assistance in pursuing OERs for their courses.

As the descriptions from inclusive instructors suggest, resource disparities can also take shape in unequal knowledge about the norms of higher education. As such, describing and explaining the rationale behind policies and procedures, for example, by providing students with a clear description of the purpose of office hours, is a key piece of an accessible syllabus. Take a moment to consider the following questions about the tools your own syllabi employ to help every student in your class have an equitable chance for success.

Reflection Questions

- Does your course currently employ multiple learning modalities and forms of assessment? How could you diversify your current approaches?
- Does your syllabus clearly articulate what students are expected to complete and when?
- Do you offer students access to resources and rationales that will help students from disparate educational backgrounds successfully navigate course requirements?
- What concerns do you have about making your course accessible? What resources does your institution offer to help address those issues?

Navigating Challenges to Inclusive Syllabus Design

The previous sections provide a road map for some of the important considerations inclusive instructors weigh when designing their courses and syllabi. They highlight many of the practices that inclusive instructors use to lay the foundation for courses that facilitate equity and belonging among an increasingly diverse student body. But there are a number of obstacles that can stand in the way of realizing these practices.

Many of these strategies are predicated on being able to anticipate the characteristics and needs of our students. The previous chapters echo the importance of getting to know who is in our classroom, and the following chapter will discuss in more detail some strategies for gathering that information at the beginning of the semester. But many of us may need to build our courses before we have access to information about our students. This can be especially challenging for new instructors, who may not be able to fall back on experience with the larger student body of an institution as a proxy for the specific students in their classroom.

One solution for this challenge is to communicate with other faculty and university staff about the characteristics of the students you are likely to encounter. Another solution is to create the basics of a syllabus that would account for the diversity of student learners along a number of dimensions but wait to finalize your syllabus until you have had time to survey your own students. This could be achieved by providing a basic overview of the course and material for the first week, while holding off the complete syllabus until the second week of the course.

Another challenge we may face in creating inclusive syllabi stems from our own position. As chapter 1 discussed, a significant impediment to inclusive teaching may be that we do not recognize our own blind spots when it comes to understanding diversity and the needs of diverse students. As the famed political journalist Molly Ivins once said, "How you see the world depends on where you stand and who you are, there's nothing any of us can do about that" (Egan et al., 2019). So, how do we overcome the biases we have in order to try and see the world from the perspective of students who may not see the world from where we stand? There are a number of useful self-assessment tools available online for instructors to try and navigate their own biases.

Even after we clear these very real hurdles, additional obstacles may challenge our ability to design inclusive courses. This chapter has already discussed how the state of the literature in your own field may limit your ability to create an inclusive reading list, as well as offering available resources to help overcome that challenge. But there are other institutional hurdles that may be harder to leap. For example, at the university level, you may be required to include certain policies and sections in a syllabus, even if they do not conform to some of the strategies inclusive teachers rely on. Your institution may also not be able to provide you with the resources, in the form of time, training, or material, to help facilitate your ability to design inclusive courses. At the level of the department, you may teach a course that uses a common syllabus, with few avenues to build the inclusive course you would like to design. Each of these represents real institutional obstacles. The epilogue will provide more strategies to navigate these challenges, discussing how a campus can work to build a culture of inclusive teaching.

Take a moment to think about which of these challenges most affect your ability to design inclusive courses and what you would need to be successful in doing so.

Reflection Questions

- What do you think some of your own biases might be when it comes to course design?
- What resources would you need to more successfully implement inclusive design principles at the course design stage? Does your institution have access to those resources? If not, where else could you find them?
- What other challenges do you face when it comes to implementing the strategies discussed in this chapter?

The Life Cycle of Inclusive Course Design

Consistent with a growth mindset approach to our teaching, the process of creating inclusive syllabi is ongoing. As inclusive instructors describe, we have the opportunity to assess, evaluate, and revise our efforts.

I continue to grow and refine courses because every group of students is unique, and I am growing too.

—Full professor, baccalaureate college, Biology

[I] review and revise the syllabus, especially course readings and videos, with the perspective of diversity in mind—are there voices that could be added and/or swapped in that would increase the representation and perspectives on the topic?

—Adjunct professor, doctorate-granting university, Education

[I create a] learner-centered syllabus; students cocreate classroom guidelines.

—Associate professor, master's college, Social Work

This can happen at several points in the lifecycle of a course. Most obviously, the creation of a new course offers a chance to build an inclusive approach from the foundation. The strategies described in this chapter should be particularly helpful when considering the design of a new course. But what about courses that are already in progress? Or courses that we have taught many times before?

Once class begins, offering opportunities for student feedback, for example through the use of midsemester evaluations, can allow us to adjust midstream. Chapter 5 will discuss strategies like these in more detail, but even here it is possible to use the syllabus as a device to foreground midcourse correction. The syllabus is an ideal place to alert students to the opportunity to provide their feedback at a predetermined point during the semester. Not only does this hold instructors accountable, but it is also another way to demonstrate to students from the outset that their voice is important in shaping the direction of the course. It is further appropriate to lay out guidelines in the syllabus that explain how you will go about making changes to a course should the need arise. Once again, in order to foster a sense of participation, you might agree not to change major deadlines, assignments, or concepts without input from students. Each of these methods provides another opportunity for the syllabus to create a foundation for inclusive pedagogy.

Finally, we have opportunities to improve our inclusive practices by revising courses at the end of the semester or the beginning of the next. In either case, student feedback can play an important role in reimagining our approaches. Perhaps one of the most common ways we might incorporate student feedback at the end of a course is by consulting course evaluations. For all of the problems associated with using student evaluations of teaching as a metric in tenure and promotion decisions, they may still provide useful evidence for instructors who wish to improve their efforts to generate equity and belonging in the classroom (or to measure whether current efforts are registering with students). It is never too late to consider how inclusivity can be structured in our course design. And once the course is in motion, there are many additional opportunities to build inclusive classrooms, as the following chapters will elaborate. Chapter 4 describes how inclusive instructors foster a welcoming environment where students feel a sense of belonging, and chapter 5 identifies specific approaches that inclusive instructors utilize during the act of teaching the course.

Key Points

- As both an early form of communication and a foundation for the course, the syllabus is one the first ways that an inclusive instructor begins to foster student belonging and equitable practices in a course.
- Inclusive course syllabi integrate diverse perspectives and course material that resonates with learners.

Inclusive instructors design courses that encourage everyone to play a role in the learning process. This includes setting the tone for the course and providing clear expectations and guidelines for inclusive participation in the classroom.

An inclusive course gives every student the tools they need to succeed. The syllabus communicates this by providing multiple modalities for learning, clear expectations, and a rationale for pedagogical choices.

Inclusive course syllabi ensure that courses are accessible to diverse learners.

The process of building an inclusive course is never complete. Inclusive instructors are always improving their course design and obtaining feedback from students to inform their efforts.

HOW DO THEY MAKE STUDENTS FEEL WELCOME?

From the very first meeting, I encourage students to think of our class as a collaborative community whose members respect one another and all contribute to the success of the course. Initially, students fill out a brief survey about their academic background as well as shar[e] a television show, sports team, hobby, podcast, or music in which they are currently interested. It asks students what name they would like to be called and which pronouns they prefer. Each student also poses one question about an artwork on the screen. This gives students the agency to decide if and what they would like to share with me and their classmates. Then students exchange surveys with the person next to them and introduce one another. The surveys circulate again and students pose another classmate's question. This activity gives each student an opportunity to make a quick connection with two others. It also sets up an environment in which students pose questions and join a collaborative discussion—two key aspects of future sessions.

—Assistant professor, doctorate-granting university, Art History

As mentioned in chapter 1, fostering a sense of social belonging in the classroom makes all students feel welcomed and supported, leading to increased motivation, improved academic performance, and a better overall learning experience. Based on our national survey data (Appendix A), we have identified key questions that inclusive instructors ask themselves to build a positive classroom environment. Similar to chapter 3, this chapter provides concrete strategies, advice, and examples that reinforce each key question. The recommended practices presented are by no means exhaustive, but rather representative of effective strategies used by inclusive instructors across experience levels, institution types, and disciplines. These key questions also hold true in face-to-face, online, and hybrid courses. Course level is an important caveat to be considered depending on your particular teaching context. An effective welcoming strategy in an introductory undergraduate course may not be ideal for a graduate seminar. Nonetheless, the key questions asked and advice given are generalizable across course types, environments, and levels. The first set of questions address unifying themes that use classroom hospitality to promote student differences, equitable practices, and positive relationships; the next group of questions carefully consider the impact timing weighs on your welcoming efforts; and the final questions help restore balance when classroom harmony is violated or disrupted. These questions will help you welcome students to the classroom, see them as they see themselves, encourage them to share their knowledge and perspectives, and allow them to flourish, not in spite of but because of their differences. We hope you are equally excited to add "welcoming instructor" to your inclusive teaching repertoire.

Reflection Questions

- What welcoming strategies have you used to build a positive classroom environment? Did they promote social belonging and equitable practices? Why or why not?

They Intentionally Create a Welcoming Classroom

An essential feature of establishing a welcoming classroom is the instructor's intentionality around creating environments where various student differences are openly acknowledged and accepted. Inclusive instructors design learning spaces to encourage and facilitate equitable participation by individuals and between students, as exercised through multiple methods of discourse. Based partially on their own knowledge bases, students should be given a space to feel empowered to share their lived experiences, personal narratives, and feelings about rules of classroom conduct that would best help them thrive. The positive relationships built from these interactions will enrich not only the classroom experience, but also inevitably translate outside of the formal classroom space. Inclusive instructors intentionally form welcoming learning communities to increase the chances for students to excel in a classroom environment that is both safe enough for them to assume their particular identities as much as possible while also being rigorous enough to challenge their comfort levels.

They Respectfully Acknowledge and Accept Student Differences

Learn and use student names (and correct pronunciation) and
. . . pronouns in [the] classroom community.

—Full professor, associate college, Biology

When we introduce ourselves at the beginning of the semester, I emphasize that students should tell me what name they go by if they do not go by the name listed on the roster.

—Associate professor, master's college, History

Learn Names, Correctly Pronounce Names, and Ask Preferred Names and Pronouns

Inclusive instructors know there are several reasons learning student names is important. Expertise from various fields, including education psychology (Murdoch et al., 2018), sociology (Smith & Malec, 1995), (Townes O'Brien et al., 2014), and biology (Cooper et al., 2017) note the impact of calling individuals by their names. It allows for better human connection and fosters more trust, empathy, and positive communication. With the power differential in higher education classrooms typically shifted toward the instructor having more power, learning and correctly pronouncing names can make students feel like valued members of the classroom community. For example, when inclusive instructors receive a new class roster they may ask for their students to confirm the pronunciation of any names that are unfamiliar and then write the phonetic spelling of the name. It is common practice for international students to adopt an English or "American" moniker. Many of these students feel it will be easier for native-English speakers to pronounce their names as they move about life in the United States. This centers the conversation on the English-speaking instructor and students and can isolate the international student. Inclusive instructors emphasize to international students that they have the right to be addressed by their preferred name and ensure everyone in the class respects this choice. If class size restricts learning every student's name, asking an individual student to share their name before reporting out can give you the chance to use their name during the particular class session (Penner, 2018). Preferred names are also critical for welcoming transgender and nonbinary students into the classroom. Recently, pronouns have garnered a lot of attention.

Several colleges and universities now have chosen name and pronoun policies that directly align with state laws, such as the New York Gender Expression Non-Discrimination Act (GENDA). Inclusive instructors can include pronouns in their email signature so that they are visible when emailing students and list them prominently on the syllabus. Students can share and do the same. To further promote the use of pronouns, many inclusive instructors undergo Safe Zone training and display their certifications in classroom or office spaces. The Safe Zone curriculum provides resources for instructors to further learn proper terminology and how to welcome LGBTQ+ students. It is important for instructors to communicate with students that although the change is honored and welcomed in the classroom, official records outside of the classroom or campus community have not been changed.

I allow students to self-identify and I self-identify at the beginning of class.

—Associate professor, master's college, Rhetoric and Composition

I ask students to complete an access needs form to inform me (and, if they choose, other students in the class) about any differences/disabilities they want to share, what supports their engagement, and how those differences can be resources to others in the course. This not only affirms student diversity and commits to respecting their differences, it also endeavors to shift the frame from difference/disability as deficit to difference/disability as resource.

—Full professor, baccalaureate college, Education

After having students complete an identity activity that fits with our curriculum, I meet with students who self-identified as a student of color, a LGBTQIA student, and sometimes other underrepresented groups depending on the context of the classroom.

—Associate professor, master's college, Education

Avoid more than just Christian religious holidays when scheduling tests.

—Academic administrator, doctorate-granting university, Anthropology

Allow Students to Self-Identify Visible and Invisible Identities

Identities are qualities, beliefs, appearances, or any other attributes that make an individual student unique. From a psychological standpoint, personal identity reflects how a student sees themself. Sociological approaches show how social identities, or the group memberships to which a student belongs, influences their learning experience (Steele & Cohn-Vargas, 2013). Inclusive instructors strive to create identity safe classrooms. Identity safe classrooms ensure students that their personal or social identities are an asset rather than a barrier to success (Steele & Cohn-Vargas, 2013). Students can choose to disclose their personal identities on an online form, in a class discussion or activity, or through an individual meeting with the instructor. Inclusive instructors are keenly aware that the most important aspects of a student's personal identity may not align with what is presumed to be their primary social identity. That is, students may not emphasize the same attributes that society has ascribed to them as important characteristics of their identities (for instance biracial or multiracial students may not identify with what others may perceive as their dominant appearance). Furthermore, some identities are readily visible while others are invisible. For example, a student whose social identity is female may self-identify more strongly as a first-generation student, eldest child, or extrovert.

Identity centrality describes the extent to which an aspect of one's identity is important to one's self-image or definition of self (Bowman & Felix, 2017). It can be measured by how central one's membership is in a particular visible (e.g., race or disability) or invisible (e.g., religion or sexuality) social identity group. The strong positive relationships that result from establishing identity safe classrooms can help students view themselves as scholars as well as their peers. Student identity centrality has been looked at in relation to success in higher education classrooms. In fact, high student identity centrality was positively related to goal commitment and higher academic persistence (Bowman & Felix, 2017). For all these reasons, allowing students to self-identify in the classroom celebrates and affirms their differences and fosters better opportunities to welcome, support, and value each student as members of the classroom community, which leads to better learning outcomes.

Design . . . the courses with every student in mind, make the best use of different educational backgrounds and experiences of the students, and most of all create a learning environment where everyone is respected and allowed to be productive to the fullest potential. That is, provid[e] students with the tools and information they need to succeed.

—Adjunct professor, associate college, Biology

[I] make sure I am truly seeing every student.

—Dean and full professor, baccalaureate college, English

Recogniz[e] and affirm . . . different life situations that may affect a student's ability to attend class, turn in assignments on time, and attend office hours.

—Survey respondent; rank, institution type, discipline not identified

I work with students who are homeless, hungry, and some who work 40–60 hours a week; I try to connect students to services and am not a jerk about late work. [I] also promote student wellness (mindfulness) practices in class.

—Full professor, master's college or university, History

Support the Whole Student Intellectually, Personally, and Socially

Students are not blank slates. They bring to the classroom their identities and lived experiences, which shape how comfortable they are and ultimately how they learn. Inclusive instructors respectfully acknowledge students as individuals and use whole student approaches to support their intellectual, personal, and social development. Whole student approaches address the emotional and social needs of students and subsequently augment the educational experience and classroom environment as is reasonably appropriate. This philosophy centers the student and recognizes academic achievement is dependent on all of the three developmental factors.

Previous academic encounters influence students' confidence and competence, which includes both formal and informal education. Inclusive instructors understand not every student has the same academic preparation outside the course prerequisites, and they take great lengths not to compare students based on prior knowledge. Instead, they help students identify strengths, challenges, and tools for success.

Personal life circumstances can bring feelings of embarrassment or shame, which can also hinder academic progress. Inclusive instructors actively work to make their classroom a safe space where students can share without judgment or pity if their basic human needs aren't being met. Savvy instructors will proactively provide access to on-campus and off-campus resources and referrals, in addition to academic resources, on syllabi and course websites. For example, students may be experiencing housing or food insecurity. A survey of approximately 86,000 students at 123 associate- and baccalaureate-granting institutions found that more than 60% of students experienced food insecurity within the past month of the study or housing insecurity/homelessness within the past 12 months of the study (Goldrick-Rab et al., 2019). These findings were more pronounced within certain student demographics, particularly students at 2-year institutions, those who identify as African American, LGBTQ+, former foster youth, independent students, students with prior criminal convictions, and veteran status (Goldrick-Rab et al., 2019). Whole student approaches require not only trust on the student's end, but also on behalf of the instructor. Inclusive instructors accept that several personal reasons may result in a student missing class and that there are no reason hierarchies. For example, a common requirement for many instructors is a note from a healthcare provider if a class is missed due to illness. A whole student approach would take into account the student may not have health insurance and be unable to provide such a note.

Social development can dramatically impact students' social belonging in classroom spaces. Inclusive instructors adopting a whole student approach recognize students reach developmental milestones at different stages depending on their social development. For example, student may experience anxiety attacks before oral presentations. Inclusive instructors might consider that the student's previous life experiences can trigger the anxiety attacks and consequently impact their academic performance. The instructor therefore consults with the student, the counseling center and the office of accessibility services to devise an equitable assessment plan that enables the student to complete their presentation. Inclusive instructors recognize flexibility can minimize student embarrassment, result in learning objectives being met, as well as address their developmental needs. The whole student approach creates student-centered and caring communities, which promotes social belonging, a sense of well-being, deeper learning, and academic success.

Understanding Various Student Differences

Inclusive instructors also recognize the importance of welcoming all of their diverse learners. Utilizing social identity research, inclusive instructors will try to better understand social factors that can promote warmth and inclusivity for a particular social group in the classroom. An example may be a veteran student. Across the country veterans in college perceive lower levels of campus support and interact less with faculty than nonveterans (National Survey of Student Engagement [NSSE], 2010). Many veterans describe their experience transitioning to college as a culture shock. According to the American Council on Education's (2018) "Toolkit for Veteran Friendly Institutions," ways that faculty can engage with this student population include identifying student veterans, encouraging them to speak about their unique experiences in class and how it relates to course content, and developing veteran-specific courses. It is also important to ask students who self-identify what they feel would be productive and invite them to participate fully in the classroom.

Reflection Questions

- How can you respectfully acknowledge and appreciate student differences in your classroom? How do you know the students feel accepted?

They Recognize Equitable Participation by Individual Students and Groups, and the Entire Class Promotes a Welcoming Classroom

Individuals

I tell the students I do not know everything and their knowledge and experience is vital to the success of the course.

—Associate professor, baccalaureate college, Biology

[I] assum[e] my students have a great deal of knowledge that I do not.

—Assistant professor, master's college, Criminal Justice

> *[I] mention . . . . that students come to class with a wealth of knowledge already and we are building on that scaffold, that they should feel comfortable taking guesses and making risks in discussion.*
>
> —Lecturer, doctorate-granting university, Biology

> *Do not ask or expect students to represent an entire group, either by look or by request.*
>
> —Academic administrator, doctorate-granting university, Anthropology

Groups

> *Assign student teams purposefully so [that] the groups are diverse but no student from an underrepresented group is isolated in a group (e.g., I try to avoid putting one Black student with three White students).*
>
> —Teaching professor, doctorate-granting university, Biology

Entire class

> *Set ground rules for class discussion.*
>
> —Assistant professor, doctorate-granting university, Linguistics and Languages

> *Make diversity and the free exchange of ideas an early discussion topic.*
>
> —Academic administrator, doctorate-granting university, Anthropology

> *Establish . . . classroom culture that promotes civil discourse.*
>
> —Associate professor, doctorate-granting university, Biology

> *[C]reate culture where it's okay to go out on a limb and be wrong.*
>
> —Full professor, baccalaureate college, Biology

> *I cocreate with students guidelines for engagement in every course, so we are intentional about cocreating a learning environment that is supportive of the particular diversity of students in that course.*
>
> —Full professor, baccalaureate college, Education

> *Students cocreate classroom guidelines.*
>
> —Associate professor, master's college, Social work

Equitable Participation by Individuals, Groups, and the Entire Class

Providing a learning environment that celebrates student differences maximizes fairness and encourages equitable participation, which helps them feel more welcomed in the classroom community. Inclusive instructors encourage equitable participation in their classrooms by acknowledging their limitations, valuing student's prior knowledge, and not singling out individuals to represent a group. When instructors openly share they do not know everything, it welcomes students to freely contribute. Inclusive instructors recognize new learning is constructed on prior student knowledge and the importance of engaging it to scaffold novel concepts and content. Prior knowledge influences individual student thinking, understanding, and problem-solving and is reflective of personal identity and not of a social identity. Verbal or nonverbal expectations for an individual student to speak for an entire group will lead to isolation and discourage participation. When encouraging participation from everyone in a small group, inclusive instructors pay special attention to ensuring that students from underrepresented groups do not to feel isolated or outnumbered. Recent work has shown group composition has a substantial impact on major persistence and group participation. When self-identified women were in female majority groups, they engaged in more verbal participation than gender parity or male majority groups (Dasgupta et al., 2015). Digital tools such as CATME can be used by instructors teaching face-to-face, online, and hybrid courses to assemble effective teams, as well as assess the degree of individual or group participation (Layton et al., 2010). Regarding the entire class, inclusive instructors set ground rules for discussions, but they also welcome student collaboration to cocreate new guidelines. The collective guidelines can be displayed to encourage discussion participation by all students, but also to serve as a reminder that student input is welcomed in the shared learning community.

Reflection Question

- What equitable participation practices are you using or can you use in a future course to make students feel more welcome in your classroom?

They Build Positive Relationships Inside and Outside the Classroom Through Faculty–Student and Student–Student Interactions

Faculty–student interactions

I also OPENLY share with [students] my multiethnic background, places I have lived, languages I speak, known genetic profile/predisposition to different diseases in my family, how my cultural upbringing influenced perceptions of different careers and life "styles," and so on. It's been very important to "introduce" myself openly to them and make it a safe environment by example.

—Full professor, doctorate-granting university, Biology

[I] mak[e] personal connections with students, explaining to them my background that is not what they might think, share that my first two test grades in college were F's, [and] share that I have ADD and dyslexia.

—Full professor, baccalaureate college, Biology

[I] giv[e] students multiple options for connecting with me outside of class.

—Associate professor, doctorate-granting university, Biology

Go see students compete, perform, and so on in their activities.

—Full professor, baccalaureate college, Biology

I also think it is important to be honest and truthful, because students can see false pretenses a mile away. Performing as an ally is very different than actually being an ally.

—Associate professor, master's college, History

Constantly remind students that some students are faster and some take more time, but the only thing that matters is the understanding.

—Assistant professor, tribal college, Mathematics

Set high standards and communicate your confidence that each student is capable of achieving them. Let your students know that you believe each has important contributions to make.

—Academic administrator, doctorate-granting university, Anthropology

Student–student interactions

[Have] interventions to increase student motivation (utility value and belonging) [and] promot[e] . . . group work to increase belonging to the class.

—Associate professor, master's college, Biology

I advocate for creating a positive social environment, interacting individually with students and encouraging them to interact with each other.

—Instructional consultant, doctorate-granting university, Faculty Development

In first year courses . . . I bring a diverse group of upper-division students to talk about their own challenges in school and how they succeeded in the hopes I can give a new student a role model.

—Senior lecturer, master's college, Engineering and Technology

Building Positive Relationships Both Inside and Outside the Classroom

One of the most prominent principles inclusive instructors demonstrate is a commitment to building positive relationships with students and facilitating positive relationships among student peers. As mentioned in chapter 2, inclusive instructors are not afraid to share their background and model the ways in which they would like to connect with students. Part of the sharing includes being open and vulnerable about challenges, particularly the notion of falling forward, as opposed to falling backward, to achieve success. Inclusive instructors share the positive benefits from negative experiences and help students build the capacity to use the technique when reflecting on their own backgrounds. Supporting students through individual interactions outside of the classroom can further support positive interactions. This may include office hours, review sessions, or attending student performances or athletic events. Inclusive instructors recognize the paramount importance of being a warm and caring ally. Having a strong sense of self identity, familiarity with power and privilege in higher education landscapes, and a willingness to advocate for institutional policies, processes, and procedures that both recruit and retain marginalized students, including BIPOC, will influence how efficacious your allyship efforts will be. It is important to be genuine and authentic and recognize that fighting systemic "-isms" can be uncomfortable but will maximize the benefits of faculty–student relationships. Student–student collaborations provide opportunities for students to encourage one another. This can be through peer, as well as near-peer, interactions. Collectively, both types of positive relationships help to create a welcoming classroom learning environment.

Reflection Questions

- How have you worked to build positive relationships with your students both inside and outside the classroom? Have these actions made your students feel more welcome?

They Can Create a Welcoming Classroom Environment at Any Time

Inclusive instructors who teach face-to-face, online, or hybrid courses recognize timing can be a valuable tool. They use evidence-based principles and strategies to make students feel welcome before the course starts, from the first day of class, within the first week, at any time throughout the course— even on the last day of class. In essence, they recognize it's never too early or late to make students feel welcome. Inclusive instructors set the tone by supplying students with a welcome address that allows them to begin familiarizing themselves with the instructor. This has the potential to quell any concerns about who the instructor is and begins the process of acclimating the students to the instructor's teaching style and approach. Inclusive instructors know their engagement with the class prior to the start of the term allows them to model community behavioral norms for everyone in the learning space and starts to build a positive relationship. The same strategies utilized at the beginning of a course can always be revisited to maintain the welcoming atmosphere throughout the term. Finally, students who feel welcomed at the conclusion of a term are confident in their competence as scholars in the greater community of practice and are more likely to walk into your classroom or office again in the future.

Reflection Question

- What can you do at the beginning, middle, or end of a course to make students feel welcome?

Before the Course Starts, They Set a Positive and Welcoming Tone

My examples all refer to online teaching: Provide a welcome statement with a positive tone, provide many resources for students who may have technical difficulties, welcome alternate views in the online discussions, [and set] course ground rules for discussions ([a] safe environment).

—Adjunct professor, doctorate-granting university, Psychology

[Create a] welcoming statement related to diversity in syllabus.

—Associate professor, doctorate-granting university, Biology

I introduce my courses with personal statements of why I think the focus is important to me and try [to] convey that enthusiasm to my students.

—Lecturer, doctorate-granting university, Women and Gender Studies

Preterm Welcome Statements and Videos

First impressions of a course and instructor can have a long-term effect on students. Inclusive instructors exhibit small behaviors early on that will leave a large welcome footprint on the classroom environment. They understand that making students feel welcome starts prior to them stepping foot into the classroom or the first log-in to the online learning environment. A welcome statement or video can be emailing to students' institutional accounts. A learning management system (LMS) site, such as Blackboard Learn, Moodle, or Canvas, can also be used to post a welcome statement or video. It should be taken into consideration that some students may have technical challenges accessing the LMS site before the course starts but usually have the technical skills to access their institutional email accounts with less difficulty. A welcome statement or video is a preview to the level of interaction and involvement expected for the duration of the course. It is important to note that a welcome statement is not synonymous with a diversity statement, although a diversity statement can have welcoming elements. A welcome statement is typically no more than one page in length. It can be used to effectively introduce yourself, your personal motivations and passion for teaching the course, the rationale for how and why you designed the course, your teaching style and approach, your commitment to student success, and any other information that would make students feel welcomed to the class.

A welcome statement or video clearly relays instructor enthusiasm. Instructor enthusiasm is widely viewed as a desirable attribute and defining quality of an effective inclusive teacher. It predicts student behavioral, cognitive, and emotional engagement; intrinsic goal orientation; and academic self-efficacy (Zhang, 2013). Specifically, a welcome video can display key nonverbal indicators of teacher enthusiasm, such as uplifting vocal delivery, shining eyes, frequent demonstrative gestures, large body movements, vibrant facial expressions, varied word selection, animated acceptance of ideas and feelings, and exuberant overall energy (Collins, 1978). Inclusive instructors transfer their enthusiasm to their students, which translates to positive behaviors and a welcoming classroom environment. A welcome statement can also be a way to invite students to collaborate on the syllabus or to take a syllabus quiz. Examples of a welcome statement and syllabus quiz questions for your modification and use have been provided in Appendices C and D.

Providing students with access to your inclusive syllabus (as discussed in chapter 3) before the course starts can serve as another greeting and can familiarize them with your learning community norms and expectations (Penner, 2018). Inclusive instructors request and incorporate inclusive instructors request and incorporate student choice before the first day of class. This deliberate precourse strategy to collaboratively design the syllabus allows feedback from students and demonstrates an instructor's willingness to share power in the classroom (Gilbert et al., 2013). This results in students feeling more comfortable interacting with the instructor and that their thoughts, interests, and suggestions are welcomed. It establishes a culture of feedback, which is further discussed in chapter 5. Additionally, a syllabus quiz is a useful low-stakes assessment that can be completed by students on their own before class begins to highlight elements that reinforce classroom cultural capital, social belonging, and inclusive course design (as discussed in chapter 5) (Chen, 2015; Raymark & Connor-Greene, 2002).

Before a course starts, inclusive instructors recognize that underrepresented students may be contemplating if they will fit in with their peers and what challenges must be overcome to succeed in the undergraduate or graduate classroom, including stereotype threat, as introduced in chapter 2. Stereotype threat is when students feel a perceived risk of confirming negative stereotypes about their social group. It stems from the cognitive imbalance that happens when a student's positive sense of self is inconsistent with the expectation that their social group should fail in a given task in an academic discipline (Rydell & Boucher, 2010). This can lead to poor academic performance in the threatened group, discouragement, and a lessened sense of belonging. As mentioned previously, several evidence-based approaches have been used to mitigate its impacts and effects. For example, self-affirmation can dramatically reduce the effects of stereotype threat and the achievement gap between African American and White students (Cohen et al., 2006). In addition to improved grades and GPAs, self-affirmation interventions bolster a greater sense of belonging (Sherman & Cohen, 2006).

Inclusive instructors who use prewelcoming strategies, like a welcome statement, can help underrepresented students self-affirm by valuing their existing knowledge and lived experiences, minimizing the perception that current success is solely dependent on prior academic preparation, access, or exposure (to which the underrepresented student may have been limited) and providing precourse resources to remedy knowledge gaps that would promote current course success. It gives the instructor a chance to relate to how the student is feeling and help them understand that their feelings as a new student are quite common. It also allows these students to begin self-affirming by capitalizing on multiple social identities, where a positive stereotype and social identity (e.g., college or graduate student and good academic performance) can help mitigate the impact of a negative stereotype (underrepresented student and poor academic performance) (Rydell & Boucher, 2010). Cultural capital is essential knowledge that students need to be successful and is an important variable of inequality in higher education classrooms (Noble & Davies, 2009). Inclusive instructors recognize cultural capital can explain variation in classroom participation by underrepresented students, and this is not reflective of academic ability or potential (Noble & Davies, 2009). They utilize prewelcome strategies like low-stakes syllabus quizzes to help demystify unspoken higher education norms and mores before the class starts and build student confidence. This allows time for underrepresented students to wear their new social identity, empower themselves, and confidently navigate standard classroom conventions. Using prewelcoming strategies that promote self-affirmation and capitalize on multiple social identities can consequently welcome all students and promote classroom belonging while simultaneously reducing stereotype threat (Noble & Davies, 2009; Penner, 2018; Rydell & Boucher, 2010).

Reflection Questions

- What elements can you include in a welcome statement or video, or syllabus quiz, that would exude enthusiasm, warmth, and welcome? How would you invite them to join your classroom community?

I conduct presemester surveys of all students in my classes, in which I ask about their goals, learning preferences, and so on.

—Full professor, master's college, History

Survey . . . students before the course begins about space, time, and pedagogy-related needs.

—Lecturer, master's college, English and Writing Studies

Preterm Assessments

A welcome statement or video provides an opportunity for inclusive instructors to share about themselves. Often inclusive instructors use preterm assessments, or preassessments, to learn more about their students and let them share. A preassessment is defined as any means used by instructors to gather information about students prior to instruction (Guskey, 2018). Instructors usually gather cognitive, affective, and behavioral information. Cognitive preassessments allow students to demonstrate what they know or can do. Affective preassessments gauge student interests, attitudes, and motivations. Behavioral preassessments focus on how students learn. Across institution types and academic disciplines, preassessments fall into three types, prerequisite, present, and preview (Guskey, 2018). Prerequisite preassessments focus on a student's prior knowledge (e.g., skills learned in previous courses), present preassessments emphasize current knowledge (e.g., existing skills and understanding), and preview preassessments help determine how much future learning occurs (e.g., skills acquired over time as evidenced by pre- and posttests).The three types of preassessments have different purposes, ask different questions, and provide different actionable information; however, they can be leveraged in the context of welcoming students.

A survey is a common preassessment tool inclusive instructors use in both face-to-face and online courses. Surveys can vary in length. A short survey can help succinctly address student goals and anticipated needs without inducing survey fatigue. A very simple one-question poll could ask "What immediate goal is this course going to help you to achieve: earning an academic degree, getting accepted to a graduate program, or securing a job?" or an open-ended question like "Why is it important for you to succeed in this course?" or "What do you want to know about me and what do you want me to know about you?" A longer survey could involve a detailed learning concept inventory. Concept inventories are tests that assess students' conceptual understanding of a subject area and are commonly used across a wide variety of STEM disciplines. They tend to include thoughtful multiple-choice items where incorrect answers are designed to reflect different depths of understanding of the particular subject area. Inclusive instructors may use the results to frontload and make available additional study resources for all students to do well. Preterm surveys allow time to tailor the course for the particular cohort enrolled. The genuine desire to collect any information that can help maximize success in the course communicates to students care, concern, and approachability, which further sets a positive and welcoming tone.

Reflection Questions

- How would you design and distribute a preterm assessment that communicates care, concern for student success, and approachability?

On the First Day of Class, They Start to Build the Classroom Community

Consider . . . the physical layout of the room to promote access/mobility and collaborative learning.

–Associate professor, special focus institution, the Arts

Ensure that the physical classroom space is inclusive for all students (e.g., are students who are alternately abled marginalized in some way?)

—Academic administrator, doctorate-granting university, Anthropology

Physical Environments That Promote Classroom Community

Inclusive instructors view the space and time before class on the first day as another opportunity to welcome students. If a student overlooked the welcome statement, welcome video, syllabus quiz, or preterm assessment, then the first time they set foot in the classroom or log in to the LMS site may be their first impression of the course. Students often arrive early on the first day of class, and inclusive instructors are cognizant of what the physical environment communicates to them. Things to consider for face-to-face courses include furniture type (desks, tables, chairs), furniture arrangement (facing forward versus clusters), space (distance between work areas), and teaching aids (placement of projectors, screens, or boards). Even a comfortable temperature and the scent in the room can place students at ease. Online courses should consider the placement of visual and auditory welcoming cues, as well as the placement of community-building activities that connect students to the course and one another.

The overall physical layout should maximize the learning and engagement of all students and support those with varying abilities. For example, an inclusive instructor may gather from a preterm survey that a student is in a wheelchair. They can then arrange with maintenance or facilities for the room to be set up in a way to promote mobility access for the student. Inclusive instructors get students talking and excited about the course. Another example is the use of tables instead of desks. Tables are known to provide easier student collaboration and can be used to facilitate classroom discussions. An inclusive instructor may use preclass discussion prompts placed on tables, such as "Welcome and introduce your neighbor" to prompt student–student interactions in the time before the instructor arrives. Inclusive instructors often arrive early to talk with students before class, which helps to further build the community.

The importance of the physical layout also extends to online classroom environments. Although most LMS have course shells and templates, inclusive instructors incorporate unique features that make the learning environment more welcoming. Four strategies can be applied to LMS site layouts that promote classroom community in these contexts. First, inclusive instructors are mindful about welcoming cues, which are the first images and text that students see when they log in to the LMS site. They strategically place welcome materials (videos or statements) and other important statements (diversity, equity, and inclusion statements) where they are readily visible. Second, they provide diverse representation of past students through videos or testimonials to engage current students. A common challenge with online courses is student engagement. This strategy nonverbally communicates that current students from various demographics are capable of completing the course. Third, inclusive instructors go beyond simply providing access to technology. They prominently display activities that lower psychological barriers in online environments, such as affirming core values. A value relevance affirmation (VRA) activity can be used to improve outcomes of identity-threatened students online (Kizilcec, Saltarelli et al., 2017). Research shows an initial VRA activity can raise grades, improve student persistence, and increase course completion rates (Kizilcec, Davis et al., 2017). A VRA activity example could be a simple 5-minute survey. Students first select their own cherished values and qualities from a predefined list the instructor creates. Next, students write how the course will help them to reinforce those values in a text box. Fourth, inclusive instructors recognize amplifying connections to the course and to students right away helps build community. For example, setting up discussion forums for common interests or professional goals is a commonly used practice to excite online students before the instructor logs on. Inclusive instructors are mindful to provide language that response times online communicate approachability and warmth in the community (e.g., responding sooner relates care or importance), as well as encourage the use of welcoming nonverbal communication like emoticons and figurative language (e.g., capitalized letters to signify excitement or agreement) (Dixson et. al, 2015).

Reflection Questions

- How can you use the physical environment before the first class starts to promote a welcoming space? What does that look like in face-to-face and online courses?

  We have an ice breaker on the first day, post bio info on a discussion forum, create groups on the first day that are used every day, share and comment on each other's success stories, and generally create an environment of respect, cooperation and fun.

  —Lecturer, doctorate-granting university, Mathematics

  At the beginning of a class or new learning experience, have the learners do an exercise in which they consider their motivation and the possibilities they envision for themselves as a result of engaging in the experience.

  —Adjunct professor, doctorate-granting university, Education

  I mention on the first day that making an environment where everyone feels comfortable and included is everyone's responsibility. I explain that everyone needs to be respectful at all times.

  —Assistant professor, master's college, Computer Science

  Discuss the importance of diversity and the need for inclusivity as an expectation for the class on the first day. We have a class activity where we come up with a code of conduct for the semester, and that code is posted on the course Web page and on the overhead during group discussions. Any deviation from the code is addressed.

  —Teaching professor, doctorate-granting university, Biology

Activities That Emphasize Diversity, Equity, and Inclusion in the Classroom Community

Inclusive instructors use low-risk first-day activities to increase student awareness of diversity in both undergraduate and graduate classrooms across various disciplines (Moore et al., 2010). This immediate increased awareness creates an environment that fosters understanding and better appreciation for the students' own experiences and their classmates. Such activities can be used to foster discussions about commonalities and differences, reveal knowledge gaps and unconscious biases, and challenge assumptions (Moore et al.,

2010). Using small group discussions, you can encourage student know their classmates, share their motivations for taking the class, ate additional community norms and expectations (Penner, 2018). Assigning a reporter for the small group is an inclusive best practice that encourages equitable participation (Tanner, 2013). This enables students to share who might not ordinarily volunteer as much as their more extroverted colleagues and allows the instructor to validate and comment on shared values between the students and themself. This is another opportunity to further develop a positive faculty–student relationship.

Inclusive instructors also take adequate time on the first day of class to welcome shared partners of the classroom teaching team, including coinstructors, teaching assistants, and supplemental instructors. This intentional acknowledgment is important for two reasons:

1. It relays to students that *everyone* in the classroom community is valued.
2. It helps to alleviate fear of failure by emphasizing prior student success and that instructor expectations are attainable and minimizes deficit models of learning.

Inclusive instructors can also use a "professor memoir" to introduce themselves. Memoirs have been shown to spark innovative and insightful responses from students and contribute to a greater sense of community in classrooms (Hollander, 2001). For example, career trajectory roadmap images allow instructors to share their educational journeys from postsecondary school, college, graduate school, and beyond. This can facilitate a discussion about academic successes, challenges, and individuals that helped guide the instructor. Inclusive instructors recognize that sharing such personal narratives helps to build trust with students.

One more issue to keep in mind when planning for the first day: Context matters. What works for first-term students might not work as well for final-term students. For example, first-year undergraduate students are unable to reflect on previous college courses. Likewise, undergraduate students in a senior seminar might already know one another, so icebreaker activities would be unnecessary for them.

Reflection Questions

- What are concrete first-day-of-class activities you can use to celebrate the diversity, equity, and inclusion in your classroom community? How can you relay to students these classroom values are important for welcoming everyone?

Within the First Week, They Maintain the Welcoming Classroom Environment

[Include] informal surveys of their cultural background, work experience, education, languages spoken, preferred foods/music/readings/sports, . . . family education, and so on.

—Full professor, doctorate-granting university, Biology

I have students privately complete a short survey at the beginning of the semester on their expectations, preferred ways of learning, and how I can best support their learning.

—Associate professor, baccalaureate college, Communications

I send an email at the beginning of the semester asking students for information they think I need to know for their success/comfort in class, for example . . . pronouns, preferences with small group work (i.e., I am female and would not be comfortable working with an all-male group), personal information (i.e., my mother just passed away), needs not addressed under ADA (i.e., I have communication and social challenges and find it beneficial if group work is very structured rather than just letting us loose on our own), and where students prefer to sit in the classroom. I give examples of my own life and encourage them to share as it will help me in my course planning.

—Survey respondent; rank, institution type, discipline not identified

I have students take a study skills inventory and a learning preference inventory at the beginning of the semester so that I can give them targeted study and test-taking strategies.

—Assistant professor, associate college, Biology

Student Information Surveys

While some inclusive instructors administer preterm surveys before the course starts, others prefer to deliver student information surveys within the first week of class for four reasons. First, after a few class meetings, more solid faculty–student and student–student relationships have been established. Therefore, student responses may be more honest, transparent, and substantive than preterm survey responses. Second, after getting to know students in the first week, the survey questions can be better tailored to the particular cohort. Third, allowing students time to complete the survey in class can improve the response rate. Fourth, some students may not have access to technology prior to the course. By administering the survey during the first week of class, students have the opportunity to use campus-available technology resources. In both time scenarios, inclusive instructors use student survey information to support social belonging and classroom equity. One such survey used at our institutions, the "Who's In Class?" form, is used to collect diversity, equity, and inclusion attributes that students bring to class. The instructor delivers the survey within the first two class sessions. Students complete it on a voluntary basis. The campus

center for teaching and learning provide an anonymous, aggregated r̵
which inclusive instructors use to design and implement teaching practices ...at
can build welcoming classroom spaces. The instructors reflect on their practices
over the semester, focusing on what seemed to work and what did not. Student
survey responses are stored only temporarily for the course and later deleted.
More detail is provided on the "Who's in Class?" form in chapter 6.

Reflection Questions

- How do you collect information about your class and use it to
  maintain a welcoming environment? Do you think there is a best
  time to do so? Why or why not?

*In an effort to reach first gen and racial minority students I . . . mandate office hours [in] smaller
classes so that everyone has the advantage of my help and advice, not just the privileged few.
I find that White middle-class kids have the cultural capital to build rapport with professors
in ways that first-gen and racial minority students cannot. With the way I approach the
classroom, I get to know all of my students and make myself available to all, not just those with
more cultural capital who have been taught to more effortlessly navigate classroom settings.*

—Visiting professor, doctorate-granting university, Sociology

Meet with each student individually at beginning of [the] semester to get to know them.

—Full professor, baccalaureate college, Biology

*Together, we use the early hours of each class to learn more about each other as individuals who
deserve our respect and support. We organize learning activities that allow for cooperation, rather
than competition, and we support learner by providing individual coaching and feedback.*

—Adjunct professor, master's college, Education

I work to establish relationships with my students early in the semester.

—Associate professor, master's college, Rhetoric and Composition

Essential Office Hours With Individual Students

Inclusive instructors recognize there are several benefits for individual students
who attend office hours. This allows for the establishment and growth of
faculty–student relationships. This can also translate to the instructor
supporting students further and taking on an active mentoring role for students who attend office hours. There is also a higher likelihood of completing
a degree, especially for underrepresented students. Scheduling extra time for
required essential office hours for each individual student promotes equitable
participation in the course and works to ensure all students have access to the
same cultural capital in the classroom.

Reflection Questions

- What are the benefits of essential office hours? How often do you need to hold them?

They Know It Is Never Too Late to Create a Welcoming Classroom Environment, Even on the Last Day of Class

After the first week of the course

> *[I] facilitate icebreakers for the first 4 weeks of class to help students get to know each other and me.*

—Survey respondent; rank, institution type, discipline unidentified

> *I create class community so that students know each other, work together, and help one another.*

—Full professor, associate college, Biology

The first half of the course

> *I send individual emails to students who are struggling early in the semester to encourage them to chat with me.*

—Associate professor, doctorate-granting university, Biology

> *Explicitly incorporate respect and listening into the participation rubric for small courses, and conduct a midquarter student reflection and check-in on this. Seek midquarter course feedback, including about ways to make the classroom environment best suited to student learning.*

—Teaching post-doc, doctorate-granting university, Biology

Throughout the course

> *[I] try to talk about myself and my journey during the semester.*

—Lecturer, Biology

Maintaining the Welcoming Classroom Environment After the First Week

All of the welcoming strategies, advice, and examples listed can be implemented at any time after the first week of the course. Inclusive instructors recognize it is important to maintain a welcoming tone throughout the course. That means they continue using community-building activities that give students agency and allow them to share and learn from one another, which reemphasizes equity and belonging. Their care and concern is ongoing, as evidenced by sending individual progress emails and collecting midcourse

feedback about the classroom environment. Inclusive instructors l
ing inspiring personal vignettes about their academic journey and l   ___,
persisted throughout the duration of the course. This fosters trust and connection with the students.

On the last day of class inclusive instructors close the course by highlighting how much students have learned, but also by thanking them for how
much they taught the instructor. This affirms student abilities and encourages them to see themselves as reaching a new scholarly milestone in the
greater disciplinary community of practice. Inclusive instructors wrap up by
asking students to reflect and give feedback on how welcomed they felt. This
feedback can be shared to make future classroom environments more inviting. The most welcoming inclusive instructors may find students take other
courses with them. By offering students to stay in touch and having drop-in
office hours for past students, they create environments where students feel
comfortable contacting them even after the current course ends.

Reflection Question

- What are ways to make students feel welcome after the first week
  of class?

They Reestablish a Welcoming Classroom Environment After a Violation or Disruption

Inclusive instructors realize that internal and external circumstances can violate
or disrupt the welcoming atmosphere in face-to-face, online, or hybrid classroom spaces. They also use evidence-based approaches that identify who or
what committed harm, acknowledge the effects, and prescribe actions to mitigate the impact on students, which reestablishes the welcoming environment.
After ground rules and expectations have been set to ensure the success of an
inclusive learning environment, opportunities for disruption may arise. These
infractions can show up at any time during the course and inclusive instructors
resolve them as quickly and completely as possible to reestablish the welcoming space. The mending of the infraction should be the work of all involved
in the learning process. Instructors have a duty to their students to do no
harm. In instances where harm is done, inclusive instructors recognize they are
responsible for making amends. Likewise, student interactions will sometimes
result in learning environments where others feel judged or unsafe. Students
must, therefore, be equipped with tools, strategies, opportunities, and spaces to
mutually and collectively resolve whatever challenges have become obstacles to

inclusive learning environments. Some approaches can be used by both faculty and students. For example, when a microaggression has occurred, Nadal's questions, the RAVEN approach, and the action framework can be used to have crucial conversations when a marginalized student has been othered and to reaffirm that they do belong in the community (see chapter 2). As recent world events reflect, barriers to a welcoming classroom can also arise from outside the classroom. In this event, expectations must be managed and curricular innovations leveraged to reinforce existing or form new learning communities, which emphasize all students are welcomed.

Reflection Questions

- What evidence-based approaches can you use to restore a welcoming classroom environment once it has been violated or disrupted? How will you gauge the impact of your efforts?

They Open Recognize Any Faculty–Student Harms and Work to Rebuild Positive Relationships

Acknowledge

Examine your background and experiences (so that you understand how your students see you!). Consider your academic traditions and the biases that they may inadvertently reinforce.

—Academic administrator, doctorate-granting university, Anthropology

[I am] open about when I do not have knowledge of one's own biases/ limitations so students know I am coming from somewhere and perhaps feel more comfortable being aware of where they come from.

—Visiting professor, doctorate-granting university, Literature

Apologize

I apologize if I know I've misspoken or neglected to address situations and ask for ways to improve my interactions with students.

—Assistant professor, doctorate-granting university, Linguistics and Languages

Act

Respond . . . to hot moments with sensitivity and taking action when observing (or perpetrating) a microaggression.

—Full professor, doctorate-granting university, Journalism, Media Studies, and Communication

Using the Stereotype Content Model to Repair Faculty–Student Harms

The stereotype content model (SCM) is a powerful social psychology theory first proposed in 2002 by Susan Fiske and others that suggests stereotypes toward particular groups arise from two variables: perceptions of warmth as well as competence. Warmth refers to friendliness, trustworthiness, likability, and sociability. It is predicted by a reference group's perceptions of a stereotyped group. Competence is the capability, assertiveness, and confidence predicted by perceptions of status, reflecting a stereotyped group's ability to put their intentions into practice. Inherent in the SCM is the notion that not all groups are the same. Some groups are viewed as more or less warm and competent. Subsequent research on a national and international scale has shown the SCM is able to predict feelings and attitudes toward a variety of different groups. Common stereotypes are shared across countries (e.g., age, disability status, citizenship status, and SES), while others are country specific (Fiske, 2018). In the United States, persistent stereotypes exist based on race, ethnicity, and religion and evoke a continuum of positive and negative emotions (Fiske, 2018).

Since the SCM is generalizable across place, level, and time, inclusive instructors in higher education use it to acknowledge and reflect on their own stereotypes, offer apologies to students who they may have harmed, and carry out actions that will reestablish a welcoming classroom space. Inclusive instructors around the country are aware they enter their classrooms with their own traditions, biases, limitations, and knowledge gaps. This can lead to inadvertent reinforcement of stereotypes through microaggressions that may violate a student's sense of social belonging and make them feel unwelcomed.

If this occurs, it must first be recognized if a positive, negative, or both kinds of stereotypes were responsible for the violation. Positive stereotype combinations with high warmth and low competence are called paternalistic prejudices (e.g., elderly and disabled students) and those with high warmth and high competence are labeled as admiration (e.g., middle class, American, and Christian students) (Fiske, 2018). Negative stereotype combinations that include low warmth and low competence are thought of as contemptuous prejudices (e.g., low-SES, immigrant, racial or ethnic minority, and Muslim students), while low-warmth and high-competence combinations are deemed envious prejudices (high-SES, Asian, and Jewish students) (Fiske, 2018). These combinations can inadvertently result in unconscious biases or conscious prejudices aimed at particular students.

Specifically, the SCM allows for unpacking the stereotype and further understanding the relationship between warmth, competence, and emotional responses. Stereotypes vary along a warmth and competence spectrum and can be contradictory (e.g., high for one variable and low for the other).

The relationship between the two variables can lead to characteristic emotional responses from the instructor in response to the stereotyped student's group. Common emotions evoked for positively stereotyped students are pity, sympathy, pride, and admiration. By contrast, the emotions evoked for negatively stereotyped students are disgust, contempt, envy, and jealousy.

Inclusive instructors also realize that harm can arise from stereotypes based on both visible and invisible student identities and have no problems apologizing. Invisible identities require special attention because the instructor may be unaware that harm was inflicted and will have to rely solely on student feedback to know it occurred. Instructors can create confidential complaint boxes, either physical or electronic, where students can share grievances. Visible student identities can include age, race and ethnicity, gender and sexuality, and differently abled status, among others. A representative list of invisible student identities can include first-generation, socioeconomic, international, citizenship, mental health, and genetic health status, as well as religious and political affiliations.

Ultimately, actions must be carried out to restore the health, well-being, and sense of social belonging in the classroom. We have provided a useful worksheet inclusive instructors use to help you articulate the stereotype and the students affected, identify which variables and emotions are involved to offer an authentic apology based on understanding, and make an action plan (Appendix E, "Stereotype Content Model-Driven Reestablishment of a Welcoming Classroom" worksheet). Examples of actions to be taken can be any of the welcoming strategies, advice, or examples mentioned previously in this chapter.

Reflection Questions

- How easy is it for you to acknowledge and apologize when you have offended a student?
- What tools do you have that can repair and restore a positive faculty–student relationship?

They Openly Recognize Any Student–Student Harms and Work to Rebuild Positive Relationships

I subscribe to the community building practices of Indigenous pedagogy—particularly creati[ng] of community standards and shared knowledge.

—Faculty developer, doctorate-granting university, Human Physical Performance and Recreation

Using Restorative Justice Pedagogy and Andragogy to Repair Student–Student Harms

Restorative justice (RJ) is a theory of justice used to repair harm and "promotes values and principles that use inclusive, collaborative approaches for being in community" (Amstutz & Mullet, 2015, p. 15). RJ is grounded in traditional indigenous ways of knowing (Ogilvie & Fuller, 2017). In this belief system, humans are not viewed as capable of existing independently. Instead, they are viewed as members of a community in close connection with one another and their environment. Therefore, all living beings are worthy and make important contributions to the well-being of the community. RJ is "victim-centered and concerned with healing harms, repairing relationships, ensuring accountability, creating opportunities to make amends, making earned redemption possible, and improving social conditions" (Gilbert et al., 2013, p. 43).

RJ principles focus on harm, accountability, and engagement (Ogilvie & Fuller, 2017). Recognizing that authoritarian classroom management interventions are known to be ineffective, inclusive instructors often utilize RJ principles in educational contexts. Restorative justice pedagogy (RJP) can empower students to use conflict resolution to solve their own problems in peer-mediated small groups through discussion with a facilitator, asking questions, and airing grievances. Concrete strategies used in small groups can include all parties involved writing in a reflection journal about the harm in a detailed way. Using active listening, the instructor or student facilitator can guide the conversation based on expressed students' needs. This activity also provides further opportunities for RJ when the facilitator can identify latent unmet needs that need to be addressed (Ogilvie & Fuller, 2017). Additionally, a talking stick can also be used to ensure equal participation for speakers and listeners (Ogilvie & Fuller, 2017).

RJP can specifically be used in higher education classrooms to reestablish a safe, caring, and welcoming environment. Since all students are considered important members of the learning community, the onus is on them to maintain harmony in the classroom. First, students who have inflicted harm must accept accountability for the harm, as well as work to understand the harm's repercussions. Second, students who have been harmed must be open and willing to discuss how the action impacted them. Third, all parties engage in critical dialogue with the facilitator about how to rectify the situation and prevent the harm from happening again in the future (Gilbert et al., 2013). As mentioned previously in this chapter, class guidelines may have been cocreated. RJP allows for a shared discussion about what actions are necessary and acceptable to realign with the mutually agreed-on guidelines. RJP helps students consider how their behavior affects others, develop a deeper sense of empathy and respect for peers, and forge community, which ultimately promotes a more welcoming classroom atmosphere (Ogilvie & Fuller, 2017).

Inclusive instructors understand RJ principles but also distinguish between RJP and restorative justice andragogy (RJA). Pedagogy generally refers to formal instructional methods used by teachers to educate students but often has underlying assumptions related to children (Gilbert et al., 2013). These instructor-centric suppositions assume learners have minimal or no relevant experience or knowledge of the subject content and passively depend on the instructor to impart knowledge. By contrast, andragogy assumes students have past knowledge based on educational and life experiences that can provide a rich framework to scaffold learning and that adults are capable of self-directed learning (Knowles, 1984b). Both approaches depend on the readiness and maturity of the student to learn and whether extrinsic or intrinsic motivating factors are present. Pedagogy and andragogy are not mutually exclusive, but rather a continuum that can often overlap (e.g., mature and highly independent children or immature and dependent adults) (Knowles, 1984b). Knowles (1984b) argues there are four key principles to effectively teach adults:

Principle 1: Create an environment conducive to communication, using a circle when possible.

Principle 2: Create a psychological climate based on mutual respect, collaborative learning, mutual trust, supportiveness, openness and authenticity, joy in learning and self-discovery, acceptance and humanness.

Principle 3: Involve students in planning, determining learning needs, and assessment methods.

Principle 4: Share responsibility for learning objectives, learning plans, learning assessment, and the classroom environment.

Inclusive instructors model and teach their students RJA in college or university-level courses by emulating authentic RJ experiences. Teaching students RJA is independent of classroom type and can be used in face-to-face, online, or hybrid courses (Gilbert et al., 2013). Principles 1 and 4 directly lend themselves to RJA and rebuilding positive relationships that have been violated in the higher education classroom.

Regarding Knowles's Principle 1, as mentioned earlier, in face-to-face courses the physical layout of the room is important for facilitating open communication and the critical dialogue necessary for RJA. Inclusive instructors know that if the physical space is designed in a way that is instructor–centered, such as forward-facing desks and chairs or tables, it will reinforce a power hierarchy and violate the basic principle of RJ that munity members are equally important. When possible, stu in a circle to engage in rich dialogue that is not directed instructor (Gilbert et al., 2013). This helps develop trust and confidence in both fellow students and the instructor, which can reestablish a safe and welcoming classroom. Since online courses lack nonverbal communication cues typified during face-to-face interactions (e.g., facial expressions or body language), inclusive instructors in this learning context teach students how to recognize both verbal and nonverbal messages when using RJA. Showing acknowledgment and responding in a timely manner to a fellow student's message mirrors active listening characterized by RJ dialogue in face-to-face environments (Gilbert et al., 2013).

Knowles's Principle 4 requires mutual responsibility for the classroom environment, which directly aligns with RJ principles. Allowing students to perform frequent group "check-ins" encourages meaningful discussions with one another and provides an opportunity to discuss harms (Gilbert et al., 2013). Inclusive instructors recognize the willingness for students to share will be variable, especially after a harm has been inflicted. However, over time it is expected trust would be restored (even if not to the initial degree) and bonds and relationships will be reformed. In online settings a "question area" that is visible to all class participants can provide aid to students seeking help or moral support by fellow students and the instructor (Gilbert et al., 2013). By contrast, "cyber cafes" allow students to interact with one another without instructor monitoring, which can promote RJA outside of class time. Both question areas and cyber cafes can minimize student isolation and promote social belonging in the classroom community after a harm.

Reflection Questions

- How easy is it for you to recognize when one student has offended another in the classroom? How comfortable are you holding individuals accountable and encouraging student dialogue? What tools do you have that can repair and restore a positive student–student relationship?

They Recognize How Events Outside the Classroom Can Impact a Student's Connection to the Classroom Community

Classroom incivility is a disruption due to disrespect or an undesirable event (Strassle & Verrecchia, 2019). Higher education research has identified several societal factors outside the classroom that may contribute to incivility. Disrespect can be due to generational shifts correlated with greater entitlement, uses of technology, increasing rates of students with psychiatric issues, and greater social acceptance of incivility (Strassle & Verrecchia, 2019). An apparent rise in classroom incivility has prompted some institutions to respond by banning the mocking of others in the classroom (Lukianoff, 2014).

Although different from faculty–student and student–student inflicted harms, inclusive instructors recognize how societal events can distract students and consequently disrupt the welcoming feeling in the classroom, such as local violence (e.g., mass school shootings), national tragedies (e.g., 9/11, George Floyd's murder and the subsequent global wave of antiracism protests sparked by the Black Lives Matter movement), and public health crises (e.g., the COVID-19 pandemic and systemic racism as pronounced by several cities and counties around the United States). In response to such events, inclusive instructors from disparate disciplines can collaborate to design multidisciplinary events that allow students to critically examine, learn from the tragedy, and form new learning communities. Recent research demonstrated how two psychology and legal professors gathered students across four classes (Social Psychology, Criminal Law, Restorative Justice, and Criminology) in an event to study the 1964 Kitty Genovese murder, which led to our modern understanding of the bystander effect (Knapp & Merges, 2017). The bystander effect is a social psychology theory that attempts to posit why an individual does not intervene in an emergency situation and why the greater the number of bystanders the less likely it is for any one of them to provide help. Using various activities throughout the event to engage and inform, three common themes emerged (Knapp & Merges, 2017):

> Theme 1: Students enjoyed having the opportunity to meet and work with students from other disciplines.

> Theme 2: Students felt that the structure of each event optimized their ability to learn from each other and from experts in each field.

> Theme 3: Students found the activities to be peer–centered and fun yet appreciated the serious nature of the events that they were celebrating.

Such curricular innovations can help students learn during a tragedy using diverse disciplinary lenses that foster new community bonds. Many survey responses revealed students enjoyed peer–peer interactions while learning how others viewed the tragedy (Knapp & Merges, 2017). They also commented that all students were engaged and efficiently worked together. Some students used a RJP strategy and simulated a RJ circle by role-playing the

participants involved in the Kitty Genovese case. Other students c
on how the tragedy inspired researchers and lawmakers to raise p
awareness of bystander apathy (Knapp & Merges, 2017).

Although the example just mentioned is based on a past event, curricular innovations that promote reestablishing welcoming classrooms can also
be adopted in real time. For example, discussions with inclusive instructors
who transitioned to remote instruction during the COVID-19 pandemic
and after George Floyd's murder revealed they planned activities that stim-
ulated deeper learning to combat students' disconnect with the classroom
community due to fears and anxieties. They designed coronavirus-related
activities that required several disciplinary insights from biological (studying the SARS-CoV-2 RNA genome), health economic (RNA genome–
based vaccine development costs and insurance coverage), and public policy
(should the most vulnerable populations have first priority access to the
vaccine) perspectives. They also designed activities around protests for racial
justice. This included antiracist education (having students take implicit bias
tests to identify unconscious biases regarding race), dissecting how the media
can shape our views on race (comparing language used in various media
outlets to describe the events immediately following George Floyd's murder,
such as riots versus rebellion/protests), a class town hall discu
and having students crowdsource antiracism resources to educ
further after class. In both instances, students were placed in
and allowed to work in virtual breakout rooms across several c
the end of the activity, each small group came back together to
larger group, and all answers were compared. Anecdotally, s
how a deeper understanding of the events helped them feel
empathy, and greater connectedness with their small group
whole. After a past or present classroom disruption, inclusive
reestablish welcoming environments through the formatio
groups in existing classroom communities.

Reflection Question

- How can you form new communities in respons
  external forces?

Key Points

Inclusive instructors across the country work hard as welcome ambassadors.
They build positive classroom environments using a variety of strategies but

agree on the same three basic tenets of making students feel welcome in higher education classrooms:

- *How* to intentionally create welcoming classroom environments by respectfully acknowledging student differences, encouraging equitable participation, and building positive relationships both inside and outside of the classroom
- *When* to create a welcoming classroom environment while recognizing that it's never too late
- *How* to reestablish welcoming classroom environments after violation or disruption by using conflict resolution approaches and community-building practices and pedagogies

All of these efforts communicate to every student that they are vital and valued members of the classroom community.

HOW DO THEY CONDUCT CLASS INCLUSIVELY?

Inclusive teaching means providing a welcoming and safe environment where individuals are recognized as valuable contributing members and a growth mindset is assumed and nurtured. It means constantly educating myself regarding pedagogical approaches and learning how to identify [my] own explicit and implicit biases so that I continue to grow and refine courses because every group of students [is] unique and I am growing too.

—Full professor, baccalaureate college, Biology

I n the previous two chapters, we have considered how inclusive instructors design a course to meet their learning objectives in an inclusive way, as well as how they make their students feel welcome in their course, especially focusing on before the course starts and throughout the duration of the course. In this chapter, we will explore how inclusive instructors apply their course design in the classroom and maintain the momentum generated early in the course throughout the duration of the course, whether that is measured in days or months. To do this, we will start by discussing foundational aspects of inclusive classroom management and progress through how teachers engage with students in an inclusive manner, utilize specific inclusive pedagogies, and assess inclusively. We will also examine the ways in which inclusive instructors acquire student feedback about the course and use this information productively to create a more equitable and inclusive classroom environment.

They Employ Foundational Inclusive Teaching Concepts and Practices

You have designed your course, created your syllabus, even had the first few class meetings, and, so far, you feel really positive about the inclusive nature of your course. You have spoken about the value of each person's perspective, modeled what you expect in terms of a respectful classroom environment, know or are getting to know the names of your students, and maybe have even found ways to learn a bit more about who the students in your classroom are. The foundation is set. Now you are tasked with helping students learn the content, concepts, and skills of whatever discipline you are teaching and maintain and grow that inclusive environment along the way. How do you do this when there is so much to be done to help students achieve learning goals? The good news is that you are not the first instructor to be faced with this challenge, and there are some foundational concepts and practices that inclusive instructors commonly use, whether they are teaching in person or digitally. These include things like student-centered learning, establishing a growth mindset, ensuring the course is accessible to all learners (incorporating universal design concepts), utilizing diverse resources, and, through it all, being explicit but also flexible. What you will come to see in the next few pages is that, in many cases, for inclusive instructors these concepts do not exist independently of one another but overlap and complement one another.

> *Inclusive teaching means making every student feel valued and respected, supporting their areas for growth, and recognizing the diverse assets they bring to the class.*
>
> —Part-time adjunct professor, associate college, Biology

They Implement Student-Centered Practices

A key tenet of successful inclusive teaching is it being student-centered, and this is seen broadly in the teaching done by inclusive instructors. In its most simple version, this means putting the students and their learning at the core of all aspects of the course. Maryellen Weimer's work on this concept has been at the forefront of this field. In her book *Learner-Centered Teaching: Five Key Changes to Practice*, Weimer (2013) contrasts teacher-centered and student-centered college teaching in terms of the role of the teacher and the student, the responsibility of learning, the balance of power in the classroom, the function of content, and the purpose and process of evaluation. In student-centered learning, the role of the teacher is more of a guide or coach than strictly a deliverer of content, and with this the power structure and responsibility of learning shifts from the instructor to the students, who have an enhanced role in determining what and how they are going to learn, but also places the onus on the students to ensure they are holding up their end of the bargain. In this context, the content and modes of evaluation serve as a means to help students learn how to learn, not just meet an end goal of what to know for a student to earn a particular grade in that course. Indeed, numerous studies have been conducted across a variety of disciplines and have broadly found that implementing the concepts of student-centered learning in the classroom leads to increased student satisfaction, motivation, knowledge acquisition, and problem-solving skills (Baxter & Gray, 2001; Chung & Chow, 2004; Kemm & Dantas, 2007; Kozar & Marcketti, 2008; Wright, 2011).

> *Inclusive teaching is learner-centered teaching that gives all students a voice and makes them feel like they belong and are respected as individuals and members of groups.*

—Full professor, doctorate-granting university, Journalism, Media Studies and Communication

They Espouse a Growth Mindset When Facilitating Learning Opportunities

Another foundational concept that inclusive teachers adopt is a growth mindset for themselves, and they seek to encourage their students to develop growth mindsets as well. The concept of a growth mindset related to learning states that intelligence is not fixed and can be developed. As evidence for this, it is well established that socioeconomic factors are one of the best predictors of academic achievement, and those with economic disadvantage tend to have depressed outcomes (Reardon, 2011). Meanwhile, there is also variation in academic success in groups of students with similar economic backgrounds, suggesting that this is not a singular effector. Interestingly, studies have shown that students fare better across socioeconomic backgrounds if they believe that their intellectual abilities can be developed (Mueller & Daveck, 1998; Stipek, 1996), and, moreover, that a growth mindset disproportionately benefits those from lower socioeconomic classes, thereby helping to close academic achievement gaps (Claro et al., 2016). Functionally, establishing a growth mindset for your course can mean a number of things. For one, explicitly discussing the concept and stating early in the course that this is your view on learning can be important to help students feel they can succeed in your course, regardless of their personal background. Part of this is acknowledging your own assumptions about what your students "should" know and correcting these through gathering relevant information from your students. The next step is providing foundational resources to all students as part of the course and allowing them to self-reflect on their need to utilize these resources with respect to what will be expected of them throughout the course. Additionally, embracing a growth mindset can mean providing opportunities for students to "fail forward" during their learning journey, be it through the use of ungraded assignments and activities, draft development, or low-stakes assessments. An important component of allowing for student growth is providing the students constructive feedback throughout their learning process. This means more than the instructor just assigning a grade, but spending time to help students identify how to improve moving forward through written responses and through conversation and modeling. In sum, establishing a growth mindset classroom culture requires not only an explicit discussion of what that is and evidence of why it is important, but also both students and instructors embracing it and acting in a way that cultivates it throughout the course.

> *I go over what a growth mindset is and encourage students to*
> *have a growth mindset and to keep working hard.*

—Assistant professor, associate college, Biology

> *[Do] not separat[e] . . . prerequisite material as "remedial" but integrat[e] it into the regular*
> *course content and provid[e] resources for students to study more. Allow . . . students to repeat*
> *work on assignments to demonstrate improvement and encourage a growth mindset.*

—Survey respondent; rank, institution type, discipline not identified

They Are Transparent About Why They Use Particular Learning Activities

Much like in chapter 3, where incorporating the rationale for course design decisions in the syllabus was discussed, inclusive instructors also apply this concept to the course content. More and more, our students don't simply want to know "what" they are going to learn, but "why" they should be learning it. With this in mind, inclusive instructors are explicit and transparent about not only what students will be learning and how, but why they will be learning it and why they will be learning it in that manner will be beneficial. This complements the growth mindset, in that explaining why students are going to be learning in a particular way, and (when possible) providing evidence of its efficacy, can lead to students to seeing a path to their own intellectual and skill growth. With this in mind, the Transparency in Learning and Teaching (TILT) higher education program was designed, which provides a simple process for ensuring transparency in the classroom and seeks to collect data on the efficacy of these practices (Winkelmes, 2014). The core concepts of TILT related to a particular assignment are three-fold:

1. Explain the purpose of the assignment.
2. Describe the task in some detail.
3. Explain the criteria for grading.

While these concepts can be applied by instructors independently in their own courses, the TILT higher education program offers training workshops, collects survey data to inform the efficacy of this work, and establishes a collaborative community aimed at enhancing teaching transparency. Indeed, several studies have found that student outcomes improve when learners understand why and how instructors had intentionally structured their learning experiences (Dunlosky & Metcalfe, 2009; National Education Association, 2013; Perry et al., 2007).

I follow the TILT model of assignment design for transparency.

—Associate professor, baccalaureate college, Communication

I use transparent assignment design using the TILT interventional methodologies.

—Full professor, master's college, History

They Use Broad Frameworks That Advance Learning for All Students

As mentioned in chapter 1 and subsequent chapters, one broad approach to support equitable and inclusive teaching is using the UDL framework. UDL is a "research-based set of principles to guide the design of learning environments that are accessible and effective for all" (CAST, n.d.b). In UDL, instructors are encouraged to provide multiple means of engagement, representation, and action and expression (Meyer et al., 2014). In terms of engagement, it is recommended that instructors recruit interest in the course material by helping students understand the value and relevance of their learning, optimizing student choice and autonomy and minimizing threats and distractions. Then this engagement requires options to be provided for this effort and engagement to be sustained and, ideally, self-regulated through goal-setting and reflection. Related to representation, UDL suggests instructors provide access to the information and skills to be learned through multiple modalities, including but not limited to text, auditory, and visual means, and supporting this perception of information with context. As for action and expression, UDL guides instructors to vary the ways that learners interact with their materials, communicate their learning, and scaffold and synthesize "lower-level" knowledge and skills into "higher-level" functions. Throughout these guidelines, it is easy to see characteristics that are common with the concept of the student-centered classroom by allowing room for students to make choices, self-regulate, and reflect. Additionally, the concept of accessibility is critical to the goals of UDL, and as such many of the practical means of applying UDL address this. For example, recording and sharing in-class lectures, captioning any videos that are used, ensuring those texts and other resources can be listened to audibly for the visually impaired, and allowing technological devices in the classroom all are actions that fit within the framework of UDL. While some of these actions may not be ones with which many college instructors have experience, most institutions have accessibility services that can help support instructors in learning how to best provide these services at both an individual student and classroom-wide level. Implementing these UDL concepts in the classroom seeks to enhance equity and promote the opportunity for all students in the classroom to succeed. Research to date suggests that UDL is indeed an effective teaching methodology for improving the learning process for students (Capp, 2017); however, additional studies are needed (using pre- and postassessments) to truly assess its efficacy in enhancing student outcomes.

Inclusive teaching incorporates but is not limited to universal design for learning (UDL). It also includes culturally responsive teaching wherein the instructor works to be conscious of bias and self-critiques and reflects on biases. It includes the classroom ([physical] or online) space, the course content, and the methodology.

—Associate professor, master's college, Rhetoric and Composition

[Inclusive teaching strategies I have used include] partnering with disability/accessibility resources on campus; making sure course materials and content are accessible, diverse, and inclusive; and creating classroom environment and guidelines for classroom discourse that emphasize the value of inclusivity for our shared learning.

—Full professor, baccalaureate college, Psychology

[I use] universal design as a principle of course content to be accessible to the maximum number of students. [I] have someone check me to make sure I interact with all students equally.

—Academic professional faculty, doctorate-granting university, Biology

I create class community so that students know each other, work together, and help one another. I provide student paper notes and my own notes (in video) for every class so that students can revisit the content. I offer many analogies to real life situations. I incorporate UDL strategies, not just in my teaching, but also in many of my assessments.

—Full professor, associate college, Biology

Survey students about their prior knowledge of the subject. Facilitate icebreakers for the first 4 weeks of class to help students get to know each other and [the instructor]. Use lecture and large discussion and small or paired discussions to provide different ways for students to interact with content. Create opportunities for students to work in teams and teach and learn from each other.

—Survey respondent; rank, institution type and discipline not identified

[I practice inclusive teaching by] incorporating universal design in assignments and lectures/discussions, [and] varied examples [and by] develop[ing] [an] open and accepting environment in the classroom.

— Assistant professor, baccalaureate college, Psychology

Reflection Question

- How do you use or envision embracing any of the following approaches in your teaching: student-centered learning, growth mindset, transparency, or UDL?

They Value Diversity in Learning

In addition to the importance of providing diverse means by which students can interact with the course material, as recommended by UDL, a major theme from the respondents to our national survey of faculty about inclusive teaching was the need to highlight the value of diversity in their class's field of study. This includes encouraging diverse student voices to be presented, heard, and considered and to be explicit about the value of these varied perspectives. It also involves the selection of resources, text, and audio/visuals from and by individuals from varied racial, ethnic, and gender backgrounds (to name just a few). Further, people and characters embedded in the learning materials (e.g., books, case studies, real-life examples) should be diversely representative, while also avoiding stereotype bias. These concepts were introduced in chapter 3 around initial course design and the construction of the syllabus, and the specific strategies inclusive instructors use in their in-person and digital classrooms are detailed next.

[I] tell the students that diversity in all respects is valued in the course [and] show the students that diversity is valued by acknowledging it throughout the course. [See the following] example[s:]

- *Provide different versions of instructional materials or activities that support the variety of viewpoints (e.g., age, culture) represented by the students in a class.*
- *Ask students to help address gaps, such as students finding and sharing images to address image or representation bias in a textbook or instructional materials created by a third party.*
- *Follow universal design for learning principles to provide multiple pathways for students to review course materials, engage with one another, and show what they know.*
- *Offer alternatives for students with technology impediments (e.g., access to devices, inconsistent connectivity).*
- *Provide clear explanations and pathways for all students to access and use academic services (e.g., tutoring, writing, library), technology services (e.g., help desk), student services (e.g., health, well-being, support for students with disabilities), and administrative services (e.g., registration, financial aid).*
- *Provide opportunities for student–student interaction that support students sharing diverse experiences and perspectives.*

—Part-time lecturer, master's college, Education

[I practice inclusive teaching by] ensuring content and resources are diverse [and by p]romoting
a growth/success/ and college-minded mindset. Promot[e] "equitable" practices versus "equal."

—Part-time visiting professor, Education

[I] create slide presentations that are accessible by UDL standards and also have various
representations of people. Create curricula that includes scholars of different backgrounds.

——Survey respondent; rank, institution type and discipline not identified

I use diverse examples and ensure my readings are from diverse perspectives and diverse authors.

—Survey respondent; rank, institution type and discipline not identified

[I use] diverse examples such as contributions of women and POC in science.

—Associate professor, doctorate-granting university, Biology

[I provide] explicit instruction of working in groups with diverse members
and how diversity is beneficial to groups. Ensure presentation images,
examples, and case studies used represent many groups of people.

—Academic professional faculty, doctorate-granting university, Biology

[I use] "[s]potlight" moments in which I highlight contributions of a wide
variety of scientists, especially those from backgrounds that are currently
underrepresented in the field. When giving examples of how to cite references,
I chose examples that have authors from a variety of backgrounds.

—Full professor, doctorate-granting university, Biology

Curat[e] readings that represent a range of experiences and expertise
and [that] come from a diverse group of authors.

—Clinical assistant professor, doctorate-granting University, Education

They Provide Structure in Their Courses

In our national study, several inclusive instructors in STEM disciplines
such as the biological sciences referred to Kimberly Tanner's 2013 article
"Structure Matters" where she provides 21 teaching strategies to attend to
individual students and promote engagement and equity in the classroom.
These range from specific practices for managing the classroom and interaction with students to being explicit and transparent about equity, to means
of collecting data and assessing the course and the students' learning. Many
of these ideas have been addressed, or will be discussed in more detail later in
this chapter, and are relevant across disciplines, but as several of our survey
respondents noted using this tool, and as have we personally seen in our own

teaching, it seemed useful to include here in the section about foundational concepts and practices.

> *Strategies that I see as specifically being more inclusive include . . . [a] variety of strategies from Kimberly Tanner's work—trying to hear every voice within a class period, using miniature white boards so that I can see every student's responses (literally), tables . . . labeled by concepts we are working on so that I'm not calling on a group by its conversationally dominant member[, and so on].*

—Adjunct professor, associate college, Biology

> *[I use] Kimberly Tanner['s] 21 strategies.*

—Lecturer, doctorate-granting university, Biology

They Are Adaptable

With the several foundational concepts, practices, and tools for inclusive teaching in the classroom we have discussed, one critical characteristic seems to permeate all of the others: adaptability. When designing a course and creating a syllabus, it is easy to envision the course exactly how you would like to see it proceed. However, it is important to appreciate that a course is not simply the content that will be covered, but it is the community of students who are going through the process of learning. And because no two students are identical, no two classes, even if covering the exact same material, should be identical. While it may be possible to learn some general information about your students during the course design process using knowledge of the student population at your particular institution, or in your particular major, relying solely on that, or worse yet, nothing related to your students at all, will do both yourself and your students a disservice. What this means is that much as the students are coming to class to learn, inclusive instructors are prepared to do the same. They learn about students, their desires and needs as related to the course, as well as what knowledge, experiences, and perspectives they can bring to the course. Then, they apply this in real time in their course. Inclusive instructors are adaptable and look at the syllabus as an important document to help support students succeed in their course but appreciate that equity is different than equality, and that since each student is unique there are times where flexibility is required for achieving the goals of an equitable and inclusive classroom.

> *Inclusive teaching is effective, holistic teaching. It means being aware that students come in with a variety of experiences and levels of preparation and being flexible and adaptable to those needs.*

—Adjunct professor, doctorate-granting university, Engineering and Technology

Recogniz[e] and affirm different life situations that may affect a student's ability to attend class, turn in assignments on time, and attend office hours.

—Survey respondent; rank, institution type and discipline not identified

Keep my eyes on each student, one by one. Mentor students' understanding and continue [to] change teaching methods to be adapted to the student's needs. Encourage work group through projects to allow different students [to] work together.

—Part-time visiting professor, doctorate-granting university, Linguistics and Language

Reflection Question

- How can you embrace diverse perspectives, structure your course, or be adaptable as you further your inclusive teaching efforts?

They Engage With Students Inclusively

Any student who has taken enough classes, and any instructor who has taught enough classes, has faced the dreaded moment when a question is asked to a classroom full of students and the only sound in response is the shuffling of feet, papers, and backpacks. Then the instructor has to make a decision: Do I provide an answer to end the awkward silence, or do I wait? Assuming the instructor makes the latter decision, eventually a student provides their thoughts, and the instructor breathes a sigh of relief as they are able to move on. But the next time this happens, what is the outcome? Commonly, it is going to be that same student who finally provides the answer. Or, maybe in your classes you have seen the opposite occur, that whenever a question is answered there are one or two students who immediately call out or raise their hand to answer the question. This scenario may not be quite as awkward, but in the end the same issue exists in both cases. Only a minority of students in the classroom are having their thoughts and voice be heard, and compounding that issue is that all too often those students whose voices are being heard are not students from marginalized groups. So how do we overcome these challenges and truly engage with our students in the classroom in an inclusive manner? There are a number of strategies that inclusive instructors have found success with to help navigate these challenges. Here, we can talk about some of the options that exist to help you find one or two that might work best for your course.

They Use Students' Names

One of the first things that sets a strong basis for inclusive interactions with students in the classroom was discussed in chapter 4, the importance of learning the names of the students in your class (or minimally having access to those names through name tents, etc.). Depending on class size this can be more or less challenging, but using the strategies set forth in the previous chapter it should be possible and can be very useful in terms of tracking who tends to speak up and who doesn't and in leveling the power structure between the instructor and the student to allow an equitable space for discussion. To this end, inclusive instructors explicitly establish a classroom environment that not only welcomes but encourages and expects to hear the ideas and perspectives of all students, because all students have value to add to the discussions, which is critical in developing a culture in which students feel comfortable speaking up.

They Use Wait Time

Once a question has been asked to the class, another important strategy inclusive instructors use is simply avoiding giving into the pressure of the silence and increasing "wait time" after posing a question to the class. The work of Mary Budd Rowe and others in this arena over a number of years has found that teachers can wait as little as 1.5 seconds (on average) after asking a question before taking a student response, providing their own, or moving forward. Even increasing this to just 3–5 seconds showed increases in both the variety of students responding, to include those who are generally more reserved or prefer to take a few moments to process the question and information before responding, and the quality of those responses (Allen & Tanner, 2002; Rowe, 1969, 1974, 1978, 1986; Tanner, 2013).

They Call on Students Equitably

Once wait time has been increased, how do inclusive instructors actually go about hearing from the students? Well, to make sure that we are not simply hearing from that one student who couldn't take the silence in the previous scenario, it is important that there is an equitable way of determining which students get to respond to a given question. For this reason, many instructors find that hand-raising is still a worthwhile practice, even in the college classroom. This simple practice that students have likely been using throughout their entire schooling career allows the instructor more control on what voices are being heard and ensures it is from a varied set of students. If there is only time for one student to respond to a given question, then the instructor can choose a student who hasn't been heard from recently in this scenario. Alternatively, the instructor could ask for thoughts from a particular area of the classroom that hasn't been a part of the conversation to that point. Ideally, there will be time allowed to hear from more than one student for most questions, in which case a classroom structure can be set where you expect to hear from two or three students about a given question before moving forward. In classroom settings of a smaller size, the "whip-around" approach, where every student has an opportunity to provide their thoughts on a topic, can be utilized (Tanner, 2013). Another approach, which can be especially useful in larger classrooms, is the random-call approach. With this approach, the instructor has either index cards or popsicle sticks, or something similar, with each student's name on them and simply randomly selects one (or more) when a question is asked. As this strategy can put a student "on the spot," it is best used when a clear classroom culture has been set that reduces the pressure of "being right" in one's answers and emphasizes the value of perspectives and ideas in a growth mindset.

> *My students come to my classroom with a staggering variety of linguistic, ethnic, and cultural backgrounds. I build in multiple stages of response to course materials so that students feel empowered to speak in class despite initial reticence due to perceived language barriers. Students respond to assigned readings and viewings in writing from home, then work in small groups (which are assembled differently each class session so that each student has the opportunity to speak with each of their classmates over the semester) to answer the same questions again in the classroom. Then, we have a large group discussion of the same questions. I've found students to be highly engaged by this process.*
>
> —Survey respondent; rank, institution type and discipline not identified

> *I use random call (by group) as to not put the spotlight on any one individual. When I occasionally use call and response I wait for multiple hands to go up so that I can hear from a diversity of students rather than just the one in the front who cannot wait to share their answer. I use name tents where students can write their preferred names so [that] I know what to call them and, by the end of the semester, I know everyone by name.*
>
> —Survey respondent; rank, institution type and discipline not identified

Reflection Questions

- Which of these strategies do you most commonly employ, if any? What is one you would like to try out in your classroom?

They Utilize Digital Technology to Support Inclusion

As technology advances, so too do the ways in which we as instructors can interact with our classes in real time. In an ever-changing arena, this currently includes programs and platforms like clickers, Poll Everywhere, Nearpod, Socratic, Kahoot, Mentimeter, Top Hat, and numerous others. This selection will certainly change and grow by the time you are reading this book, but the important thing is that there are options available that an instructor can examine for use in their class. Technology platforms come with numerous potential benefits related to their versatility. First, they can be particularly useful for those with auditory disabilities. Many allow students to respond anonymously and for those responses to be shared in that anonymous manner to the class. This can be a good way for an instructor to hear from all students while also removing the pressure on anyone particular student. This may, in fact, actually lead to students being willing to discuss their ideas further, once they see they are not the only student with a particular opinion (or, alternatively, advocate for a stance that was less popular in the class). Some of the technological audience response systems also allow for the instructor to collect data to be reviewed outside of class time, both on the class as a whole and individually, which may allow targeted educational interventions where appropriate (McGivern & Coxon, 2015). Importantly, if not adequately considered, the use of technology for gathering student responses can potentially also detract from a truly inclusive classroom if access to the technology that is needed to respond is not ubiquitous. To overcome this obstacle, there are options. One, the necessary technology can be provided to all students in the form of clickers. If this is not possible, or the technology being used employs the students own technology (e.g., smartphone, tablet, laptop, etc.), then it will be important that in advance of the activity the instructor anonymously collects information regarding if all students have the ability to bring that technology to the classroom, for example by using a survey like "Who's In Class?" which is explained in more detail in chapter 6. If there are indeed students who do not have the ability to bring the necessary technology to the classroom, then the instructor can either provide "extra" devices for anyone who would like to borrow one that day (in a way that does not shame or single out students who do borrow these devices) or could determine if it is appropriate to alter the activity into a format where students pair up and then respond together on a shared device. Research has shown that the use of audience response systems is generally well-received by students as a learning tool and can be particularly beneficial in empowering otherwise "reluctant participators" to participate (Graham et al., 2007; Gubbiyappa et al., 2016; Sarvary & Gifford, 2017). Further, for instructors who are concerned that introducing or allowing personal technological devices (e.g., cell phones) in their classroom will have negative impacts by increasing cell phone usage unrelated to the class during class time (Morrell & Joyce, 2015), at least one study has looked into this and has found that this was not the case (Moorleghen et al., 2019). Inclusive instructors have also found ways to accomplish some of these same goals in cases where technology is unavailable or may actually decrease the inclusivity of the course. An example of this can be seen in the use of analog clickers that consist of color-coded response cards, such as those used by Dr. Edward Prather in his astronomy courses at the University of Arizona (TILT, n.d.).

> *[Inclusive teaching strategies I employ include] using anonymous polling to "hear" how the entire class is doing.*
>
> —Part-time lecturer, doctorate-granting university, Biology

Reflection Questions

- What benefits do you see for using digital technology-based audience response systems specifically in your class? What disadvantages? If you haven't used these before, what is one particular topic your class explores that these might be most useful for?

They Acknowledge Various Forms of Engagement

While here we are discussing ways in which students are sharing their opinions audibly or through technology, it is important to note that inclusive instructors also acknowledge that student engagement in a course does not only present itself in this manner. This may be especially relevant for digitally delivered courses. As detailed in chapter 3, inclusive instructors make sure they communicate with their class what the expectations for participation are for that particular course. In fact, this represents an opportune way to involve students in guideline creation at the beginning of the course, so they not only are aware of the expectations but have agency in their creation, and those agreed-on expectations for engagement can be incorporated into the syllabus itself. Then, following these guidelines throughout the duration of the course will maintain that inclusive and equitable environment so that all students can be successful.

> *Participation can take many forms (not just speaking, but also active listening, notetaking that is shared, responding to other students' work, etc.) to allow for and affirm a diversity of ways of contributing.*
>
> —Full professor, baccalaureate college, Education

Reflection Question

- What do you expect from your students in terms of participation in the classroom?

They Utilize Specific Teaching Methods That Promote Inclusivity

While there is significant evidence that shows that achievement gaps exist in higher education in both in-person and digital classrooms, there have been limited studies that explore the pedagogical approaches that reduced these gaps in a controlled manner. Here we will examine instances where there is data that supports the use of various course structures and pedagogies in reducing achievement gaps across the student population in higher education. While a number of these studies have occurred in STEM-fields, it is likely that the approaches to teaching are applicable across disciplines.

Their Courses Have High Structure

A 2014 study by Eddy and Hogan specifically disaggregated student data by racial groups and first-generation status to address the idea that the level of course structure may impact achievement across these groups. Through this disaggregation, this study extended the work of Freeman et al. in 2011, which found that increased course structure improved student performance broadly. In the 2014 study, course structure was categorized as low, moderate, or high, where low was traditional lecture, moderate allowed for 15–40% of class time devoted to student-centered activities or interaction, and high had greater than 40% of the class time for these student engagement activities (as well as increased use of graded preparatory and review assignments). Examining student performance across these three levels of structure found that increased course structure (to a moderate level of structure) enhanced exam performance of all students but disproportionately enhanced the exam performance of Black and first-generation students. Indeed, the achievement gap for Black students was reduced by 50%. Eddy and Hogan (2014) noted this finding that pedagogical decisions can influence the achievement of students' subpopulations differentially has also been seen in other studies in physics (Beichner, 2007) and psychology (Kim, 2008), emphasizing the importance of considering pedagogical methods in creating inclusive and equitable classrooms.

They Implement Active Learning Approaches

As course structure choices that increase student participation and engagement during class time led to improved performance in traditionally lower-achieving student populations, this suggests that utilizing student-centered, active learning approaches can not only broadly enhance student performance (as reviewed in Michael, 2006) but also promote a more inclusive classroom. In 2020, Theobald et al. conducted a meta-analysis of 15 studies looking at examination scores and 26 studies examining failure rates, totaling over 50,000 students, and found that active learning decreased achievement gaps in underrepresented minorities and low-income students by 33% and 45% for each respective metric. Indeed, in our own teaching, we have examined the role of serious gaming as a means of active learning in the STEM fields and found that females made a larger knowledge gain utilizing this methodology than did their male counterparts (Addy et al., 2018). Our experiences, and those of many of the respondents to our national survey of faculty on inclusive teaching, note positive experiences related to inclusivity and equity with various other active learning pedagogies, including but not limited to case studies, problem-based learning (PBL), classroom jigsaws, team-based learning (TBL), classroom debates, interactive lectures, process-oriented guided inquiry learning (POGIL), and think-pair-share activities. As can be seen in their descriptions that follow, many of these activities utilize small groups and collaborative learning, a process that has been found to be broadly effective in enhancing student achievement (Johnson et al., 2000). Further, while many of these pedagogies were developed for face-to-face courses, all of them can be applied in a synchronous online learning environment using breakout group functions available on most video messaging platforms, and most can be utilized even in asynchronous online environments.

Case study learning employs a narrative or real-life example where information and/or data is provided relevant to a problem presented to the characters in the case itself. Students are often required to understand the problem and read the case to acquire the necessary information to come to an educated conclusion or solution to the problem presented. This may occur through a series of smaller, more directed questions or a more open-ended problem-based activity. The case study method of learning seeks to employ various aspects of Bloom's taxonomy and, if designed properly, particularly target the upper levels of application, analysis, evaluation, and potentially creation. Particularly when multiple cases are used over the duration of a course, cases with a diverse set of characters and situations can enhance how students of diverse backgrounds may be able to connect to the material. The

National Center for Case Study Teaching in Science (University of Buffalo Libraries, 2020) and the SAGE Business Cases (SAGE, 2020) represent reviewed and vetted collections that can be used in higher education teaching in their respective disciplines.

PBL is a method where instead of being provided information that can then be used to solve problems, like in case studies, students are instead provided a real-world problem first, often complex and open-ended in nature, and tasked with determining what they need to learn in order to solve it. These learning activities can take place over various timelines depending on the topic, from a single class session to the entirety of the course. PBL is commonly done with students working in teams and thus can leverage the diverse assets the group members bring to the team. Even when done individually, PBL helps minimize the power difference in the classroom, as the students themselves acquire ownership in what and how they learn. Examples of how PBL has been applied in STEM fields, and opportunities for implementation, can be found in the New England Board of Higher Education Problem Based Learning Projects website (New England Board of Higher Education, 2020). Importantly, aspects of PBL can be incorporated into various teaching methods, some of which are described next.

POGIL is a variation of PBL, where the faculty provide the necessary data for students (in small groups) to discover key concepts for themselves with little direct guidance from the instructor. Related to the "process-oriented" component of POGIL, the instructor intentionally considers what process skills are important to develop in their students, and, oftentimes, the students are asked to reflect on their learning process during or after the activity itself. As the instructor interacts with students during the activity, and reviews process-based reflections after the activity, they are better able to understand their student population and adapt future learning activities appropriately. The POGIL website not only provides more information about this pedagogy, but also implementation tutorials and curricular materials for fields including psychology, computer science, and others (POGIL, 2020).

Classroom jigsaws are a cooperative learning technique that often employ aspects of PBL while also making students dependent on each other in order to succeed. This method was first developed in 1971 by Elliot Anderson as a way to combat racial bias, and the basis is that students are divided into groups and each member of that group is required to specifically learn only a percentage of the topic being explored and then come back to their group and share what they have learned. The group as a whole then is assessed either through their ability to solve a problem they were tasked with through a quiz or another means. There is only one student responsible for becoming an expert in a certain part of the content initially, yet students are assessed on all aspects; each student in the group has an implicit value for all others. Additional information about this pedagogy and tips for implementation across disciplines is accessible at the Jigsaw Classroom (2020) website.

TBL is a specific teaching strategy that uses a three-step process to achieve learning goals, which starts with preclass preparation, in-class readiness assurance testing, and an application-based activity. The preclass preparation asks the students to use materials, commonly provided by the instructor, to explore concepts related to the topic being examined in advance of coming to class. Then, the initial portion of the class session is devoted to individual and then team-based assessment, both of which count toward the individual student's grade but are geared at assuring that the students, individually and as a team, are ready to apply their learning. The third step asks students to apply their learning, commonly in a means similar to the PBL methods described. An overview of this pedagogy as well as relevant resources can be found at the Team-Based Learning Collaborative (2020) website.

Interactive lectures are classes in which the instructor intentionally incorporates engagement opportunities for students to participate and interact directly in the material. For example, in a mathematics course, after an instructor has explained a particular analysis, time is allowed for students to work on applying that analysis in a practice problem, followed by discussion. In other disciplines, this may take different forms. One commonly noted method inclusive instructors we surveyed used was to employ "think-pair-share," where after lecture or readings students were posed with a question that they were to spend time thinking about individually, then pair up with one or more other students to brainstorm together, and then share the conclusions they have come to with the class. This is particularly effective from an inclusivity perspective, as when each student gets an opportunity to share their thoughts with other students in the class in a low-stakes situation, different ideas can be evaluated in the pairings, and then there are opportunities for those more willing to share with the larger class.

Building on some of the benefits of think-pair-share, classroom debates task students with arguing for or against controversial stances relevant to the classroom content. There are many ways in which classroom debates can be organized, whether there are several breakout groups that are all debating topics simultaneously or whether teams of students work to develop an argument together about one of several specific topics and the debate occurs with two teams debating opposing sides of the same topic in front of the class. By doing this in teams, it again allows an initial lower-stakes opportunity for all voices to be heard and for that message to be incorporated into what is presented in the argument in front of the class, without forcing any one individual student to speak in this forum.

[I use] think-pair-share and other student-centered activities interspersed wit

—Full professor, baccalaureate cou...

My courses are active, with a variety of strategies that support a diversity of learners (jigsaws, etc.) and small-group work dominating course time.

—Adjunct professor, associate college, Biology

[I use] small group projects [and] problem-based learning activities.

—Associate professor, master's college, Education

Reflection Questions

- Which of the active learning strategies that you have never implemented before would you like to incorporate into your teaching? Which class and for which topic would you implement it?

They Use Technology Inclusively

As technology advances, and its implementation in the classroom expands, instructors in higher education are looking to employ these tools in inclusive ways. To this end, a 2016 study by Meredith Warren showed the efficacy of utilizing student-centered technology in enhancing student participation and high-quality understanding in the humanities. Further, a study in utilizing technology-enabled active learning in introductory physics courses found that this learning approach appealed more to females (an underrepresented population in the field) than it did to males, suggesting the potential for its use to narrow learning gaps between genders (Ruey et al., 2011). Later in this chapter we will discuss assessing students in an inclusive way, but the use of daily in-class, online testing as a formative means of learning in large lecture classes not only yielded an overall improvement in exam performance by approximately half a letter grade above controls, but also reduced the achievement gap between social classes by 50% (Pennebaker et al., 2013). Technology use plays a particularly important role in hybrid and online courses. As mentioned previously, it has been shown that achievement gaps exist in the online course context across disciplines. A 2019 study by Gavassa et al. conducted a comparative study of a single course taught by the same instructor in three formats: low-structured face-to-face, highly structured hybrid (50% face-to-face and 50% online), and moderately structured fully online. Interestingly, in this course exam scores were lowest for all students in the low-structured face-to-face course, while Hispanic and Black students had higher scores in the highly structured hybrid course, confirming the findings of the 2014 study by Eddy & Hogan that course structure impacts achievement gaps and suggesting that the hybrid course format may be especially beneficial to certain underrepresented groups. Other studies have identified that achievement gaps exist in massive open online course (MOOCs), specifically related to gender, geography, and social identity (Kizilcec & Halawa, 2015; Kizilcec et al., 2017). These gaps were able to be reduced by including short activities known to lessen social identity threats (e.g., writing about personal values related to their course) or those geared at increasing a sense of belonging in the course (e.g., reading testimonials from advanced learners who had similar experiences), concepts that were introduced as broadly important in chapters 1 and 2. There is mounting evidence that similar pedagogical activities that require students to reflect on their learning, especially related to their personal values, can also be effective at reducing achievement gaps in face-to-face courses (Harackiewicz et al., 2016). This study by Harachiewicz et al. (2016) examined the achievement gaps in underrepresented minority and first-generation students in STEM fields by implementing utility-value interventions where students wrote about the personal relevance of course materials and reduced the achievement gaps seen in the course by 61%. Many of the teachers responding to our national survey on inclusive teaching also mentioned utilizing reflective writing and utility value interventions as being beneficial to inclusivity in their own courses.

> *[I employ] interventions to increase student motivation (utility value and belonging) and allow . . . students space to describe connections meaningful to them with others.*
>
> —Associate professor, master's college, Biology

> *[We do] values affirmation exercises (talking about how students' values motivate their learning) [and focus on] affirming identity and belonging through exercises that place students in the role of scientists/experts.*
>
> —Associate dean, master's college, Environmental Studies and Forestry

> *[I start the day with] brief reflective questions to begin class, [where students] write on [their] own, then share with partner or in small group.*
>
> —Part-time lecturer, baccalaureate college, Biology

They Use Multiple Modalities to Enhance Student Learning

Regardless of discipline or course format, the core concepts of the now classical works of Benjamin Bloom's "Learning for Mastery" that achievement gaps are diminished when varied instructional methods are utili.. true. Evidence indicates that the positive effects of utilizing multiple n. of instruction, directed by formative assessment, not only increases achievement outcomes, but also confidence in learning, in-class engagement, and attitudes toward learning (Guskey, 2007). In our own classes, we have seen the benefit of diversifying instruction in how our students respond to the course through anecdotal and evaluative feedback. Further, instructors who responded to our national survey indicated their intentionality about utilizing assorted instructional activities in their own courses. As such, the best specific pedagogy for creating an equitable and inclusive classroom may be using a variety of pedagogies.

My courses are active, with a variety of strategies that support a diversity of learners (jigsaws, etc.) and small-group work dominating course time. Strategies that I see as specifically being more inclusive include the following:

- *Preclass structured reading guides that students fill out (terminology and conceptual)*
- *Reflection letters, three per semester, to open communication with students about goals and barriers for the course (I used to do required office hours but am an office-less adjunct now)*
- *A variety of strategies from Kimberly Tanner's work—trying to hear every voice in a class period, using miniature whiteboards so that I can see every student's responss (literally), tables . . . labeled by concepts we are working on so that I'm not calling on a group by its conversationally dominant member, [etc.].*

—Adjunct professor, associate college, Biology

I employ a variety of activities (silent writing time; options to share or keep writing to one's self; choice of assignments; creative modes of expression; activities that involve movement; etc.) so that students can focus on engaging with the material and one another.

—Full professor, baccalaureate college, Education

Reflection Questions

- Take one specific topic you address in a course that you have taught and think about the method you have utilized to teach that concept. What is another instructional approach you could use to teach that same concept? Would it be possible to implement both pedagogical choices in your class, and do you think that would benefit your students?

They Conduct Inclusive Assessment

A significant component of most college courses is the assessment of student learning. Historically, student assessment in higher education has most commonly been in the form of examinations. However, whether standard examinations represent the most inclusive means of assessment, and what the format, style, and expectations of those exams should be, is an ongoing debate. So what do inclusive instructors think about assessment?

They Consider the Length and Timing of Assessments

One consideration in terms of examination format is the rate at which students need to answer questions to complete the exam. In the 1950s, Frederic Lord explored the question of whether examinations that required faster or slower answer rates were more valid in terms of assessing student learning. This study found that there was no inherent difference in their validity but with the caveat that a general conclusion could not truly be reached without considering a specific exam, its content and question number, and the amount of time to administer the exam (Lord, 1953). In 1996, a study by Parr et al. suggested that "unspeeded" exams were a more equitable means of assessment, especially considering students with disabilities (Parr, 1996). More recently, a study by Tijmstra and Bolsinova (2018), which focused on how to analyze questions students did not answer due to time restrictions, suggested that the practical considerations of time limits on exams are necessitated by the desired outcomes of the course. If answering questions in a particular amount of time was important for the discipline, then a timed test would be most appropriate, with appropriate consideration given to the number of questions and amount of time allowed. Alternatively, if speed of response was not of particular importance, then an untimed test (or not counting any unanswered questions when assessing an exam) would be more appropriate (Tijmstra & Bolsinova, 2018). With such understanding, assessments such as take-home exams and authentic assessments that resemble the real-world application of students' learning become not only viable but potentially preferable. And if a timed exam is to be given, it is vital that the instructor work with the accessibility services at their institution to allow for any accommodations necessary for the students in their class.

They Carefully Choose Their Question Styles

Another consideration when creating an examination is the type of questions that are offered. A 2017 study by Hubbard et al. examined how multiple true-false (MTF) versus free-response (FR) questions reveal student understanding of concepts. Their findings suggested that MTF was best at revealing students who had mixed conceptions (some correct and some incorrect), while FR questions were particularly useful at identifying the completeness, or incompleteness, of students' understanding of a concept. In the end, the authors recommended the use of hybrid examinations that combined multiple question formats to get the broadest and most accurate assessment of student learning.

They Allow for Immediate Feedback and the Retaking of Exams

Some instructors who prioritize student mastery of the material in their courses find it beneficial to offer students multiple chances to take an exam until they earn a grade they are satisfied with. This can occur through taking the same exam over from start to finish, from redoing specific questions they had not earned full credit on the first time through, or by taking alternative examinations on the same material. Indeed, with these concepts in mind, the immediate feedback assessment technique (IF-AT) was developed. IF-AT exams (commonly multiple choice), have a student respond to a question by scratching off a selected answer, and they are immediately shown whether that answer is correct (often by revealing a star). If they did not answer correctly, then they can reevaluate their thinking and try to answer again, but with the fact that it was not their first answer still readily apparent to the instructor for grading purposes. The benefit of the IF-AT method is that students leave the exam immediately knowing the correct answer, which is known to support learning. Moreover, a study found that implementing the IF-AT method reduced student test anxiety (Dibattista & Gosse, 2006). This overarching strategy of multiple attempts on an exam or question fits nicely in the growth mindset and learner-centered approaches discussed previously.

They Include Student-Created Exam Questions

Another strategy that fits with the concept of making examinations learning tools themselves is involving students in the creation of the exam questions. In a first-year seminar that an author of this book teaches, the "final examination" for the course occurs throughout the entirety of the semester, with each class session starting with a student-created question. At the beginning of the semester, each student chooses a day they will be responsible for creating a question they believe represents one of the most critical concepts from the previous class. The student creating the question must provide it to the instructor in advance of the class and go through a collaborative revision process with the instructor to ensure the question represents what the student felt was important and is framed appropriately for other students to respond to. Once finalized, that question is then delivered to the class. Students are then assessed on both the questions they created and the questions that they answer through the semester. We have personally seen this method enhance students' feelings of ownership in their learning, as well as their belonging to the class. Further, this method helps to diminish the classroom power structure between instructor and student. A study examined this same concept in a single session as opposed to semester-long examination format and found that student written exams improved question relevance and aided in managing exam-related stress while also being perceived as more challenging (Corrigan & Craciun, 2013).

They Leverage Technology When Testing

Finally, related to examination modes of assessment, the increasing ability for instructors to leverage the power of technology is something that inclusive instructors are considering and utilizing in their courses. An article by Williams et al. (2014) focusing on English (UK) universities notes how while pedagogical changes to support individuals with learning difficulties have seen significant changes, assessment methods have not. In their study, they look specifically at the use of untimed online assessment methods and conclude that standard examination practices unfairly disadvantage an increasing proportion of students (those with specific learning difficulties) and that online assessment methods can provide a more equitable mechanism for student assessment.

> *I offer untimed, online assessments that they can take as many times as they want until they get a grade they want—these are very difficult, so students do them many times. The grades students get on these assessments are not the same as their course averages, and many of my lower-achieving students do better on these because of their work ethic.*

> —Full professor, associate college, Biology

They Offer Alternatives to Traditional Exams

While we have discussed items to consider in making more inclusive examinations, we have not yet addressed how inclusive instructors view the place for examinations as inclusive and equitable. It is fair to say that many inclusive instructors utilize examinations in their courses; however, that is not to say that all do. And, moreover, the proportion of a course grade that is exam dependent can vary significantly. Indeed, there is some evidence that moving away from grading schemes that emphasize high-stakes exam scores over more low-stakes methods of assessment can help close achievement gaps. For example, a study found that the performance of females in STEM fields, a group that historically shows lower outcomes, improved by utilizing mixed assessment methods, including group participation, low-stakes quizzes and assignments, and in-class activities (Cotner & Ballen, 2017). Interestingly, even the performance gap on exams in these courses decreased with the assessment diversification. These authors posited that their findings likely extend beyond females in STEM and that the microclimate of classrooms related to assessment methods can impact success rates for various underrepresented groups in various fields. So what are the other types of activities that can be assessed toward a student earning a grade in your course? Almost any other activities that are done in the class, including problem sets, oral presentations, group activities, case studies, skill demonstrations, research papers, reflections, quizzes, and in-class participation, among others, are ripe for assessment and being considered as important factors in forming a final course grade for a student. What is clear is that inclusive instructors use various forms of assessment in their courses and carefully design them to be equitable. Further, with any assessment utilized, it is critical that the instructor identify if it is meant to be formative (i.e., determining how a student is learning material and supporting that learning through ongoing feedback) or summative (i.e., evaluating how much has been learned) and ensure that the timing and method of assessment is appropriate for the purpose. Inclusive instructors will often emphasize formative assessments so that their students have multiple chances of learning that are not high stakes and help students achieve the learning goals.

> *[I] hav[e] a clearly articulated course structure that includes daily assignments and regular low-stakes formative assessments [and use] early summative assessments worth [a] lower percetnage of the course grade than later assessments.*

—Lecturer, doctoral-granting university, Biology

> *Utiliz[e] formative assessment and various types of summative assessments. Hav[e] transparent assignments.*

—Full professor, doctorate-granting university, Journalism, Media Studies and Communication

> *[I place] significant emphasis on formative assessment techniques (low and hi tech) [and use] varied assessment techniques incentivizing preparation for classroom activities.*

—Lecturer, doctoral-granting university, Biology

They Use Inclusive Grading Strategies

Inclusive instructors seek to utilize grading strategies that are the least biased and support the learning of diverse students. To this end, one question that an instructor should consider prior to conducting any form of assessment, and share with their students, is whether their grading strategy is based on student performance relative to others in the class (norm referenced) or purely on their individual achievement (mastery based or criterion referenced) (Bond, 1996; Huitt, 1996). With norm-referenced grading, an individual grade is compared to the group at large, most commonly with the anticipation of a bell curve, where most students earn an intermediate grade with smaller populations earning higher and lower grades. In criterion-referenced grading, each student is assessed independently of their ability to master the material and skills on a specific predetermined set of criteria. In this method, it is formally possible that all students earn A's or F's or anywhere in between. A study by Smeding et al. (2013) examining Psychology undergraduates at a French institution found that the achievement gap due to SES was decreased by employing mastery-based assessment. While this study provides strong reasoning to consider utilizing criterion-referenced grading, either strategy may be appropriate depending on the course and desired outcomes, and, indeed, it is possible to combine the approaches in a process that clusters or groups student performance even before assigning grades.

The goal is success for all students, not ranking students on a normal distribution.

—Lecturer, doctoral-granting university, Psychology

Inclusive teaching is creating a welcoming classroom environment for ALL students, having high expectation with support for students who need it to be successful, and differentiating content presentation, learning activities . . . that accommodate each student's learning style, and options for demonstrating mastery.

—Adjunct instructor, master's college, Psychology

I employ student self-assessment and cocreated grading criteria so that students with different needs, styles, preferences, strengths, and challenges can engage in a variety of ways and demonstrate their learning in different ways.

—Full Professor, baccalaureate college, Education

When it comes to the actual grading of assignments and examinations, where possible it is inclusive to use the blinded method, where the assessor does not know whose work they are assessing. This helps to reduce any potential conscious or unconscious biases that might exist, either based on the student's past work or any other factors.

[I] use blind grading practices and inform students of such.

—Full professor, undergraduate college, Biology

In the discussions in this section, we considered assessment in the context of grades. We would be remiss to not note that some inclusive instructors are minimizing grading in their courses by utilizing self- or peer-review processes, authentic assessments, or instituting "grade-free zones" in their courses, or even moving fully to "ungrading." Ungrading does not necessarily mean that instructors do not review and provide feedback on student work through the course; in fact, it generally focuses on these aspects but removes the attaching of grades to that work, as it looks at the assignments as a means for learning not assessment. At institutions that require course grades, some inclusive instructors have turned that process over to the students themselves, asking students to self-reflect, determine, and justify their own course grade. In these cases, the power dynamic between instructor and student is clearly diminished, which can positively influence the classroom community and learning throughout the duration of the course. There are also a number of institutions that have moved away from grading entirely, currently including schools like Hampshire College, Antioch University, and others. Additionally, there are institutions that maintain course grades but in a deemphasized manner supplemented by narrative evaluations, currently including Reed College and Sarah Lawrence College. A number of these institutions specifically state a focus on student growth and constructive learning as a reason for their nontraditional assessment models.

Reflection Questions

- Think about one means of assessment you implemented in your last course. Hypothetically reformat that assessment or its delivery in an alternative way based on the information in this section. What advantages might there be to this new version? What challenges do you foresee? Do the advantages outweigh the challenges?

They Acquire Student Feedback Throughout the Semester

Returning to the foundational concept of inclusive teaching being student centered, it is critical to acquire student feedback on their experiences in the course and use that feedback productively. This gives all students a voice. Most institutions of higher education have a system for end-of-course student evaluations, which are commonly standardized across the institution. When appropriately reviewed and considered by the instructor, these evaluations can indeed be useful in revising, updating, and improving a course for the next time it is taught. However, inclusive instructors suggest relying solely on end-of-course evaluations has two major detractions: first, that it does not allow the instructor to be responsive in real time, and second, that the next time the course is taught, it will not be with the same student community, and as such those evaluations may not be as relevant. Further, although not called out explicitly in the study, evaluations are vulnerable to biases. In chapter 2 it was noted how even as early as during the creation of the syllabus an instructor can embed opportunities for student feedback throughout the course, and in so doing make students aware that they have agency in the course structure and design from the beginning. Indeed, a major theme of instructors responding to our national survey on inclusive teaching was the need for, and use of, early, in-course student evaluations.

> *[I] conduct an observation/midsemester feedback session to get feedback from students about how the class is helping them learn and what can be done to improve it.*

—Part-time instructional consultant, master's college, English

> *[I] seek midquarter course feedback, including about ways to make the classroom environment best suited to student learning.*

—Teaching post-doctoral fellow, doctorate-granting university, Biology

> *[I] ask students about their experiences with the course material. I check in with students regularly to get feedback on how to improve teaching.*

—Assistant professor, baccalaureate college, Nursing

They Acquire Feedback During the Course

Indeed, articles in the literature also support this idea of collecting student feedback during the course itself, be it regularly throughout the semester, at the end of learning units, or at the midsemester mark (Golding & Adam, 2016; Griffin & Cook, 2009; Santhanam & Hicks, 2004). Moreover, the literature speaks to using this feedback not simply to evaluate one's teaching, but rather to improve it. This again harkens back to a key tenet of inclusive teaching in the classroom: adaptability. Inclusive teachers, like their students, employ a growth mindset and take a reflective approach to how they view their evaluations and then can use that data as formative feedback to be employed in near real time in the same course the feedback came from (Golding & Adam, 2016). Alternatively, if instructors hold negative perceptions of evaluations, and believe that student evaluations are flawed and poor indications of teaching quality, they are unlikely to be able to utilize

the feedback to improve (Aleamoni, 1999; Smith, 2008).
ceive that there are barriers to their success in a course, then it be..
instructor who seeks to be inclusive to respond to this, either by ada..
their classroom or discussing with the class why certain instructional methodologies are being utilized. Even if alterations cannot be made, this allows
for students to feel heard, gain ownership in the course, and understand why
certain pedagogical choices have been made.

> *I solicit anonymous midterm feedback and make changes to the course based*
> *on those suggestions (or explain why I can't make a requested change).*

> —Associate professor, baccalaureate college, Communications

> *Students are engaged around the course outcomes and feedback is welcomed. Students*
> *feel a sense of ownership of the learning within the inclusive teaching environment.*

> —Director of assessment, doctorate-granting university, Education

Reflection Questions

- How often do you receive formal (anonymous or otherwise) feedback
  from your students about the course? When do you receive such
  feedback? Would it be beneficial to receive more feedback from the
  students or at a different time?

They Use Varying Methods for Acquiring Feedback

So how do inclusive instructors acquire student feedback during their course
term? The short answer is that there are multiple options, and inclusive
instructors can and do utilize the methods that are most appropriate for their
course and student population. One method commonly applied is the survey
method. This can be done either in person or online (potentially through
course management software) and can be implemented anonymously or with
the option for students to identify themselves if desired. In general, it is good
practice to collect feedback anonymously, as they may not feel comfortable
being honest with feedback that may be seen as critical when they are still in
the ongoing course. Another means of acquiring student feedback is through
reflective writing assignments that ask the students not only to reflect on
what they learned, but also how they experienced their learning. Depending
on course structure, these assignments may be graded, or perhaps low stakes
to ungraded. Some students may feel more able to clearly articulate their
perspectives through talking about them rather than writing or completing a

survey. Indeed, we saw several respondents to our national survey on inclusive teaching mention that they make themselves available for these one-on-one conversations outside of class time and are explicit about office hours not being only for course content discussions but also for student feedback about the learning process, including both what is working for them and (especially) what is not. While some students may be confident enough to have these one-on-one conversations, that may not be the case for all students. In cases where in-person discussions are considered valuable but there is concern that all voices may not be heard equally, the use of student representatives who converse with subsets of students across the classroom community can be useful. When this approach is implemented, instructors have often had the "representative" positions be voluntary and ideally rotate to include other students throughout the course timeline. One thing that inclusive instructors do really well is appreciate that they are not alone in the endeavor of trying to provide the best learning environment for their students. With that in mind, collaborating with other colleagues or instructional consultants at their institution's center for teaching and learning (if present), can be a useful way to acquire anonymous feedback from students. The classic saying "you scratch my back and I will scratch yours" is quite applicable here, and finding a colleague who can come to your class to collect feedback in turn for you doing the same in their class can be very useful indeed. In the end, it is important to realize that collecting feedback from students about their learning is in many ways similar to supporting their learning in the first place, and offering and encouraging various means by which students can provide feedback to you will likely lead to the most robust and useful responses.

> *I have a clear teaching philosophy and approach to inclusion and accessibility stated in my syllabus and I discuss this with students on the first day. I make myself available after class and during office hours with the explicit invitation of feedback about the learning environment and issues of access and accommodation.*

> —Assistant professor, master's college, Anthropology

> *[I provide] multiple avenues for feedback (i.e., formal/informal/anonymous or in person).*

> —Associate dean, master's college, Environmental Studies and Forestry

> *Inclusive teaching means using classroom pedagogical strategies that aim to help all students feel empowered to learn, valued in the classroom, and expect to be capable of success. When possible it's good for these strategies to be research validated, though many are based also on some mix of instructor experience, student feedback, and common sense.*

> —Full professor, baccalaureate college, Physics

Reflection Question

- What is a method of gathering student feedback you are not currently using that you would want to apply in your course?

Key Points

- Inclusive instructors are student centered, embrace a growth mindset, ensure transparency in their assignments, and use principles of course design that can support learning, value diversity, and exhibit adaptability.
- In the teaching strategies that they implement in the classroom, inclusive instructors engage students inclusively in their learning, strive to use assessment measures that are fair and unbiased, and continually seek feedback from their students to modify their approaches.

In chapters 3–5 we have explored the process of designing and implementing an inclusive and equitable course, from constructing a syllabus to creating a welcoming environment during the first few course meetings, to, here in chapter 5, utilizing recommended practices for engaging with students in the classroom, instructional activities, assessment, and feedback acquisition throughout the duration of the course. We used our own experiences, published research, and the responses to our national survey of higher education instructors on inclusive teaching to inform these conversations. In the Epilogue, we will explore how we in the field of higher education can go from inclusive courses to more wide-spanning inclusive environments at a departmental, school or divisional, and institutional level.

PART THREE

DEVELOPING AND
SUSTAINING A CULTURE
OF INCLUSIVE TEACHING

6

USING A TOOL TO SUPPORT
INCLUSIVE TEACHING

*[The form helps instructors by][b]eing more aware of the population of students they
are teaching any how to better implement class content based on this. It allowed my
professor to get to know me, and it may make students feel more comfortable going to
that professor for help during office hours or even in class. I liked it because it made
me feel like my professor knew me for me and not just as another number.*

—Student feedback on "Who's in Class?" form

B y now we hope you have a sense of what inclusive instructors do with
regard to designing their course syllabi, fostering a welcoming learning environment, and choosing which teaching approaches to implement. In this chapter we describe the "Who's in Class?" form, a tool that
can support inclusive instructors in designing equitable courses (see Figure
6.1). In our experience the majority of students have appreciated when their
instructors implement the form, and the instrument serves as an excellent
starting point for instructors teaching for the first time or those who have
been teaching for many years, as information pertains to the students in each
unique class.

As touched on in various parts of the book, starting in chapter 1, inclusive instructors recognize the critical importance of understanding who
their learners are with regard to the social identities, equity and inclusion
challenges, perspectives, and other attributes that they bring to the course.
A major initial challenge that inclusive instructors face in learning these
aspects about their students is that diversity can be both visible and invisible,
and they do not want to make assumptions about their learners. To address
this concern, they provide opportunities for students to share their diverse
attributes. The "Who's in Class?" form is such a tool that provides a venue for
students to voluntarily and anonymously describe aspects about themselves
that can impact how they learn in a course.

Figure 6.1. The "Who's in Class?" form.

This form gives you the opportunity to share aspects of your social identity and other attributes that can help your instructor know how to better support overall learning in this course. Please be aware that you are *not* obligated to complete this form. The information collected will be aggregated, held anonymous, and used to help foster an inclusive and equitable classroom.

Course name: _____

Instructor's last name: _____

Semester (e.g., Spring 2025): _____

Please answer the questions that follow. As a reminder, you are not obligated to answer any of the questions. The goal of this questionnaire is to help me understand who is in class so that I can support your success.

Section I. Select all that apply.

Y N

❑ ❑ I work on or off campus. The number of hours that I work per week is

_____.

❑ ❑ I play on a varsity athletics team at this institution.

❑ ❑ I live off campus. My commute time is _____.

❑ ❑ I am over 25 years of age.

❑ ❑ I am on active duty or a veteran.

Section II. Select all that apply.

Y N

❑ ❑ I have a mobile device with Wi-Fi capability.

❑ ❑ I have a laptop or desktop computer that I can use for classwork.

❑ ❑ I am financially capable of purchasing all of the materials needed for this class (e.g., textbooks) without hardship.

❑ ❑ I am Pell eligible, meaning that my family income level allows me to qualify for federal Pell grants.

❑ ❑ I receive other forms of financial aid in significant amounts.

(continues)

Figure 6.1. (*continued*)

Section III. Select all that apply.

Y   N

❑   ❑   I have a disability, either invisible or visible. Here is more information that I would like to share about my disability: _____

❑   ❑   Other health concerns that I would like to share are _____.

❑   ❑   I am a "quiet" student, meaning that I reenergize from having time alone.

❑   ❑   I engage in religious or spiritual practices that may impact my ability to attend class. More specifically, I would like to share _____.

❑   ❑   I engage in religious or spiritual practices that may impact my performance in class. More specifically, I would like to share _____

❑   ❑   I have dependents I take care of outside of school.

❑   ❑   My preference for class assignments is to complete them by typing rather than handwriting.

❑   ❑   Other factors that may impact my experiences in this class are _____
_____.

Section IV. Select all that apply.

Y   N

❑   ❑   I am a first-generation student (i.e., neither of my parents obtained a bachelor's degree at a 4-year institution).

❑   ❑   One of my parents obtained a bachelor's degree at a 4-year institution.

❑   ❑   Both of my parents obtained a bachelor's degree at a 4-year institution.

❑   ❑   I have a sibling who has or is currently attending a 4-year institution.

Section V. Answer the questions that follow.

My racial/ethnic background is _____.

My gender identity is _____.

My sexuality is _____.

The pronouns I use are _____.

My nationality/country of origin is _____.

English is not my first language. My proficiency level is (e.g., beginning/intermediate/advanced for listening/speaking/writing/reading) _____.

(*continues*)

Figure 6.1. (*continued*)

> **Section VI. Additional social identities or personal attributes that are not included in the previous sections that I would like to share are as follows:**
>
> _____
>
> _____
>
> _____
>
> _____
>
> **Section VII. Personal connections with the material that relate to my social identity or other personal attributes that I would like to share are as follows:**
>
> _____
>
> _____
>
> _____
>
> _____
>
> **Section VIII. My expectations for inclusivity (an equitable, welcoming environment) in this course are as follows:**
>
> _____
>
> _____
>
> _____

Tool Design

In the first phase of designing the tool, our research team, consisting of faculty as well as an educational developer, considered attributes related to equity and inclusion that can implicate students' ability to meet the learning outcomes of a course. We deliberated on the content and drafted a preliminary version of the tool. In the next phase, the team invited feedback from students, including those selected as peer advocates in an organization focused on social justice and diversity, equity, and inclusion, as well as staff in multicultural affairs offices and faculty. We used this next round of feedback to further refine the tool. We next invited instructors to use the tool in various types of courses using particular guidelines, as indicated later in this chapter. Because this was part of a research investigation, institutional research approval was sought and the project considered exempt. The tool is designed for instructors who have a baseline understanding and appreciation for major principles in inclusive teaching, such as bias awareness, stereotype threat, and microaggressions, and seek to be more inclusive in their instruction. We recommend that before using this tool all instructors undergo such professional development so as not to reinforce bias.

Implementing the Tool

The "Who's in Class?" form was initially administered in a survey software platform with controls set to anonymous and a link distributed to the instructor for administration in their course. The data were only provided to instructors in aggregate to minimize the chances of identifying students. The instructor was given a link to the report with the data that allowed them to monitor student responses in real time.

Instructors were asked to administer the form through correspondence to students in the first week of classes. They were welcome to send the initial correspondence prior to the start of classes and were asked to send at least one reminder email. The instructors were to indicate that the instrument was nonmandatory and anonymous and to explain the rationale behind why they were using it. Based on our experience, this worked fairly well, and we have further recommendations for usage. We encourage multiple modes for disseminating the invitation to complete the form through email and a LMS as well as allowing class time for explanation and completion of the form, if possible.

Interpreting Student Responses and Making Changes

As the information from this form is relevant to, and intended to enhance, the particular offering of the course it is implemented in, it is important that the analysis of its results occur early in the course timeline. At the end of the first week the instructors were encouraged to reflect on how they would make changes in their course based on their students' responses. This discovery process proved to be a welcome new challenge for them. They created an action plan and met with staff from the center for teaching and learning to discuss the changes they would make to their courses given their newfound learning of the attributes their diverse learners bring to the course.

Feedback and Reflections During the Semester

Instructors were encouraged to explicitly let students know the changes they made to the course based on feedback received without revealing any information not appropriate to share with the class. Otherwise, students may not have been aware that there were changes made due to these factors to be inclusive of all learners. While teaching the course instructors were also encouraged to keep a digital or physical journal and record their perceptions of the impact of their inclusive teaching approaches on student learning. They were also encouraged to ask students for midsemester feedback using open-ended questions, similar to those described in chapter 4.

Case Applications

Following are scenarios that instructors may encounter in their classes after administering the form and examples of small modifications they can make in their course syllabi and teaching practices to foster inclusion. Please note that for simplicity, in many of the scenarios only one factor implicated is presented, but any combination of factors is more likely, given the intersecting identities and other attributes that diverse students bring to their classes. After the findings are introduced for a particular example, reflect on the changes you would make if presented with the scenario as the instructor of record and afterward review some sample actions.

Financial Hardship

Findings: There are students in the course who cannot easily purchase required materials and who are Pell eligible and recipients of financial aid. There are also students who do not have laptops. The instructor teaches a STEM (science, technology, engineering and math) course with a high-cost textbook that is a useful learning resource to help students meet their course objectives.

Modifications: Because there are students facing financial hardship, the instructor carefully brainstorms what they can do to make the course materials more accessible to all students. The instructor has a few copies of the textbook in their office. They decide to place them on reserve in the library and let the students know so that they can check them out. The instructor makes a long-term plan to investigate the use of an open access textbook. Because laptops are not required by all students at the institution, the instructor also ensures that any student-centered learning activities do not require all students to bring a laptop to class.

Learning Accommodations

Findings: An instructor discovers that a few students in the class have a fairly common learning accommodation that allows them to have extra time on assessments in a distraction-reduced environment. This information was actually obtained from the Office of Accessibility Services and confirmed on the "Who's in Class?" form.

Modifications: The instructor ensures that there is ample time for the students to take all assessments with the amount of time needed. Additionally, the instructor decides to make one test a take-home exam to give students flexibility in completion. This take-home assessment is designed to still test conceptual understanding in a fair manner.

Cocurricular Involvement and Obligations

Findings: An instructor discovers that they have a large number of student athletes in a course who have time conflicts with office hours during certain times of the day because of practice or games.

Modifications: The instructor alters the office hours by extending time so that student athletes have the most likelihood of being able to attend. Additionally, the instructor, knowing students are parts of sports teams, applies various course concepts to a number of areas, including sports. At the institution there are also tutoring services for athletes and nonathletes for which the instructor makes the class aware. Lastly, for a final ethnography course project the instructor gives students the choice of which questions they can ask and the location where they can make their observations, as consistent with UDL. Some student athletes choose to make observations in their sports settings.

First-Generation Students

Findings: Based on the "Who's in Class?" form, there are several first-generation students in a large enrollment course. Many of the students responding, in addition to not having a parent obtain a bachelor's degree, also did not have siblings or other relatives.

Modifications: At the beginning of the course the instructor shares how they were a first-generation student and what they did to navigate through college. To build a welcoming classroom environment the instructor also invites previous students, some of whom are first-generation students, on what they did to help them be successful in the course. The instructor ensures that all information on the course is explicitly explained and decides to provide even more opportunities for low-stakes assessments for students to be able to practice course quizzes and assessments. On the syllabus and verbally the instructor shares all resources available for first-generation students and all learners to support their academic success on campus.

Diverse Countries of Origin and English-Language Learners

Findings: The "Who's in Class?" form reveals that there are students from diverse countries of origin in an online class. There are also several students whose native language is not English.

Modifications: After carefully reviewing the syllabus, the instructor decides to incorporate culturally responsive materials in the content of the course. The instructor also uses principles of UDL to give students the choice to apply class projects to their own cultures. The instructor ensures that there is closed captioning for all microlecture recordings so that all students can have a visual representation rather than only verbal representation.

Learners Who Self-Identify as Being Quiet

Findings: For a face-to-face discussion-based course, the instructor discovers that many students identify as being quiet students. The course topics at times can also be controversial.

Modifications: The instructor wants to ensure that quiet students find their voice in the classroom and carefully redefines what participation in the course means. The instructor decides to also give students the option to post to an online discussion board where quieter students may be more likely to contribute to give multiple options. The instructor also decides to use ample wait-time after asking questions, employs activities such as think-pair-share periodically to allow for active learning, in addition to smaller-scale interactions, has students respond in writing to prompts rather than verbally, and uses polling software that enables equitable participation.

Religious Observances

Findings: There are several students in the course who have religious observances that conflict with course activities and assessments.

Modifications: The institution has a nondiscrimination policy around students with religious observances. They are to let their instructor know of their conflicts within the first 2 weeks of the semester. In anticipation of this, the instructor carefully designed the course syllabus so that major assignments do not conflict with major religious observances. The instructor also tells the class that if any students do have a conflict due to a religious observance to let them know in advance. This policy is listed on the course syllabus. For these students, the instructor allows some flexibility in due dates and course obligations so that students can meet the learning goals of the course.

Learners From Groups Underrepresented in the Discipline

Findings: An instructor teaching in a discipline where there is underrepresentation of various racial and ethnic groups finds that there are a number of students with such social identities in their class.

Modifications: The instructor views this diversity as an asset and the scenario as a perfect opportunity to help all learners feel welcome in the discipline. The instructor implements a values affirmation exercise for learners before assessments and affirms the identities of these students on a personal level, as well as validates their lived experiences, to minimize stereotype threat. The instructor also integrates a variety of examples of those who contribute to the field and are of diverse racial and ethnic backgrounds.

Learners Identifying as LGBTQ+

Findings: Some students completing the "Who's in Class?" form identified as LGBTQ+.

Modifications: The instructor, out of a genuine desire to support all learners, completed Safe Zone training. During the course the instructor affirmed the identities of all students, including those who were LGBTQ+. They respectfully used pronouns and also carefully integrated readings in the curriculum from diverse authors, including those that identified as LGBTQ+.

Learners With Seemingly Similar Backgrounds

Findings: When an instructor implements the "Who's in Class?" form they find that those students who respond do not exhibit a lot of noticeable variation in sections I through V of the instrument. Most students fall in major demographic group categories of privilege. Minimal information is provided in the open-ended questions of the form as well.

Modifications: The instructor decides to follow-up on the form on students' course-specific prior knowledge, conducts a few formative assessments, and finds significant variation. To benefit all students, and particularly those with limited prior experience with the material, the instructor posts a variety of tutorials and activities on foundational material on the LMS that students can freely review at any point. The instructor also integrates a variety of readings from diverse authors, fields, and perspectives in the course.

Additional Recommendations

Instructors Can Tailor the Form
There may be additional items you may want to know about your students. Instructors can therefore add questions and tailor the form accordingly.

Instructors Are Encouraged to Use Other Means to Better Understand the Attributes Learners Bring to the Course
The "Who's in Class?" form is one tool to help instructors design more inclusive instruction, but it need not be the only one. Inclusive instructors can also use additional feedback mechanisms, such as assessing prior knowledge, as illustrated in the previous example focused on learners with seemingly similar backgrounds or, as discussed in chapter 4, essential office hours. Typically information regarding accommodations will be provided by accessibility services; however, some students may choose not to disclose disabilities through formal institutional procedures and only mention them on the form anonymously.

Instructors Should Delete Student Response Data After the Course Ends
Student responses, though anonymous, should be used during the course solely for the purposes of the instructor designing an inclusive learning experience. Also, the tool was not meant for instructors to store student responses for the long term, but rather delete them at the conclusion of the course.

Reflection Questions

- How could you utilize or adapt this tool for courses that you teach?
- With whom could you partner as you administer the tool to discuss your action plans and obtain feedback?

Key Points

- Understanding the diverse attributes that students bring to the classroom is critical for inclusive course design and implementation of inclusive teaching approaches.
- By adapting and administering a tool such as the "Who's in Class?" form early on in a course, instructors can have a better sense of such attributes and tailor instruction to ensure that it is equitable and fosters a sense of belonging.

7

CONCLUDING THOUGHTS

I n this book we highlight how equitable learning experiences and a sense of belonging are critical for students to thrive at institutions of higher education. Applying this to teaching signifies that courses, whether face-to-face, hybrid, or fully online, are designed to support a diverse student body to help all learners reach their potential. Inclusive instructors recognize that student diversity enhances the learning experience for everyone, and they affirm students' social identities and take responsibility for creating inclusive learning experiences. Inclusive instructors outline a clear plan to ensure student success even before the course starts. The content of their courses is reflective of diverse contributions and perspectives and is accessible to their learners. They utilize a variety of strategies that help their students feel welcome in the class and ensure that even if discord occurs they restore a positive course climate. They are student-centered in their approaches to learning. We also highlight how there is not one approach to inclusive teaching. There are many strategies and practices that can be adopted to support diverse learners.

We also captured what inclusive instructors do to create equitable, welcoming learning environments for their students. We facilitated active reflection on the content to encourage instructors to advance their inclusive teaching efforts and include all chapter reflection questions in aggregate in Appendix B. Given the many competing obligations of teaching, we recommend that instructors ask these questions of themselves periodically regardless of their level of teaching experience to help sustain a mindset of inclusive teaching. Additionally, we challenge instructors to reflect on how inclusive instruction manifests within their teaching philosophy and what more they would like to learn or implement in their courses to make them more equitable and inclusive.

We emphasize that while there are general principles that underlie inclusive teaching, the choice of which strategies to utilize may be influenced by disciplinary-, institutional-, course-, and instructor-related factors. Some inclusive teaching approaches, such as creating a roadmap for a course and learning students' names, apply broadly, while others are more relevant for particular courses. Similar to many other instructional approaches, there is no one-size-fits-all strategy for inclusive teaching. In deciding which methods to employ, we recommend that all instructors keep contextual factors in mind.

Measuring the impact of inclusive teaching efforts is also of importance to ensure such approaches foster equity and belonging. We encourage instructors to examine the general assessment data that can be gathered on their learners or to perform a scholarship of teaching (SoTL) project in their courses. Either may be chosen depending on whether the intent is to gather data for the instructor's own usage (assessment project) or publish more generalizable data that is disseminated in a scholarly manner (SoTL project). For example, as an assessment project, instructors can analyze data on student grades to determine if achievement gaps are evident between diverse groups of learners within their courses. When instructors use effective inclusive teaching approaches and control for confounding factors, such gaps should lessen. Analyses may also involve examining themes from student comments on course evaluations in classes that did not utilize inclusive teaching approaches and those that did to determine if there is evidence that students felt a sense of belonging in the class. Inclusive instructors benefit from using a variety of approaches to gather feedback on their efforts.

We hope this book has inspired and encouraged you to reflect on how to become an inclusive instructor, how to enhance your current inclusive teaching practices, or how to develop initiatives and policy at your institutions. Being an inclusive instructor is a continual process that involves making active, intentional pedagogical choices for each iteration of every course taught. Inclusive instructors take ownership and claim that their job is never done while they continue to interact with students. Future instructors may continue to grapple with the principles in this book in anticipation of teaching students. They should continue to seek relevant resources for pedagogical growth so that when the opportunity is presented for them to teach a course they will have an appropriate foundation. A variety of professional development opportunities are listed in the Epilogue as examples. Current instructors who are already teaching, as well as more experienced instructors, can always grow and learn more from their colleagues, modifying their pedagogical choices to account for diverse learners. As the demographics of higher education continue to change, being responsive and adaptable will be integral in supporting our learners. As described for other frameworks, such as culturally responsive pedagogy, inclusive instructors see reflection on teaching efforts as an important process, ground their decisions on actual evidence of what their students need, are flexible and will consider alternatives when appropriate, perceive classroom practices from their own point of view as well as that of their learners, and identify where they need to learn more (Rychly & Graves, 2012). Embracing each of these aspects can help instructors become more inclusive in their teaching.

Consider the following statement from Armstrong (2011):

> There is plenty to be nervous about when it comes to envisioning your formerly "neutral" classroom as a swarm of complex human interactions where social issues are in motion, lessons about equity are being learned, and assumptions about ability or human value are being reinforced or challenged. If your academic discipline or your personal experience has not empowered you to confidently address this dynamic system, it can feel like the best advice is to shut your eyes and never think about it again because it is just too difficult, too sticky, and too risky to take into account. But many instructors actually do this kind of work well, and they do it well most of the time. Not just the Professors of Ethnic Studies and Global Studies, but lots of instructors in many different fields.
>
> How is that possible? It is not that these instructors are necessarily gifted with some supernatural flair for human relations, or some mystical ability to interact with people in ways that empower them, or because they intuitively know how to make students "feel good." Rather, it is because such faculty know how— and the "how" is not necessarily about the content of their courses or even their own identities. Rather, they have learned how to do it—that is, they have gained knowledge of and become skilled at deploying pedagogical strategies for inclusivity within the complex social moment that is "the classroom." Put another way: there really is research on this stuff—serious, scholarly, substantive research—and there really are best practices. And there are instructors who make it their business to know the research and to try the best practices. We don't expect our students to start doing experiments in a chemistry lab without instruction, and we don't imagine they can just begin painting in oils without some guidance. Why, then, do we persist in the expectation that faculty can, by sheer force of will and lots of good intentions, easily manage the complex work of promoting an equitable classroom climate without a little input, guidance, knowledge, and help from the experts? (pp. 54–55)

Being an inclusive instructor is an ongoing process that involves learning, mistakes, persistence, reflection, and a willingness to adapt teaching practices to a diverse student population. Student populations will likely continue to evolve in higher education, and inclusive instructors continue to face emergent issues that impact equitable learning, such as what we experienced with COVID-19 and calls against anti-Black racism. This work requires a continual dedication and commitment and consideration of one's own teaching practices within the context of student diversity. Although self-work and reflection is critical, inclusive teaching is well worth the effort to provide all of our students the opportunity to achieve their educational goals.

Developing and Sustaining a Culture of Inclusive Teaching

To my understanding, inclusive teaching incorporates instructional strategies that promote respect for the varied characteristics among all learners; strategies that help each student learn, grow, achieve, and make a vital contribution to the classroom culture.

—Adjunct instructor, master's college, Education

Throughout the book we explored a number of actions that inclusive instructors take in their courses. In this final section we describe the role that everyone—instructors, administrators, and students—can play to develop and sustain a culture of inclusive teaching at their institution. Critical aspects for developing a culture of inclusive teaching include providing access to and seeking resources that promote community understanding of what inclusive teaching looks like when practiced, community willingness to adopt inclusive teaching practices, and institutional policies and procedures that advance inclusive teaching efforts.

Developing a Culture of Inclusive Teaching

Key components for developing a culture of inclusive teaching include raising awareness of concerns around inclusion, providing visible support to instructor change agents who lead their peers in adopting such practices, and providing resources through professional development to encourage more widespread adoption. This process can be informed by the diffusion of innovations theory (Rogers, 2003). This theory suggests that individuals come to adopt innovations at different rates and that some forms of evidence may be more effective at encouraging adoption than others. For example, there will be those who will innovate (innovators), others who will quickly adopt such innovations (early adopters), and yet others who might take more time and evidence to adopt (laggards), as well as those in between (the early and late majorities).

Applying the principles of this theory, the factors that may influence instructor adoption of inclusive teaching may include awareness of what inclusive teaching looks like when implemented in a course, perceptions of the relative advantage of using inclusive teaching in, how compatible inclusive teaching is to current teaching practices, how simple such strategies are to incorporate and whether there are available supports, how easy they are to test, and whether others will be able to observe the results of their efforts. Professional development experiences focused on inclusive teaching can support instructors by encouraging a reflective process on the first four aspects of this theory. The significance of implementing equitable teaching practices can be emphasized in sessions where inclusive instructors articulate why using them is integral to student learning and their effectiveness as a teacher. Students can also be invited to voice the importance of the inclusive teaching efforts of their instructors at such sessions. Additionally, educational developers or others facilitating the sessions can share relevant research in support of inclusive instruction, some of which is integrated throughout this book. Instructors can also share their personal journeys, the steps they took to implement inclusive teaching practices, and how they tried it out in their courses. These may include lessons learned from the experience and advice to others. Educational developers can provide helpful tips on the small steps that can be taken to enhance inclusive teaching efforts. For example, instructors typically need not transform an entire course to ensure that it is inclusive. In this sense professional development can provide a supportive setting for instructors to work through their process of adoption. Larger-scale institutional commitments to inclusive teaching can address the final attribute of the diffusion of innovations theory, whether efforts will be visible to others, and will be discussed in the subsequent paragraphs.

Internal Professional Development Focused on Inclusive Teaching

> *[Attend] professional development workshop[s] on inclusive teaching strategies . . .*
> *[and] other professional development workshops that, though not specifically about*
> *inclusive teaching, disseminate inclusive techniques. My institution is majority-*
> *minority; this sometimes means that there's not enough focus on what inclusivity*
> *means and looks like (people assume it's already/inherently inclusive), but it also*
> *means that inclusive teaching is necessary to effectively work with students.*
>
> —Instructional consultant, master's college, English

In institutions across the United States, professional development is typically performed by centers for teaching and learning; offices dedicated to equity, diversity, and inclusion; and departments, suggesting that the responsibility of who provides such support differs across institutions. Individual faculty also often play roles in providing professional development for their peers by sharing their expertise and experiences. We posit here that inclusive teaching is the collective responsibility of all members of the institution who contribute to the institutional mission around teaching and learning. Depending on an institution's stage with regard to the adoption of inclusive teaching, available resources, and goals, a variety of professional development approaches can be considered, from individual events to more intensive and sustained experiences. Further, efforts may have different audiences, such as future or current instructors or those who teach courses in an online environment. Following are example sessions that can be considered individually as part of a series or be more intensive professional development activities that can encourage and support instructor awareness and adoption of inclusive teaching. Instructors looking to advance inclusive teaching can seek opportunities for such sessions.

Topics for Series Sessions

Institutions can run an inclusive teaching series involving community-wide sessions centered around the topics of equity and belonging in teaching and learning. These sessions can invite the larger college or university community into a broader dialogue around inclusive teaching and can be run as panel discussions with instructors or students, interactive activities, or in other formats such as with case examples. Following are several topical sessions that have potential to be implemented in a short time frame of less than 2 hours. The first two support the conceptualization and significance of inclusive teaching while the remainder traverse a variety of topics important to consider in equitable and inclusive instruction. This list is not exhaustive, and there are other creative approaches that can be used for sessions focused on inclusion. To maximize impact, each session can encourage participants to be reflective about their teaching and start to develop short- or long-term action plans for how they will consider implementing such practices in their own teaching.

Important principles in inclusive teaching

There are general concepts in inclusive teaching that at a foundational level are important and that all who teach or will teach students should be aware and professionally develop. Three important concepts are defining inclusive teaching, understanding the role of privilege, and developing an awareness of and mitigating biases. The following sessions, "Characterizing Inclusive Instruction," "The Role of Privilege in Inclusive Teaching," and "Recognizing, Mitigating and Addressing Biases" are sample sessions.

Characterizing inclusive instruction

A significant challenge for many instructors in their beginning stages of learning about inclusive instruction is defining what the term signifies. For example, how do the principles of diversity, equity, and equality apply to inclusive teaching? We introduced such terminology in chapter 1. To help participants conceptualize each term, they can be charged to define each in a small group. Then they can next be invited to consider and individually reflect on what each term means to them in their own teaching, as well as discuss their challenges, goals, and hopes for being an inclusive teacher.

The role of privilege in inclusive teaching

Design . . . a course and its assignments so that students from underprivileged backgrounds can succeed on a more equitable footing with their classmates . . . and engender . . . a classroom climate that allows students to bring their full selves into class activities and discussions.

—Survey respondent; rank, institution type, discipline not identified

One of the major barriers to inclusive teaching reported by instructors is a lack of awareness that there are differences between learners that must be considered to promote effective teaching (Addy et al., in press). This ideology of colorblindness, as described in earlier chapters, can include not being aware of how student privilege can impact the ability to learn in a course. Certain moments, such as the COVID-19 pandemic and the related emergency switch to remote teaching, can show the influence of privilege on student learning and success in a course. Because the transition occurred so abruptly, some students lacked access to courses because they did not have a laptop, did not have access to Wi-Fi, had to work to support their families, had added responsibilities to watch siblings, did not have a dedicated space to join synchronous sessions, and experienced other challenges that were directly related to their privilege. Even in brick-and-mortar courses students may lack financial means to afford course materials, may need to support themselves and families and have less time to work, or experience many of the other circumstances that can impact their achievement and sense of belonging.

A session dedicated to exploring how students can vary according to their amount of privilege, discussing the issue in a local institutional context, and proposing strategies can raise awareness. Facilitators can define privilege and inclusive teaching or invite participants to come up with their own definitions, arrange participants in small groups, as appropriate, and run an activity such as "Privilege for Sale" (Safe Zone Project, 2020b). After running this activity, facilitators can hold a group discussion on why they chose the various privileges. Facilitators can ask participants to describe the relationship between privilege and inclusive teaching, particularly with students at their institution. Then participants can review case examples that are realistic, where they will need to come up with recommendations for how an instructor can be more inclusive, and discuss them as a large group.

Recognizing, mitigating, and confronting biases

Inclusive teaching means using approaches that are not biased against particular groups
of students. It's basically about giving everyone a chance to
learn and to demonstrate their learning.

—Postdoctoral researcher, baccalaureate college, Biology

In addition to privilege awareness, another topic that is a critical aspect of building a culture of inclusion is being aware of assumptions held about others and preventing their harmful impacts. Participants in a national study described how their colleagues' lack of awareness of their personal biases was a major barrier to them implementing inclusive teaching approaches (Addy et al., in press). As mentioned in chapter 2, inclusive instructors are aware of their own biases and mitigate their impacts. A session focused on preventing the harmful impacts of implicit bias might start with participants defining bias, exploring their own biases, and equipping them with strategies if they witness bias in their own courses.

With regard to recognizing and mitigating implicit biases, various strategies described in the literature have mostly been done in laboratory research settings, and more work is needed to fully understand the efficacy of such approaches in real-life settings. Worth mentioning, however, is the research on the strategies that has been conducted to date regardless of the setting. For example, "discounting commonly held stereotypes, using context to influence implicit responses, changing the way an out-group member is evaluated and categorized, using context to change the level of threat evoked to an out-group, using motivation to change responses to an out-group, encouraging people to take responsibility for their implicit biases" are some described by the Equality Challenge Unit (ECU, 2013). Given that bias in the classroom is apparent and has been described in the literature, additional instructors can also be equipped with tools to help navigate incidents should they come up with students (Boysen & Vogel, 2009). One method is the confronting prejudiced responses (CPR) model, devised by Ashburn-Nardo et al. (2008). This model helps individuals determine whether action should be taken for a particular discriminatory event.

Inclusive course design

There are various basic elements of a course, such as the choice of what content to include, the expense of course materials, and accessibility of materials, that can be intentionally designed to be inclusive of learners. Professional development in course design can help instructors design an inclusive course.

Culturally sustaining pedagogy

[Include] practices and content that include as many viewpoints as possible from non-Western authors/scholars/persons presented with a critical consideration of privilege and oppression.

—Teaching fellow, doctorate-granting university, English

A remarkable aspect of higher education is the cultures in which our students bring to the course. Inclusive instructors view such cultures as an asset and carefully integrate them in their courses. A session focused on culturally sustaining pedagogy may equip instructors with pedagogical tools that help them develop a sense of the cultures represented in their classrooms and reflect on their courses to propose learning experiences that can make them more culturally relevant to their learners.

Developing an affordable course

Regardless of institution type, not all students may have the financial means to purchase course materials that can directly impact their academic success in a course. For example, students who cannot afford a textbook may choose to not buy it for a class and rely on other freely available materials. However, these other materials may be insufficient for their learning. In inclusive course design, an instructor reflects on the cost of materials for a course, seeking ways to lower the financial burden of course materials. This may involve exploring the usage of open educational materials, open-source software, or other ways to reduce costs. A session devoted to creating an affordable course can involve instructors examining their course syllabi and exploring other options for their course materials. For example, this may involve searching for open-access textbooks, software, or other materials that are of no or low cost. Librarians with expertise in electronic materials can be very valuable in cofacilitating these sessions. Further, inclusive instructors who utilize OERs can also choose to share their own experiences.

Creating accessible courses

I have attended a workshop on how to design a CougarView course accessible to students of different types of disability.

—Associate professor, tenured, master's college, Computer Sciences

Educat[e] on how to make PPT slides more accessible to blind students.

—Associate professor, tenured, doctorate-granting university, Public Health

Designing course materials that all learners are capable of accessing, regardless of whether they have accommodations, is an inclusive practice. Principles of UDL can be explored in this type of session in addition to ways of ensuring that digital materials are accessible (Tobin & Behling, 2018). Offices of Accessibility Services and Instructional Technology can be particularly relevant partners for this type of session. Instructors can develop plans for designing, or during the session adapt course materials such as PDF files or video files so that they are accessible to all learners.

Building community in inclusive classrooms. There are a variety of sessions that can support instructors in fostering a classroom community.

Developing collaborative course guidelines

In order to build community in inclusive classrooms, it is important that guidelines for how the class will interact are established at the beginning of the course, as mentioned in chapter 4, so that all members can equitably contribute to the course. An effective practice in educator development is modeling the actual practice that will occur. In this type of session, facilitators can consider modeling this process by having participants develop collaborative guidelines for that particular session and later implement a similar process to their own courses. Instructors who have developed collaborative classroom guidelines can consider obtaining the permission of their students and sharing examples of what these guidelines might look like for various course types, such as seminar and lecture courses.

Teaching inclusively in an online environment

While various inclusive teaching concepts used in brick-and-mortar classrooms can apply to courses taught online, there are some aspects important to consider in a virtual environment. Such a session might explore aspects such as building community online in both synchronous (live) and asynchronous online class sessions, encouraging the engagement of all learners in online discussion forums, creating accessible course content on an online platform, and other relevant topics such as providing welcoming videos and video feedback. This type of session can be delivered online and, again, use modeling to highlight various effective teaching practices. For example, participants could be added into a LMS and role-play the student experience in using a discussion form or other tool. Further, this session presents opportunities for collaboration with instructional technology offices at an institution.

Inclusive Practices for Diverse Learners

Inclusive teaching encompasses a number of things, but at its core it is a pedagogical philosophy that seeks to eliminate barriers to learning and increase accessibility. This inclusion may take the form of eliminating barriers based on race, ethnicity, gender sexuality, ability status, religion, etc. It also means being attentive to first-generation or low-income concerns and trying to make course materials and strategies transparent and accessible to students.

—Assistant professor, master's college, English

Running sessions dedicated to inclusion challenges faced by specific populations of diverse learners at an institution demonstrates the importance of supporting all students and can generate a number of strategies and partnerships that can advance inclusive teaching efforts. The integration of student-faculty pedagogical partnership models, where students are involved in these discussions and provide recommendations and feedback, can enhance their effectiveness. More information and sample sessions incorporating student partners can be found in the article "Where Are the Students in Efforts for Inclusive Excellence?: Two Approaches to Positioning Students a Critical Partners for Inclusive Pedagogical Practices" (Cook-Sather et al., in press).

First-generation students

The number of first-generation students continues to rise across colleges and universities (Skomsvold, 2014). Although definitions of first-generation students can vary, here we describe them as students who are the first in their families to pursue a bachelor's degree. Understanding barriers that first-generation students can face in navigating the college experience and the assets they bring can be used to design more inclusive learning experiences. A variety of possibilities exist for increasing awareness of obstacles that first-generation students can face in college, including case examples where participants devise recommendations for supporting first-generation students, hearing their actual testimonies and advice .

Sexual orientation and gender identity

Institutions may offer Safe Zone training or sessions with similar goals to bring awareness to the issues that LGBTQ+ students can experience in their learning environments and recommendations for how to become allies (Safe Zone Project, 2020a). Such sessions can be offered in partnership with institutional offices devoted to diversity and inclusion. Providing insight into the experiences of students excluded from cisheteronormative culture, as well as taking intentional actions toward inclusion, can support a welcoming classroom environment.

Inclusive STEM education

In many science, technology, engineering and math (STEM) disciplines there is underrepresentation of females and students of color. Designing classrooms that are inclusive of such learners and encouraging their success is critical. Professional development experiences directed at inclusive STEM education may involve active learning strategies for teaching larger introductory courses and other challenges of teaching practice, such as effective problem-solving, integrating diversity into curricula, encouraging belonging, and providing academic support for learners studying in STEM disciplines.

Religious or spiritual identity

Students of different religions may have observances or traditions that can impact the classroom. Considerations for religion can be discussed, such as not administering assessments on major religious holidays and being flexible for students who have particular observances or practices, such as fasting or praying, and how they may impact their experience in the classroom. College chaplains and other religious and spiritual organizations may be appropriate campus partners for such sessions.

Measuring impact

Instructors may also be interested in measuring the impact of their inclusive teaching efforts to determine whether they are promoting student equity and belonging. An initial session can focus on the design of an assessment or scholarship of teaching and learning project. A variety of books are available to step through project design, including *Engaging in the Scholarship of Teaching and Learning: A Guide to Develop a Project from Start to Finish* by Bishop-Clark and Dietz-Uhler (2012). Given that such projects are typically ongoing, instructors can seek further support from a center for teaching and learning, if available, and seek discipline-based resources or organizations and journals focused on the scholarship of teaching and learning, such as the International Society for the Scholarship of Teaching and Learning.

Reflection Question

- What topics related to inclusive teaching would you most benefit from exploring during a professional development experience? If on-campus professional development is not available, consider books, initiatives facilitated by other institutions, and resources that can support your efforts.

Intensive Professional Development

> *My institution provides reading circles, ongoing training institutes, online modules,*
> *course design training—all dedicated to inclusive teaching. They also offer student panel*
> *presentations with students from traditionally marginalized identity groups. These*
> *panels allow the students to share their biggest challenges with faculty directly.*
>
> —Faculty adjunct developer, doctorate-granting university,
> Human Physical Perforamce and Recreation

Sessions offered one time have their own value; however, intensive professional development experiences can engage participants in more immersive experiences and have the potential for more impact. We define *intensive professional development* as those that extend beyond a single event lasting less than a day. Following are a few examples.

Faculty learning communities focused on inclusive teaching

> *Our teaching center is sponsoring two faculty learning communities this semester on*
> *inclusive pedagogy. The new director of that center also incorporates inclusive/diversity-*
> *related programming into other programming she runs whenever possible. The Office of*
> *Social Equity also regularly offers Safe Space training and other diversity-related professional*
> *development for employees across campus that includes some teaching tips for faculty.*
>
> —Survey respondent; rank, institution type, discipline not identified

Faculty learning communities are communities of practice with instructors who engage in ongoing experiences around a particular pedagogical topic (Cox, 2004). While they vary in implementation, they can be composed of eight to 12 instructors who meet regularly, facilitating a faculty learning community around diversity, equity, and inclusion, or a particular specialized topic. These communities may engage in a variety of efforts such as the following:

- Reviewing literature and recommended practices around inclusive teaching
- Having opportunities to share their inclusive teaching efforts and troubleshoot challenges in the classroom
- Designing scholarship of teaching and learning or assessment projects to measure impact
- Observing one another's classrooms and reflecting on teaching

Student Partnerships in the Classroom

Our Faculty Development Center is engaged in a year-long effort to support inclusion and belonging. We brought an internationally known speaker to start the year, began a student-faculty partnership program that targets first-generation and students from equity-seeking groups, are sponsoring a 2-day symposium on teaching for inclusion and belonging, and are supporting a faculty fellow whose focus is on using design principles to encourage more inclusive practices.

—Associate professor, director, master's college, Social Work

Students can be excellent partners for inclusive teaching efforts in the classroom. They can be trained to observe classrooms and provide helpful feedback to instructors to advance teaching excellence. There are resources such as *Pedagogical Partnerships: A How-to Guide for Faculty, Students, and Academic Developers in Higher Education* by Cook-Sather et al. (2019) that can be useful for instructors who are interested in partnering with students on their teaching.

Inclusive Teaching Circles

[Current initiatives include] [o]ngoing needs assessment, [and] diversity and inclusion faculty fellows provide workshops and resources on inclusive teaching.

—Assistant professor, educational developer, doctorate-granting university, Linguistics and Languages

Institutions may provide funding for interested faculty to engage in year-long fellowships focused on inclusive teaching. These fellowships can take on a variety of forms, which may involve more deeply learning and exploring the literature related to the pedagogical topic of interest, participating in external professional development experiences to learn more, and leading initiatives such as faculty learning communities and other sessions for the institution.

Intensive Institutes

Immersive experiences involving multiday intensive institutes can prepare instructors to implement inclusive teaching practices in their courses. These institutes may involve multiple interactive sessions focused on inclusive teaching, such as those previously described.

Teaching Circles

Instructors teaching similar courses can also partner with one another to form a teaching circle where they take time and create a space to share their experiences with inclusive teaching and consider implications for their practice.

Community Reads

> *There are multiple book groups each semester wherein faculty read and discuss books on inclusive teaching. Some popular titles have been* Teaching to Transgress; Exploring Race in Predominantly White Classrooms; *[and]* Universal Design in Higher Education.
>
> —Associate professor, tenured, master's college, Rhetoric and Composition

There can be much gained through the shared experience of a community reading of a book or of articles around the topic of inclusion and then reflecting on how to integrate such learned principles into teaching practice. Reading groups have many options. The facilitation of chapters can be rotated among participants, and discussions can focus on applying the content of the book to classroom teaching.

Reflective Teaching Experiences on Inclusive Teaching

Teaching squares or triangles:
Teaching squares or teaching triangles programs involve instructors partnering with one another in sets of four (squares) or three (triangles). The instructors are typically from different disciplines and visit and observe at least one of their group member's courses, focusing not on giving feedback but rather on reflecting on their own teaching practices. All observations are collegial and confidential. Anne Wessely from St. Louis Community College is credited with first developing the Teaching Squares program. Participants often write a reflection based on their experiences and may have an opportunity to share as a community. Such reflections can focus on inclusive teaching.

External Professional Development Focused on Inclusive Teaching

> *Sadly, there are none [opportunities for professional development focused on inclusive teaching]. I have to rely on conferences . . . [and] professional contacts, but mostly just informal discussions with my favorite colleagues.*
>
> —Associate professor, tenured, doctorate-granting university, Sociology

Not all colleges and universities have the capability to run dedicated programming focused on inclusive teaching. Instead, instructors at such institutions can consider other opportunities to enhance their development until their institutions can obtain resources and build necessary structures and supports. These may involve engagement in symposia, conferences, institutes and webinars, and MOOCs focused on topics specific to inclusive teaching.

Faculty had the opportunity to participate in the Association of College and University Educators' online course in effective teaching practices.

—Visiting professor, Education

The Association of American Colleges and Universities has a specific area of focus on diversity, equity and student success (AAC&U, 2020). They offer a variety of resources, including programs, institutes, reports, and other featured publications, as well as webinars on related topics that instructors can utilize for free if their institution is a paying member. The Association of Public and Land-Grant Universities (APLU, 2020) has a commission for access, diversity, and excellence that also offers relevant resources and supports. The American Association of Community Colleges (AACC, 2020) similarly has a commission on diversity, inclusion and equity. Other organizations, such as the Association of College and University Educators (ACUE, 2020), provide professional development opportunities for instructors focused on evidence-based teaching.

A leading organization for preparing STEM graduate students and postdoctoral fellows is the Center for the Integration of Research, Teaching and Learning (CIRTL, 2020), whose mission is to "enhance excellence in undergraduate education through the development of a national faculty committed to implementing and advancing effective teaching practices for diverse learners as part of successful and varied professional careers (para. 4)." One of their value statements is inclusive excellence and innovation, or "critical examination of data, scholarly reflection, and collective review are our standards of excellence. We innovate for mutual improvement of inclusive educational practices" (CIRTL, 2020; para. 10). CIRTL offers trainees a variety of resources including online courses and a variety of other experiences focused on inclusive teaching.

Conferences focused on teaching and learning, whether local, regional, or national, may offer sessions around inclusive teaching. Further, many disciplinary organizations have dedicated time at conferences or workshops around inclusive teaching.

A variety of institutions also offer massive online courses on inclusive teaching or certificate programs focused on inclusive teaching. For example, Columbia University has offered the "Inclusive Teaching Supporting All Students in the College Classroom" online course (edX, 2020). Cornell University (n.d.) has offered the "Teaching & Learning in the Diverse Classroom MOOC."

There are many resources outside of the institution that can support inclusive teaching efforts; however, institutional commitment is at the heart of developing a culture of inclusive teaching. Each of these professional development experiences can be targeted toward specific groups, such as trainees like graduate students and postdoctoral fellows, or all faculty at an institution.

Reflection Question

- Identify professional development experiences that address inclusive teaching you could further explore, whether at your institution or beyond.

Inclusive teaching, to me, means understanding, welcoming, and meeting the needs of whoever chooses to take the class that I am teaching. Understanding or seeking to understand issues around varying abilities, cultures, and identities and implementing practices to "level the playing field" is, to me, the essence of inclusivity in teaching.

—Survey respondent; rank, institution type, discipline not identified

Sustaining a Culture of Inclusive Teaching

As expressed by the respondents in the national study, lack of institutional commitment to inclusive teaching is one of the largest barriers to implementation (Addy et al., in press). Lacking support from colleagues or administration is a barrier to the adoption of inclusive teaching approaches. Institutional commitment is reflective of strategic plans around equity, diversity, and inclusion, as well as resources and support structures in place that support inclusion. When there is institutional commitment to inclusive instruction, there is evidence through artifacts such as strategic plans, diversity statements, as well as financial resources and professional development opportunities.

Strategic Goals for Inclusive Excellence

At the institutional level, a commitment to inclusive excellence is a key element in the strategic plans of colleges and universities, and is evidence of actionable steps being taken to accomplish such goals. Incorporated in such plans are explicit references to the critical importance of inclusive learning experiences, and that inclusion is a collective campus effort and not the work of a single individual or office. Hired instructors become enculturated into a place that values inclusive teaching, have resources to advance their efforts, and teach at the institution because of these shared values.

Diversity and Inclusion Statement

Accompanying such plans is a diversity and inclusion statement, which attests to the value and importance of having a diverse faculty, staff, and student body and the inclusion of all members of the campus community. As mentioned in chapter 3, there can be value in including a campus-wide diversity and inclusion statement in a course syllabus, voicing the importance of the principles in it, and abiding by them in the course. As a case example, the University of Baltimore Maryland County (UMBC) has historically been an innovator in supporting the educational experiences of disadvantaged students, especially those in STEM disciplines (Hrabowski et al., 2019; Summers & Hrabowski, 2006), which has also been replicated at other institutions (Domingo et al., 2019). The UMBC diversity and inclusion vision statement in 2020 indicates, "Our UMBC community redefines excellence in higher education through an inclusive culture that connects innovative teaching and learning, research across disciplines, and civic engagement. We will advance knowledge, economic prosperity, and social justice by welcoming and inspiring inquisitive minds from all backgrounds." When an instructor articulates the value of such a statement to their students and how the course will abide by these principles, and reiterates the ideas during the course, this can be quite powerful in fostering an inclusive classroom climate.

Professional Development Focused on Inclusive Teaching

Additional commitment to inclusive teaching, as described earlier, includes professional development opportunities available to instructors to learn more about and discuss inclusive teaching efforts. The institution may have a center for teaching and learning that implements such programming, as aligned with the institution's strategic goals, or possibly a faculty affairs or multicultural education office that supports such efforts. There are multiple structures in place for instructors that support their inclusive teaching efforts.

Student Supports for Inclusion

There are also student supports in place from a student's matriculation into the institution until graduation. This may look like inclusive recruitment practices enacted by admissions offices, financial aid support, spaces and groups of belonging on campus, and supports for academic success.

Financial Resources Allocated Toward Inclusive Teaching

Financial investment from an institution is further evidence of a commitment to inclusive teaching. This may include specific grants to which faculty can apply to support pedagogical efforts to inclusive teaching in their courses. An institution may also offer funding for instructors to obtain professional development outside of the institution to enhance their inclusive teaching efforts. One example of institutional commitment to funding inclusive teaching efforts is the Maricopa Millions project enacted by the Maricopa Community Colleges (n.d.) to make courses more affordable. This project involved increasing the number of instructors using OERs such as open-access textbooks and other materials in their courses that are of no or minimal costs to students. The course schedule also indicates which courses utilize OER. The first 5 years of this program yielded a savings of over $11,500,000 for students. Instructors with the Maricopa Community College system can apply for a development grant and participate in this initiative that highlights financial commitment. There may also be evidence of external funding opportunities that enhance pedagogical efforts toward inclusion, for example, the Howard Hughes Medical Institute Inclusive Excellence grant.

Diversity, Equity, and Inclusion Topics Integrated Into Standing Meetings

At institutional faculty, school/college/division, and departmental meetings, diversity, equity, and inclusion (DEI) can be added as a standing agenda item to signify its importance. Each meeting can start with opening remarks about an issue related to DEI and a discussion about how faculty can be responsive toward such issues on campus.

Inclusive Teaching Embedded in Rewards Systems

Perhaps one of the most impactful steps toward sustaining an inclusive culture in an institution is embedding it in the rewards system. Colleges and universities who have taken the next step and integrated evidence of effective inclusive teaching into criteria for promotion and tenure review have the potential to enable a culture of inclusive teaching like no other. One critique to this we have seen is "Will this be genuine effort?" We suspect we may always run into the conundrum of the authenticity of inclusive teaching efforts to some degree, but having particular pedagogical structures in place can have the power to support all learners in reaching their learning goals and also potentially transform mindsets around the value of inclusive teaching at our colleges and universities when successes are witnessed. The University of Oregon is a case example of such efforts. The institution defines teaching excellence as "Inclusive, Engaged and Research-Led" (University of Oregon, 2020). They characterize inclusive teaching as the following:

> Inclusive teaching engages and values every student and attends to the social and emotional climate of the class. A broad philosophy that should be realized in each and every UO course by each and every UO teacher, inclusion is enacted through particular choices faculty make in their presentation of self and content and through deliberate ways of drawing on assets each student brings to the classroom.

For example, UO faculty might . . .

- convey that each student brings valuable assets and goals to their work.
- introduce the instructor's own intellectual journey and process of expert thought.
- use course materials that represent the racial, ethnic, gender, ability, intellectual, and socioeconomic diversity of the field and the contested and evolving status of knowledge.
- deploy a range of methods to engage students and bring out their strengths.
- address students by their chosen names and pronouns; this includes finding ways to use names in large-classes and online fora.
- know students' goals for their learning and find ways to connect the concerns of the course to students' own concerns.
- maximize student motivation by leveraging students' sense of the relevance, rigor, and supportiveness of a course—and of their own self efficacy within it.
- build classroom community, including establishing clear expectations around classroom engagement.
- design courses with physical and content accessibility in mind.

The University of Oregon also transformed their course evaluations process to provide feedback both from students and the instructor on inclusive teaching efforts.

Reflection Questions

- What is some evidence for institutional commitment to inclusive teaching that you have witnessed at your current institution or other institutions where you have been employed?
- Are there additional artifacts of commitment you have observed that have not yet been described that you can add to this list?

Key Points

- Moving toward excellence in inclusive instruction necessitates more than a public statement. There should be evidence of commitment.
- Artifacts illustrating institutional commitment to inclusive teaching include strategic plans describing how the college or university supports the learning of a diverse student body, the structures in place for supporting instructors in implementing inclusive teaching efforts and an inclusive student experience, financial commitment to inclusive teaching efforts, and the integration of inclusive teaching in institutional reward systems.

The content of this book was informed by data gathered in a multipart survey study of a national sample of 306 instructors from diverse institution types and disciplines. Respondents included 180 females, 174 individuals who self-identified as White and non-Hispanic, 118 tenured or tenure-track faculty, 175 full-time faculty, 97 faculty who worked at a doctorate-granting institution, and 162 faculty who had participated in professional development activities that focused on inclusive teaching. Respondents were from 44 different academic disciplines. Study participants completed the inclusive teaching questionnaire, which consisted of 18 Likert scale items, eight open-ended questions, and an array of demographic questions. The questionnaire, specific methods of data collection, and analysis are described in detail in Addy et al. (in press). The first part of the study examined the predictors of inclusive teaching at the time the survey was administered, perceived barriers to implementation, and perceived actions that could advance inclusive teaching efforts at colleges and universities.

This book draws from study data exploring instructor definitions of inclusive teaching and the reported strategies utilized in their courses. The comments that are presented in this book are direct quotes to the responses from the following open-ended questions:

- Please define what inclusive teaching means to you.
- Please list any inclusive teaching strategies that you use in your courses.
- Describe any inclusive teaching initiatives at your institution. Please be sure to only provide general information that does not identify your institution.

Such data, in addition to the coauthors' personal experiences with inclusive teaching and research on inclusive teaching, largely undergirds the narrative of this book and the quotes utilized.

Following is a list of all reflection questions for each chapter that may be used as a discussion guide for each of the chapters of the book.

Chapter 1: The What and Why of Inclusive Teaching

- What is (are) your institutional culture(s) around equitable and inclusive teaching practices? How would you respond if asked what inclusive teaching meant to you?
- What are the percentages of first-generation students at the institution(s) in which you teach? Regardless of whether this information is readily available, consider inviting your students in a brave way to share whether they are first-generation students.
- Are adult learners enrolled at the institution(s) in which you teach? In your classes? Why are they in school? What life experiences and factors can impact their success?
- What course-related factors are important for you to consider if students in your course have limited financial means or time to study?
- What are some accommodations that your learners have needed in the past or with which you have personal experience?
- What are equity issues in your discipline? How are they being addressed?
- What are the relative numbers of international students at your institution(s)? From which countries do they originate? Regardless of whether this information is readily available, consider inviting your students in a brave way to share whether they are international students and develop an understanding of cultural norms that may implicate their classroom success.

- Identify any services provided on your campus(es) to support students with mental health concerns. Consider working with counseling services to determine how to identify such students.
- What are the religious affiliations of students at your institution(s)? Which major observances or traditions may need to be considered when designing learning experiences?
- Who are your learners? What diversity assets do they bring to the classroom? What challenges can they face with inclusion?
- Based on these studies, what actions can instructors take that might help promote inclusion in the classroom setting with regards to social belonging?
- What factors should an instructor keep in mind when designing an equitable course?
- Reflect on your beliefs about equity and inclusion. What motivates you to read this book to learn more about inclusive teaching practices?
- How can each of these frameworks support an inclusive classroom experience for diverse learners?

Chapter 2: What Do They Know About Being Inclusive?

- Does your institution have an office devoted to institutional research? If so, seek out any demographic information can provide about the students at your college or university. On first glance, what if any relationships do you see between the institutional data and the students within your courses? Is there any information available on students in your department or program major or minor that could inform your teaching efforts?
- How can you better understand the attributes and social identities your learners bring to your courses?
- What are problems with the deficit model in higher education?
- What are some assets your diverse learners bring to your course?
- How can you affirm the social identities of all students, including those most susceptible to stereotype threat?
- Have you ever witnessed or been the victim of a microaggression in a teaching and learning setting? As an instructor, how can you be proactive in addressing these in your courses?
- How can instructor empathy for students help foster a more inclusive classroom environment?

- What does or might a holistic approach to learning look like to you in a course setting?
- What are some next steps you can take toward becoming more inclusive in your teaching?

Chapter 3: How Do They Design an Inclusive Course?

- What is your main goal when writing a syllabus? What do you expect it to accomplish?
- Does your approach to the syllabus mirror any of the models described?
- What changes would you need to make to your syllabus in order for it to reflect the strengths of the different approaches? What do you think is currently missing or underdeveloped from those models?
- Do you typically think about making your course inclusive—creating the conditions for educational equity and belonging—when you first begin to design your syllabi?
- If so, at what stage of course design do you consider inclusivity?
- What are you currently doing to try and design your syllabus to reflect inclusive teaching?
- What perspectives does your syllabus already include? Whose voices do you think are currently missing from your syllabus?
- What would you need to do to include those missing voices?
- Does your syllabus currently use inclusive, warm language? How could you change the tone and language of your syllabus to reflect these goals?
- Does your syllabus clearly articulate both rights and responsibilities for instructors and students?
- Does your syllabus convey a clear explanation for participation in the classroom? Does it meaningfully convey to students that all voices are not only welcome but critical for the learning process?
- Does your course currently employ multiple learning modalities and forms of assessment? How could you diversify your current approaches?
- Does your syllabus clearly articulate what students are expected to complete and when?
- Do you offer students access to resources and rationales that will help students from disparate educational backgrounds successfully navigate course requirements?
- What concerns do you have about making your course accessible? What resources does your institution offer to help address those issues?

- What do you think some of your own biases might be when it comes to course design?
- What resources would you need to more successfully implement inclusive design principles at the course design stage? Does your institution have access to those resources? If not, where else could you find them?
- What other challenges do you face when it comes to implementing the strategies discussed in this chapter?

Chapter 4: How Do They Make Their Students Feel Welcome?

- What welcoming strategies have you used to build a positive classroom environment? Did they promote social belonging and equitable practices? Why or why not?
- How can you respectfully acknowledge and appreciate student differences in your classroom? How do you know the students feel accepted?
- What equitable participation practices are you using or can you use in a future course to make students feel more welcome in your classroom?
- How have you worked to build positive relationships with your students both inside and outside of the classroom? Have these actions made your students feel more welcome?
- What can you do at the beginning, middle, or end of a course to make students feel welcome?
- What elements can you include in a welcome statement or video, or syllabus quiz, that would exude enthusiasm, warmth, and welcome? How would you invite them to join your classroom community?
- How would you design and distribute a preterm assessment that communicates care, concern for student success, and approachability?
- How can you use the physical environment before the first class starts to promote a welcoming space? What does that look like in face-to-face and online courses?
- What are concrete first-day-of-class activities you can use to celebrate diversity, equity, and inclusion in your classroom community? How can you relay to students these classroom values are important for welcoming everyone?
- How do you collect information about your class and use it to maintain a welcoming environment? Do you think there is a best time to do so? Why or why not?

- What are the benefits of essential office hours? How often do you need to hold them?
- What are ways to make students feel welcome after the first week of class?
- What evidence-based approaches can you use to restore a welcoming classroom environment once it has been violated or disrupted? How will you gauge the impact of your efforts?
- How easy is it for you to acknowledge and apologize when you have offended a student? What tools do you have that can repair and restore a positive faculty–student relationship?
- How easy is it for you to recognize when one student has offended another in the classroom? How comfortable are you holding individuals accountable and encouraging student dialogue? What tools do you have that can repair and restore a positive student–student relationship?
- How can you form new communities in response to disruptive external forces?

Chapter 5: How Do They Conduct Class Inclusively?

- How do you use or envision embracing any of the following approaches in your teaching: student-centered learning, growth mindset, transparency, or UDL?
- How can you embrace diverse perspectives, structure your course, or be adaptable as you further your inclusive teaching efforts?
- Which of these strategies do you most commonly employ, if any? What is one you would like to try out in your classroom?
- What benefits do you see for using digital technology-based audience response systems in your class? What disadvantages? If you haven't used these before, what is one particular topic your class explores that these might be most useful for?
- What do you expect from your students in terms of participation in the classroom?
- Which of the active learning strategies (case studies, PBL, POGIL, classroom jigsaws, interactive lectures, think-pair-share, classroom debates) that you have never implemented before would you like to incorporate into your teaching? Which class and for which topic would you implement it?
- Take one specific topic that you address in a course you have taught and think about the method you have utilized to teach that concept.

What is another instructional approach you could use to teach that same concept? Would it be possible to implement both of these pedagogical choices in your class, and do you think that would benefit your students?

- Think about one means of assessment you implemented in your last course. Now, hypothetically reformat that assessment or its delivery in an alternative way based on the information provided. What advantages might there be to this new version? What challenges do you foresee? Do the advantages outweigh the challenges?
- How often do you receive formal (anonymous or otherwise) feedback from your students about the course? When do you receive such feedback? Would it be beneficial to receive more feedback from the students, or at a different time?
- What is a method of gathering student feedback you are not currently using that you would want to apply in your course?

Chapter 6: Using a Tool to Support Inclusive Teaching

- How could you utilize or adapt the Who's in Class? Form for courses that you teach?
- With whom could you partner as you administer the tool to discuss your action plans and obtain feedback?

Epilogue: Developing and Sustaining a Culture of Inclusive Teaching

- What topics related to inclusive teaching would you most benefit from exploring during a professional development experience? If on-campus professional development is not available, consider books, initiatives facilitated by other institutions, and resources that may support your efforts.
- Identify professional development experiences in inclusive teaching that you could further explore, whether at your institution or beyond.
- What is some evidence for institutional commitment to inclusive teaching that you have witnessed at your current institution or other institutions at which you have been employed?
- Are there additional artifacts of commitment you have observed that have not yet been described that you can add to this list?

F ollowing is an example of a welcome statement that instructors can use to engage with students before the term starts.

Dear Students,

Welcome to Term 20XX Intro Course! My name is Professor (Last Name) and I will be your instructor for the next XX weeks. Let me start by telling you a little about me. I have a graduate degree in discipline X from (R1 Research University). My bachelor's degree is in discipline Y and from (Selective Liberal Arts College). My partner and I spend weekends volunteering in our community and watching football (Go Team!). In a former life, I was a spoken word poet and known to play a terrific pizzicato piece on my violin. I can't wait to learn more about what knowledge, experiences, and talents you're bringing to our classroom community.

My course goal is to help you develop a new appreciation for (subject matter) and spark your desire to learn more about the subject after you leave every class! I'm so excited to teach this course because (motivation(s)). You may be excited, but also a little nervous, too. I understand there is a lot of new material to learn and you want to do well. I took this course when I was at the same academic stage as you, and I had similar feelings. Don't worry. We'll start from your individual baseline knowledge and build from there. You're walking into the course with important foundational knowledge and lived experiences! The course will be conducted using (LMS) and everything for your success can be found at (course website). I've listed many resources to help you review important topics that we'll cover throughout the (term). You will be able to login a month before the course starts in case you'd like to get a head start.

Every course here at (R1 Research University) requires a significant time commitment from you. I expect you to spend at least (quantity) hours per week working on the material. While there is a significant amount of reading and problem-solving, I have worked to make it enjoyable, interesting, relevant, and applicable to your daily life. Are there any hot topics you're yearning to learn about? I invite you to send me an email from now until the first 2 weeks of class with your suggestions. I've reserved the last week of class on the syllabus to teach student suggested topics.

If you find yourself having trouble with any of the course content at any point, please contact me as soon as possible. I'm here to help you. My preferred contact method is email. My goal is to respond to messages within 24 hours between 9:00 a.m. and 6:00 p.m., Monday through Friday. However, sometimes unforeseen life circumstances may arise. If you do not receive a response back within a 24-hour time frame, please resend the message with a reminder.

It's true that you will learn a lot from me this term. However, learning is a two-way street. I'm looking forward to learning a lot from, and working with, you!

With enthusiasm,

(Preferred instructor name)

(Contact number)

(Institutional email)

F ollowing is an example of a syllabus quiz that can be used by the instructor to engage with students before the term starts.

Preferred instructor name, Term 20XX Intro Course, Current Institution
In the following you will see frequently asked questions about your instructor and the course. All of the answers are stated in the syllabus, except open-ended questions. Correct answers are in bold.

1. *What is the preferred name of the instructor? Pick all that apply.*
   a. *First Name*
   b. *Last Name*
   c. *Mr. or Ms. First Name*
   d. *Mr. or Ms. Last Name*
   e. **Professor Last Name**
   f. **Dr. Last Name**

2. *Where can you learn more about the Institution's preferred name policy and request a name change?*
   https://diversity.institution.edu/preferred-name-policy/

3. *What is your instructor's preferred method of contact and a realistic response time on weekdays between 9:00 a.m. and 6:00 p.m. throughout the term?*
   a. *Email and instantly*
   b. **Email and 24 hours**
   c. *Telephone and instantly*
   d. *Telephone and 24 hours*

4. *What is your instructor's preferred method of contact and a realistic response time on weekends between 9:00 a.m. and 6:00 p.m. throughout the term?*
   Email, however, your instructor does not respond to emails over the weekend. She/he/they will respond on Monday morning at 9:00 a.m. Your instructor strives to balance work and life and believes you should too.

2. *Where can you find helpful advice on proper etiquette to email this, or any, instructor?*
  Link to advice article about proper protocol to email your instructor
3. *When and where are office hours? Pick all that apply.*
   a. **Mondays, Wednesdays, and Fridays from 12:00–2:00 p.m. in the instructor's office**
   b. *Tuesdays and Thursdays from 12:00–2:00 p.m. in the instructor's office*
   c. *Mondays, Wednesdays, and Friday from 12:00–2:00 p.m. at another location on campus*
   d. *Tuesdays and Thursdays from 12:00–2:00 p.m. at another location on campus*
   e. **By appointment in the instructor's office**
7. *How do you sign up for office hours to get the instructor's help with specific topics and concepts?*
   a. *Just walk in*
   b. **Use the scheduling site link**
8. *What are essential office hours and why has your instructor cleared their schedule especially for you?*
   These are the time blocks that the instructor schedules for you to come to office hours to discuss your background, goals, successes, and challenges and to receive tips and advice on how to finish the course strong.
9. *Which of the following are needed to do well in this course? Pick all that apply.*
   a. *Prior knowledge from high school*
   b. *Perfect grades in previous college classes*
   c. **Successfully pass the prerequisite courses**
   d. **Dedicate at least 9 hours per week to the current coursework (including studying alone, studying in groups, individual tutoring, peer tutoring, and office hours)**
10. *Why did your instructor choose your current textbook? Pick all that apply.*
    a. **It is clear and rigorous.**
    b. **Its price was reasonable.**
    c. **It emphasizes active learning.**
    d. **It provides diverse representation of scholars in the field.**
    e. **It focuses on helping students understand key concepts in the field.**
11. *What are the instructor's expectations of you in this course?*
    a. **Attendance: Make every effort to attend all classes on time. If you can't make it on time for any reason, come to class and maximize learning in the time that is left.**

b. *Sickness/illness: If you are not feeling well, please notify the instructor BEFORE class and stay home to take care of yourself.*

c. *Assigned readings: All assigned readings should be read before coming to class.*

d. *Problems: This text was selected for its many types of questions. You should be able to answer questions in a chapter, as well as the end-of-chapter questions. These types of questions are similar to quiz and exam questions.*

e. *Work as many problems as you can, both alone and in groups. If you want the instructor's assistance solving a particular problem, please let them know and they can discuss the solution with you.*

f. *Class participation: Active listening skills, activities, and discussion participation, and respect for our classroom is expected and encouraged at all times.*

g. *Assignment submissions: Assignments should be submitted in class and/or on the LMS site by the specified deadline.*

h. *Lecture documents: All lecture documents will be available on the LMS site for the following week every Friday by 5:00 p.m. Everyone is expected to check weekly before coming to class.*

i. *Cell phone policy: Cell phones are permitted during class; however, their use should be restricted to class-related materials. They must be turned to silent or vibrate during class time.*

j. *Laptop and other device policy: Laptops and other devices are permitted during class; however, their use should be restricted to class-related materials.*

12. *How can you share your expectations of the instructor in this course? Pick all that apply.*

   a. *Email*

   b. *Office hours and essential office hours*

   c. *Anonymous suggestion box section of the LMS*

   d. *Anonymous suggestion box provided in class each session*

13. *Approximately how many hours per week should you be working outside of the class to be successful in this course?*
   Average number of hours

14. *Why is getting enough sleep critical for being successful in this course?*
   Various supporting evidence

15. *When are assignment due dates?*
   Various dates

16. *How can I share an assignment idea that I liked a lot in past or current courses with my instructor? Pick all that apply.*
    a. *Tell a friend*
    b. **Email the instructor**
    c. *Write it in your journal*
    d. **Talk with the instructor**
17. *Is late work accepted?*
    a. **Yes, you may use your flex passes**
    b. **No**
18. *Are there extra credit opportunities?*
    a. **Yes, within the guidelines described in the syllabus**
    b. *No*
19. *How can I add a topic that I'm interested in to the tentative schedule listed at the end of the syllabus? Pick all that apply.*
    a. *Tell a friend*
    b. **Email the instructor**
    c. *Write it in your journal*
    d. **Talk with the instructor**
20. *If I disagree with my classmate's point of view, I can (Pick all that apply):*
    a. *Cut them off*
    b. *Scream at them*
    c. *Talk about the conversation outside of the classroom*
    d. **Talk calmly and engage in respectful critical dialogue**
    e. **Refer to the class discussion guidelines we cocreated as a class**

APPENDIX E

Stereotype Content Model-Driven Reestablishment of a Welcoming Classroom Worksheet

(Adapted from Fiske, 2018)

The worksheet that follows can be used by inclusive instructors to rebuild a positive faculty–student relationship if it has been disrupted by faculty-held stereotypes that harmed a student. It will help the instructor to do the following:

1. Acknowledge the positive or negative stereotype and identify personal background, biases, and experiences that shaped the view.
2. Identify all the student demographics that have been harmed.
3. Analyze which emotions are evoked by the stereotype and reflect on how it contributed to the harm.
4. Decide on what actions to take to repair the harm and possible outcomes.

Stereotype?		
Positive or negative?		
Affected student(s)?		
	High competence	**Low competence**
High warmth	Emotions evoked:	Emotions evoked:
Low warmth	Emotions evoked:	Emotions evoked:

Actions	Direct action(s): Indirect action(s):
Expected outcomes	

ABOUT THE AUTHORS

Tracie Marcella Addy is associate dean of teaching and learning at Lafayette College in Easton, PA, where she oversees the Center for the Integration of Teaching, Learning, and Scholarship and partners with faculty across disciplines and ranks on their teaching efforts. She is an invited speaker and scholar on topics related to teaching and learning. She holds a PhD from North Carolina State University, MPhil from Yale University, and BS from Duke University.

Derek Dube is an associate professor of biology and director of the Center for Student Research and Creative Activity at the University of Saint Joseph (CT). His scholarship and publication record range from laboratory research in microbiology and virology to development of educational materials and research on pedagogical practices in STEM fields. He earned his PhD in Microbiology from the University of Virginia and a BS in Biology from James Madison University.

Khadijah A. Mitchell is the Peter C.S. d'Aubermont, M.D. Scholar of Health and Life Sciences and assistant professor of biology at Lafayette College. Her award-winning scholarship addresses the causes and consequences of cancer health disparities in underrepresented populations. Mitchell's teaching and public health leadership roles promote both education and health equity. She earned her PhD in Human Genetics and Molecular Biology from the Johns Hopkins School of Medicine, a graduate certificate in Health Disparities and Health Inequalities from the Johns Hopkins Bloomberg School of Public Health, an MS in Biology from Duquesne University, and a BS in Biology from the University of Pittsburgh.

Mallory E. SoRelle is an assistant professor of public policy at the Sanford School of Public Policy at Duke University. Her research and teaching interests explore how public policies influence intersectional forms of socioeconomic and political inequality in the United States. SoRelle holds a PhD in American Politics from Cornell University, a Master of Public Policy from Harvard University's Kennedy School of Government, and a BA with honors from Smith College.

REFERENCES

Addy, T. M., Dube, D., Croft, C., Nardolilli, J. O., Paynter, O. C., Hutchings, M. L., Honsberger, M. J., & Reeves, P. M. (2018). Integrating a serious game into case-based learning. *Simulation & Gaming, 49*(4), 378–400. https://doi.org/10.1177/1046878118779416

Addy T. M., Reeves P. M., Dube D., & Mitchell K. A. (In press.). What really matters for instructors implementing equitable and inclusive teaching approaches. *To Improve the Academy.*

Aleamoni, L. M. (1999). Student rating myths versus research facts from 1924 to 1998. *Journal of Personnel Evaluation in Education, 13*(2), 153–166. https://doi.org/10.1023/A:1008168421283

Allen, D, & Tanner, K. (2002). Approaches to cell biology teaching: questions about questions. *Cell Biology Education, 1*(3), 63–67. https://www.lifescied.org/doi/pdf/10.1187/cbe.02-07-0021

American Association of Community Colleges. (2020). *Home page.* https://www.aacc.nche.edu

American College Health Association. (2018). *Spring 2018: Reference group executive summary.* https://www.acha.org/documents/ncha/NCHA-II_Spring_2018_Reference_Group_Executive_Summary.pdf

American Council on Education. (2018). *A toolkit for veteran friendly institutions.* https://www.acenet.edu/Documents/Veterans-Toolkit-2018.pdf

American Psychological Association. (2020). *Intersectionality.* https://apastyle.apa.org/style-grammar-guidelines/bias-free-language/intersectionality

Amstutz, L. S., & Mullet, J. H. (2015). *The little book of restorative discipline for schools: teaching responsibility, creating caring climates.* Good Books.

Angelou, M. (2014). *Rainbow in the cloud: The wit and wisdom of Maya Angelou.* Random House.

Aragón, O. R., Dovidio, J. F., & M. J. Graham. (2017). Colorblind and multicultural ideologies are associated with faculty adoption of inclusive teaching practices. *Journal of Diversity in Higher Education, 10*(3), 201–215. http://dx.doi.org/10.1037/dhe0000026

Armstrong, M. A. (2011). Small world: Crafting an inclusive classroom (no matter what you teach). *Thought and Action*, 51–61. http://www.nea.org/assets/docs/2011TandAArmstrongFINAL.pdf

Aronson, B., & Laughter, J. (2016). The theory and practice of culturally relevant education: A synthesis of research across content areas. *Review of Educational Research, 86*(1), 163–206. https://doi.org/10.3102/0034654315582066

Aronson, J., Lustina, M. J., Good, C., Keough, K., Steele, C. M., & Brown, J. (1999). When White men can't do math: Necessary and sufficient factors in stereotype threat. *Journal of Experimental Social Psychology, 35*(1), 29–46. https://doi.org/10.1006/jesp.1998.1371

Ashburn-Nardo, L., Morris, K. A., & Goodwin, S. A. (2008). The confronting prejudiced responses (CPR) model: Applying CPR in organizations. *Academy of Management Learning & Education, 7*(3), 332–342. https://www.jstor.org/stable/40214552

Association of American Colleges & Universities. (n.d.). *Diversity, equity, and student success.* https://www.aacu.org/diversity-equity-and-student-success

Association of College and University Educators. (2020). *About.* https://acue.org/about/

Association of Public & Land-Grant Universities. (n.d.). *Access, diversity & excellence.* https://www.aplu.org/members/commissions/access-diversity-and-excellence/index.html

Baecker, D. L. (1998). Uncovering the rhetoric of the syllabus: The case of the missing I. *College Teaching, 46*(2), 58–61. https://doi.org/10.1080/87567559809596237

Banks, J. A. (1993a). Approaches to multicultural curricular reform. In J. A. Banks & C. A. Banks (Eds.), *Multicultural education: Issues and perspectives* (2nd ed.) (pp. 3–24). Allyn & Bacon.

Banks, J. A. (1993b). The canon debate, knowledge construction, and multicultural education. *Educational Researcher, 22*(5), 4–14. https://doi.org/10.3102/0013189X022005004

Baxter, S., & Gray, C. (2001). The application of student-centered learning approaches to clinical education. *International Journal of Language & Communication Disorders, 36*(1), 396–400. https://doi.org/10.3109/13682820109177918

Beichner, R. (2007, March). The Student-Centered Activities for Large Enrollment Undergraduate Programs (SCALE-UP) project. In E. F. Redish and P. J. Cooney (Eds.), *Research-Based Reform of University Physics, 1*(1), 1–42. https://www.compadre.org/Repository/document/ServeFile.cfm?ID=4517&DocID=183

Bishop-Clark, C., & Dietz-Uhler, B. (2012). *Engaging in the scholarship of teaching and learning: a guide to develop a project from start to finish.* Stylus.

Bond, L. (1996). Norm- and criterion-referenced testing. *Practical Assessment, Research & Evaluation, 5*(2), 1–3. https://doi.org/10.7275/dy7r-2x18

Booker, K. C., & Campbell-Whatley, G. (2019). Student perceptions of inclusion at a historically Black university. *Journal of Negro Education, 88*(2), 146–158. https://www.jstor.org/stable/10.7709/jnegroeducation.88.2.0146?seq=1

Bowman, N. A., & Felix, V. (2017). It's who I am: Student identity centrality and college student success. *Journal of Student Affairs Research and Practice, 54*(3), 235–247. https://doi.org/10.1080/19496591.2017.1331853

Boysen, G. A., & Vogel, D. L. (2009). Bias in the classroom: Types, frequencies, and responses. *Teaching of Psychology, 36*(1), 12–17. https://doi.org/10.1080/00986280802529038

Bye, L., Muller, F., & Oprescu, F. (2019). The impact of social capital on student wellbeing and university life satisfaction: A semester-long repeated measures study. *Higher Education Research & Development, 39*(5), 898–912. https://doi.org/10.1080/07294360.2019.1705253

Calhoun, C. (2009). The undergraduate pipeline problem. *Hypatia, 24*(2), 216–223. https://doi.org/10.1111/j.1527-2001.2009.01040.x

Capp, M. J. (2017). The effectiveness of universal design for learning: A meta-analysis of literature between 2013 and 2016. *International Journal of Inclusive Education, 21*(8), 791–807. https://doi.org/10.1080/13603116.2017.1325074

CAST. (n.d.a.). CAST: *Our work.* http://www.cast.org/our-work#.W_2JRxNKii4

CAST. (n.d.b.). *CAST home page.* http://www.cast.org/

CAST. (n.d.c.). *The UDL guidelines.* http://udlguidelines.cast.org

Center for First-Generation Student Success. (2019). *First-generation college students: Demographic characteristics and postsecondary enrollment.* https://firstgen.naspa.org/files/dmfile/FactSheet-01.pdf

Center for the Integration of Research, Teaching and Learning Network. (2020). *About CIRTL.* https://www.cirtl.net/about

Chávez, A. F., Guido-DiBrito, F., & Mallory, S. L. (2003). Learning to value the "other": A framework of individual diversity development. *Journal of College Student Development, 44*(4), 453–469. https://doi.org/10.1353/csd.2003.0038

Chen, B., Thompson, K., Sugar, A., & Vargas, J. (2015). Syllabus quiz. In B. Chen, A. deNoyelles, & K. Thompson (Eds.), *Teaching online pedagogical repository.* University of Central Florida Center for Distributed Learning.

Chung, J. C. C., & Chow, S. M. K. (2004). Promoting student learning through a student-centered problem-based learning subject curriculum. *Innovations in Education & Teaching International, 41*(2), 157–168. https://doi.org/10.1080/1470329042000208684

Claro, S., Paunesku, D., & Dweck, C. S. (2016). Growth mind-set tempers the effects of poverty on academic achievement. *Proceedings of the National Academy of Sciences of the United States of America, 113*(31), 8664–8668. https://doi.org/10.1073/pnas.1608207113

Cohen, G. L., Garcia, J., Apfel, N., & Master, A. (2006). Reducing the racial achievement gap: A social-psychological intervention. *Science, 313*(5791), 1307–1310. https://doi.org/10.1126/science.1128317

Cohen, G. L., Garcia J., Purdie-Vaughts V., Apfel N., & Brzustokski, P. (2009). Recursive processes in self-affirmation: Intervening to close the minority achievement gap. *Science, 324*(5925), 400–403. https://doi.org/10.1126/science.1170769

Cole, D., & Ahmadi, S. (2003). Perspectives and experiences of Muslim women who veil on college campuses. *Journal of College Student Development, 44*(1), 47–66. https://doi.org/10.1353/csd.2003.0002

Collins, M. L. (1978). Effects of enthusiasm training on preservice elementary teachers. *Research in Teacher Education, 29*(1), 53–57. https://doi.org/10.1177/002248717802900120

Cook-Sather, A., Addy, T. M., DeVault A., & Litvitskiy, N. (In press.). Where are the students in efforts for inclusive excellence?: Two approaches to positioning students as critical partners for inclusive pedagogical practices. *To Improve the Academy.*

Cook-Sather, A., Bahti, M., & Ntem, A. (2019). *Pedagogical partnerships: A how-to guide for faculty, students, and academic developers in higher education.* Elon University Center for Engaged Learning. https://doi.org/10.36284/celelon.oa1

Cooper, K. M., Haney, B., Krieg, A., & Brownell, S. E. (2017 , October 13). What's in a name? The importance of students perceiving that an instructor knows their names in a high-enrollment biology classroom. *CBE Life Sciences Education, 16*(1). https://doi.org/10.1187/cbe.16-08-0265

Cooper, P., & Cuseo, G. (1989). The course syllabus. *Teaching Newsletter California State University at Dominguez Hills, 2*(4), 1–4.

Cornell University. (n.d.). *Center for Teaching Innovation: Teaching & learning in the diverse classroom MOOC.* https://teaching.cornell.edu/tldc-mooc

Corrigan, H., & Craciun, G. (2013). Asking the right questions: Using student-written exams as an innovative approach to learning and evaluation. *Marketing Education Review, 23*(1), 31–36. https://doi.org/10.2753/MER1052-8008230105

Cotner, S., & Ballen, C. J. (2017). Can mixed assessment methods make biology classes more equitable? *PLOS One, 12*(12), e0189610. https://doi.org/10.1371/journal.pone.0189610

Covarrubias, R., Valle, I., Laiduc, G., & Azmitia, M. (2018). "You never become fully independent": Family roles and independence in first-generation college students. *Journal of Adolescent Research, 16*(1). https://doi.org/10.1187/cbe.16-08-0265

Cox, M. D. (2004). Introduction to faculty learning communities. *New Directions for Teaching and Learning, 2004*(97), 5–23. https://doi.org/10.1002/tl.129

Crenshaw, K. (1989). Demarginalizing the intersection of race and sex: A Black feminist critique of antidiscrimination doctrine, feminist theory and antiracist politics. *University of Chicago Legal Forum, 1989*(1), 139–167. https://chicagounbound.uchicago.edu/uclf/vol1989/iss1/8

Danielson, M. (1995, April 19–23). *The role of the course syllabi in classroom socialization.* Paper presented at the Annual Meeting of Central States Communication Association, Bloomington, IN. https://files.eric.ed.gov/fulltext/ED387845.pdf

Dasgupta, N., Scircle, M. M., & Hunsinger, M. (2015). Female peers in small work groups enhance women's motivation, verbal participation, and career aspirations in engineering. *Proceedings of the National Academy of Sciences, 112*(16), 4988–4993. https://doi.org/10.1073/pnas.1422822112

Davis, B. G. (1993). *Tools for teaching.* Jossey-Bass.

Davis, S., & Schrader, V. (2009). Comparison of syllabi expectations between faculty and students in a baccalaureate nursing program. *Journal of Nursing Education, 48*(3), 125–131. https://doi.org/10.3928/01484834-20090301-03

Dean, K. L., & Fornaciari, C. J. (2014a). Creating masterpieces: How course structures and routines enable student performance. *Journal of Management Education, 38*(1), 10–42. https://www.learntechlib.org/p/157035/

Dean, K. L., & Fornaciari, C. J. (2014b). The 21st-century syllabus: Tips for putting andragogy into practice. *Journal of Management Education, 38*(5), 724–732. https://doi.org/10.1177/1052562913504764

Dekker, S., Lee, N. C., Howard-Jones, P., & Jolles, J. (2012). Neuromyths in education: Prevalence and predictors of misconceptions among teachers. *Frontiers in Psychology, 3*(429), 1–8. https://doi.org/10.3389/fpsyg.2012.00429

Denton, A. W., & Veloso, J. (2018). Changes in syllabus tone affect warmth (but not competence) ratings of both male and female instructors. *Social Psychology of Education, 21*(1), 173–187. https://doi.org/10.1007/s11218-017-9409-7

Dibattista, D., & Gosse, L. (2006). Test anxiety and the immediate feedback assessment technique. *The Journal of Experimental Education, 74*(4), 311–328. https://doi.org/10.3200/JEXE.74.4.311-328

Dika, S. L., & D'Amico, M. M. (2015). Early experiences and integration in the persistence of first-generation college students in STEM and non-STEM majors. *Journal of Research in Science Teaching, 53*(3), 368–383. https://doi.org/10.1002/tea.21301

Dixson, M. D., Greenwell, M. R., Rogers-Stacy, C., Weister, T., & Lauer, S. (2017). Nonverbal immediacy behaviors and online student engagement: Bringing past instructional research into the present virtual classroom. *Communication Education, 66*(1), 37–53. https://doi.org/10.1080/03634523.2016.1209222

Domingo, S., Sharp, S., Freeman, A., Freeman, T., Jr., Harmon, K., Wiggs, M., Sathy, V., Panter, A. T., Oseguera, L., Sun, S., Williams, M. E., Templeton, J., Folt, C. L., Baron, E. J., Hrabowski, F. A., III, Maton, K. I., Crimmins, M., Fisher, C. R., & Summers, M. F. (2019). Replicating Meyerhoff for inclusive excellence in STEM. *Science, 364*(6438), 335–337. https://doi.org/10.1126/science.aar5540

Dunlosky, J., & Metcalfe, J. (2009). *Metacognition.* SAGE.

Dweck, C. S. (2006). *Mindset: The new psychology of success.* Random House.

Eberly, M. B., Newton, S. E., & Wiggins, R. A. (2001). The syllabus as a tool for student-centered learning. *Journal of General Education, 50*(1), 56–74. http://jan.ucc.nau.edu/~coesyl-p/syllabus_cline_article_4.pdf

Eddy, S. L., & Hogan, K. A. (2014). Getting under the hood: How and for whom does increasing course structure work? *CBE—Life Sciences Education, 13*(3), 453–468. https://doi.org/10.1187/cbe.14-03-0050

eDX. (2020). *Inclusive teaching: Supporting all students in the college classroom.* https://www.edx.org/course/inclusive-teaching-supporting-all-students-in-the

Engel, J., (Director, Writer, Producer), Egan, J. (Producer), & Vandervoort, C. (Producer). (2019*). Raise hell: The life and times of Molly Ivins* [Film]. Magnolia Pictures.

Equality Challenge Unit. (2013). *Unconscious bias and higher education.* https://www.ecu.ac.uk/wp-content/uploads/2014/07/unconscious-bias-and-higher-education.pdf

Espinosa, L. L., Turk, J. M., Taylor, M., & Chessman, H. M. (2019). *Race and ethnicity in higher education: A status report.* American Council on Education.

Filback, R., & Green, A. A. (2013). *Framework of educator mindsets and consequences.* https://rossier.usc.edu/files/2013/08/Educator-Mindsets-and-Consequences-Table-Filback-Green-2013.pdf

Fiske, S. T. (2018). Stereotype content: Warmth and competence endure. *Current Directions in Psychological Science, 27*(2), 67–73. https://doi.org/10.1177/0963721417738825

Fiske, S. T., Cuddy, A. J. C., Glick, P., & Xu, J. (2002). A model of (often mixed) stereotype content: Competence and warmth respectively follow from perceived status and competition. *Journal of Personality and Social Psychology, 82*(6), 878–902. https://doi.org/10.1037/0022-3514.82.6.878

Freeman, S., Eddy, S. L., McDonough, M., Smith, M. K., Okoroafor, N., Jordt, H., & Wenderoth, M. P. (2014). Active learning boosts performance in STEM courses. *Proceedings of the National Academy of Sciences, 111*(23), 8410–8415. https://doi.org/10.1073/pnas.1319030111

Freeman, S., Haak, D., & Wenderoth, M. P. (2011). Increased course structure improves performance in introductory biology. *CBE Life Sciences Education, 10*(2), 175–186. https://doi.org/10.1187/cbe.10-08-0105

Gannon, K. (2018, February 27). A case for inclusive teaching. *The Chronicle of Higher Education.* https://www.chronicle.com/article/The-Case-for-Inclusive/242636

Gavassa, S., Benabentos, R., Kravec, M., Collins, T., & Eddy, S. (2019). Closing the achievement gap in a large introductory course by balancing reduced in-person contact with increased course structure. *CBE—Life Sciences Education, 18*(1), 1–10. https://doi.org/10.1187/cbe.18-08-0153

Gay, G. (2010). *Culturally responsive teaching: Theory, research, and practice* (2nd ed.). Teachers College Press.

Gilbert, M. J., Schiff, M., & Cunliffe, R. H. (2013). Teaching restorative justice: Developing a restorative andragogy for face-to-face, online and hybrid course modalities. *Contemporary Justice Review, 16*(1), 43–69. https://doi.org/10.1080/10282580.2013.769305

Ginsberg, M. B., & Wlodkowski, R. J. (2009). *Diversity and motivation: Culturally responsive teaching in college* (2nd ed.). Jossey-Bass.

Golding, C., & Adam, L. (2016). Evaluate to improve: Useful approaches to student evaluation. *Assessment & Evaluation in Higher Education, 41*(1), 1–14. https://doi.org/10.1080/02602938.2014.976810

Goldrick-Rab, S., Baker-Smith, C., Coca, V., Looker, E., & Williams, T. (2019). *College and university basic needs insecurity: A national #RealCollege survey report.* https://hope4college.com/wp-content/uploads/2019/04/HOPE_realcollege_National_report_digital.pdf

Good, C., Rattan, A., & Dweck, C. S. (2012). Why do women opt out? Sense of belonging and women's representation in mathematics. *Journal of Personality and Social Psychology, 102*(4), 700–717. https://doi.org/10.1037/a0026659

Gopalan, M., & Brady, S. T. (2019). College students' sense of belonging: A national perspective. *Educational Researcher, 49*(2), 134–137. https://doi.org/10.3102/0013189X19897622

Graham, C. R., Tripp, T. R., Seawright, L., & Joeckel, G. (2007). Empowering or compelling reluctant participators using audience response systems. *Active Learning in Higher Education, 8*(3), 233–258. https://doi.org/10.1177/1469787407081885

Griffin, A., & Cook, V. (2009). Acting on evaluation: Twelve tips from a national conference on student evaluations. *Medical Teacher, 31*(2), 101–104. https://doi.org/10.1080/01421590802225788

Grunert, J. (1997). *The course syllabus: A learner-centered approach*. Anker.

Gruttadaro, D., & Crudo, D. (2012). *College students speak: A survey report on mental health*. National Alliance on Mental Illness. https://www.nami.org/getattachment/About-NAMI/Publications-Reports/Survey-Reports/College-Students-Speak_A-Survey-Report-on-Mental-Health-NAMI-2012.pdf

Gubbiyappa, K. S., Barua, A., Das, B., Vasudeva Murthy, C. R., & Baloch, H. Z. (2016). Effectiveness of flipped classroom with poll everywhere as a teaching-learning method for pharmacy students. *Indian Journal of Pharmacology, 48*(7), S41–S46. https://doi.org/10.4103/0253-7613.193313

Guo, S., & Jamal, Z. (2007). Nurturing cultural diversity in higher education: A critical review of selected models. *Canadian Journal of Higher Education, 37*(3), 27–49. https://files.eric.ed.gov/fulltext/EJ799706.pdf

Guskey, T. R. (2007). Closing achievement gaps: Revisiting Benjamin S. Bloom's "learning for mastery." *Journal of Advanced Academics, 19*(1), 8–31. https://doi.org/10.4219/jaa-2007-704

Guskey, T. R. (2018). Does pre-assessment work? Educators must understand the purpose, form, and content of pre-assessments to reap their potential benefits. *Educational Leadership, 75*(5), 52–57. http://www.ascd.org/publications/educational_leadership/feb18/vol75/num05/Does_Pre-Assessment_Work%C2%A2.aspx

Haak, D. C., HilleRisLambers, J., Pitre, E., & Freeman, S. (2011). Increased structure and active learning reduce the achievement gap in introductory biology. *Science, 332*(6034), 1213–1216. https://doi.org/10.1126/science.1204820

Habanek, D. V. (2005). An examination of the integrity of the syllabus. *College Teaching, 53*(2), 62–64. http://dx.doi.org/10.3200/CTCH.53.2.62-64

Harackiewicz, J. M., Canning, E. A., Tibbetts, Y., Priniski, S. J., & Hyde, J. S. (2016). Closing achievement gaps with a utility-value intervention: Disentangling race and social class. *Journal of Personality and Social Psychology, 111*(5), 745–765. https://doi.org/10.1037/pspp0000075

Harnish, R. J., & Bridges, K. R. (2011). Effect of syllabus tone: Students' perceptions of instructor and course. *Social Psychology of Education, 14*(3), 319–330. https://doi.org/10.1007/s11218-011-9152-4

Harrington, C., & Thomas, M. (2018). *Designing a motivational syllabus: Creating a learning path for student engagement*. Stylus.

Hollander, S. A. (2001). Taking it personally: The role of memoirs in teacher education. *Electronic Journal for Inclusive Education, 1*(5), 1–8. https://corescholar.libraries.wright.edu/cgi/viewcontent.cgi?article=1034&context=ejie

hooks, b. (1994). *Teaching to transgress: Education as the practice of freedom*. Routledge.

Hrabowski, F. A., Rous P. J., & Henderson P. H. (2019). *The empowered university: Shared leadership, culture change, and academic success*. Johns Hopkins University Press.

Hubbard, J. K., Potts, M. A., & Couch, B. A. (2017). How question types reveal student thinking: An experimental comparison of multiple-true-false and free-response formats. *CBE Life Science Education, 16*(2). https://doi.org/10.1187/cbe.16-12-0339

Huitt, W. (1996). Measurement and evaluation: Criterion- versus norm-referenced testing. *Educational Psychology Interactive,* Valdosta State University. http://www.edpsycinteractive.org/topics/measeval/crnmref.html

Imad, M. (2020, June 3). Leveraging the neuroscience of now. *Inside Higher Ed.* https://www.insidehighered.com/advice/2020/06/03/seven-recommendations-helping-students-thrive-times-trauma

Ives, J., & Castillo-Montoya, M. (2020). First-generation college students as academic learners: A systematic review. *Review of Educational Research, 90*(2), 139–178. https://doi.org/10.3102/0034654319899707

Jigsaw Classroom. (2020, May 22). *The jigsaw classroom.* https://www.jigsaw.org/

Johnson, D. W., Johnson, R. T., & Stanne, M. B. (2000). *Cooperative learning methods: A meta-analysis.* University of Minnesota Press.

Jordt, H., Eddy, S. L., Brazil, R., Lau, I., Mann, C., Brownell, S. E., King, K., & Freeman, S. (2017). Values affirmation intervention reduces achievement gap between underrepresented minority and White students in introductory biology classes. *CBE Life Sciences Education, 16*(3), 1–10. https://doi.org/10.1187/cbe.16-12-0351

Jury, M., Smeding, A., Stephens, N. M., Nelson, J. E., Aelenei, C., & Darnon, C. (2017). The experience of low-SES students in higher education: Psychological barriers to success and interventions to reduce social-class inequality. *Journal of Social Issues, 73*(1), 23–41. https://doi.org/10.1111/josi.12202

Kaplan, D. M., & Renard, M. K. (2015). Negotiating your syllabus: Building a collaborative contract. *Journal of Management Education, 39*(3), 400–421. https://doi.org/10.1177/1052562914564788

Kemm, R. E., & Dantas, A. M. (2007). Research-led learning in biological science practical activities: Supported by student-centred e-learning. *FASEB Journal, 21*(5), A220. https://doi.org/10.1096/fasebj.21.5.A220-b

Kim, H. S. (2008). Culture and the cognitive and neuroendocrine responses to speech. *Journal of Personality and Social Psychology, 94*(1), 32–47. https://doi.org/10.1037/0022-3514.94.1.32

Kizilcec, R. F., Davis, G. M., & Cohen, G. L. (2017). *Towards equal opportunities in MOOCs: Affirmation reduces gender and social-class achievement gaps in China.* https://rene.kizilcec.com/wp-content/uploads/2017/02/kizilcec2017towards.pdf

Kizilcec, R. F., & Halawa, S. (2015). Attrition and achievement gaps in online learning. *Proceedings of the Second ACM Conference on Learning @ Scale, 57–66.* https://doi.org/10.1145/2724660.2724680

Kizilcec, R. F., Saltarelli, A. J., Reich, J., & Cohen, G. L. (2017). Closing global achievement gaps in MOOCs. *Science, 355*(6322), 251–252. https://doi.org/10.1126/science.aag2063

Knapp, S., & Merges, R. (2017). An evaluation of three interdisciplinary social science events outside of the college classroom, *College Teaching, 65*(3), 137–141. https://doi.org/10.1080/87567555.2016.1244655

Knowles, M. S. (1984a). *The adult learner: A neglected species* (3rd ed.). Gulf Publishing.

Knowles, M. S. (1984b). Introduction: The art and science of helping adults learn. In M. Knowles & Associates (Eds.), *Andragogy in action: Applying modern principles of adult learning* (pp. 1–24). Jossey-Bass.

Knowles, M. S. (1990). *The adult learner: A neglected species* (4th ed.). Gulf Publishing.

Knowles, M. S., Holton, E. F., & Swanson, R. A. (2005). *The adult learner: The definitive classic in adult education and human resource development* (6th ed.). Elsevier.

Kohn, A. (1993). *Punished by rewards: The trouble with gold stars, incentive plans, A's, praise, and other bribes.* Houghton Mifflin.

Kosmin, B. A., & Keysar, A. (2015). *National demographic survey of American Jewish college students 2014: Anti-Semitism report.* Trinity College. https://digital-repository.trincoll.edu/cgi/viewcontent.cgi?referer=https://scholar.google.com/scholar?hl=en&as_sdt=0%2C31&q=jewish+students+discrimination+college&btnG=&httpsredir=1&article=1133&context=facpub

Kozar, J. M., & Marcketti, S. B. (2008). Utilizing field-based instruction as an effective teaching strategy. *College Student Journal, 42*(2), 305–311.

Ladson-Billings, G. (2006). "Yes, but how do we do it?" Practicing culturally relevant pedagogy. In J. G. Landsman & C. W. Lewis (Eds.), *White teachers diverse classrooms: Creating inclusive schools, building on students' diversity, and providing true educational equity* (pp. 33–46). Stylus.

Layton, R. A., Loughry, M. L., Ohland, M. W., & Ricco, G. D. (2010). Design and validation of a Web-based system for assigning members to teams using instructor-specified criteria. *Advances in Engineering Education, 2,* 1–28. https://files.eric.ed.gov/fulltext/EJ1076132.pdf

LeViness, P., Bershad, C., & Gorman, K. (2017). *Association for University and College Counseling Center directors annual survey.* https://www.aucccd.org/assets/documents/Governance/2017%20aucccd%20survey-public-apr26.pdf

Lipson, S. K., Lattie, E. G., & Eisenberg, D. (2019). Increased rates of mental health service utilization by U.S. college students: 10-year population-level trends (2007–2017). *Psychiatric Services, 70*(1), 60–63. https://doi.org/10.1176/appi.ps.201800332

Lord, F. M. (1953). Speeded tests and power tests—An empirical study of validities. ETS *Research Bulletin Series, 1953*(2), i–9. https://doi.org/10.1002/j.2333-8504.1953.tb00228.x

Lowther, M. A., Stark, J. S., & Martens, G. G. (1989). *Preparing course syllabi for improved communication.* National Center for Research to Improve Postsecondary Teaching and Learning.

Lukianoff, G. (2014). *Unlearning liberty: Campus censorship and the end of American debate.* Encounter Books.

Marcis, J. G., & Carr, D. R. (2003). A note on student views regarding the course syllabus. *Atlantic Economic Journal, 31*(1), 115–116. https://link.gale.com/apps/doc/A99933291/AONE?u=duke_perkins&sid=AONE&xid=a92dd24c

Maricopa Community Colleges. (n.d.). *Open educational resources.* https://www.maricopa.edu/current-students/open-educational-resources

Marken, S. (2020, January 7). *About a quarter of U.S. adults consider higher ed affordable.* Gallup. https://www.gallup.com/education/272366/quarter-adults-consider-higher-affordable.aspx

Martin, N. D., Spenner, K. I., & Mustillo, S. A. (2017). A test of leading explanations for the college racial-ethnic achievement gap: Evidence from a longitudinal case study. *Research in Higher Education, 58*(6), 617–645. https://doi.org/10.1007/s11162-016-9439-6

Matejka, K., & Kurke, L. B. (1994). Designing a great syllabus. *College Teaching, 42*(3), 115–117. https://doi.org/10.1080/87567555.1994.9926838

McAllister, G., & Irvine, J. J. (2002). The role of empathy in teaching culturally diverse students: A qualitative study of teachers' beliefs. *Journal of Teacher Education, 53*(5), 433–443. https://doi.org/10.1177/002248702237397

McGivern, P., & Coxon, M. (2015). Student polling software: Where cognitive psychology meets educational practice? *Frontiers in Psychology, 6*(55), 1–3. https://doi.org/10.3389/fpsyg.2015.00055

McKeachie, W. J. (2002). *McKeachie's teaching tips: Strategies, research, and theory for college and university teachers.* Houghton Mifflin.

Meyer, A., Rose, D. H., & Gordon, D. (2014). *Universal design for learning: Theory and practice.* CAST.

Michael, J. (2006). Where's the evidence that active learning works? *Advances in Physiology Education, 30*(4), 159–167. https://doi.org/10.1152/advan.00053.2006

Miyake, A., Kost-Smith, L. E., Finkelstein, N. D., Pollock, S. J., Cohen, G., & Ito, T. A. (2010). Reducing the gender achievement gap in college science: A classroom study of values affirmation. *Science, 330*(6008), 1234–1237. https://doi.org/10.1126/science.1195996

Moore, S., Wallace, S. L., Schack, G., Thomas, M.S., Lewis, L., Wilson, L., Miller, S., & D'Antoni, J. (2010). Inclusive teaching circles: Mechanisms for creating welcoming classrooms. *Journal of the Scholarship of Teaching and Learning, 10*(1), 14–27. https://files.eric.ed.gov/fulltext/EJ882122.pdf

Moorleghen, D. M., Oli, N., Crowe, A. J., Liepkalns, J. S., Self, C. J., & Doherty, J. H. (2019). Impact of automated response systems on in-class cell phone use. *Biochemistry and Molecular Biology Education, 47*(5), 538–546. https://doi.org/10.1002/bmb.21257

Morrell, L. J., & Joyce, D. A. (2015). Interactive lectures: Clickers or personal devices? *F1000 Research, 4*(64). https://doi.org/10.12688/f1000research.6207.1

Mueller, C. M., & Dweck, C. S. (1998). Praise for intelligence can undermine children's motivation and performance. *Journal of Personality and Social Psychology, 75*(1), 33–52. https://doi.org/10.1037/0022-3514.75.1.33

Murdoch, Y. D., Hyejung, L., & Kang, A. (2018). Learning students' given names benefits EMI classes. *English in Education, 52*(3), 225–247. https://doi.org/10.1080/04250494.2018.1509673

Murphy, M., Steele, C. M., Gross, J. J. (2007). Signaling threat: How situational cues affect women in math, science, and engineering settings. *Psychological Science, 18*(1), 879–885. https://doi.org/10.1111/j.1467-9280.2007.01995.x

Nadal, K. (2014). A guide to microaggressions. *Cuny Forum, 2*(1), 71–76. https://advancingjustice-la.org/sites/default/files/ELAMICRO%20A_Guide_to_Responding_to_Microaggressions.pdf

National Center for Education Statistics. (n.d.). *Students with disabilities.* https://nces.ed.gov/fastfacts/display.asp?id=60

National Education Association. (2013). Using assessment wisely. *NEA Higher Education Advocate, 30*(1), 6–9. https://tilthighered.com/assets/pdffiles/Transparency%20in%20Learning%20and%20Teaching.pdf

National Survey of Student Engagement. (2010). *Major differences: Examining student engagement by field of study—annual results 2010.* Indiana University Center for Postsecondary Research. https://files.eric.ed.gov/fulltext/ED512590.pdf

Nelken, M. L. (2009). Negotiating classroom process: Lessons from adult learning. *Negotiation Journal, 25*(2), 181–194. https://doi.org/10.1111/j.1571-9979.2009.00219.x

New England Board of Higher Education. (2020, May 22). *Problem based learning projects.* https://www.pblprojects.org/

Nieto, S. (1999). *The light in their eyes: Creating multicultural learning communities.* Teachers College Press.

Noble, J., & Davies, P. (2009). Cultural capital as an explanation of variation in participation in higher education. *British Journal of Sociology of Education, 30*(5), 591–605. https://doi.org/10.1080/01425690903101098

Ogilvie, G., & Fuller, D. (2017). Restorative justice pedagogy in the ESL classroom: Creating a caring environment to support refugee students. *TESL Canada Journal, 33*(10), 86–96. https://doi.org/10.18806/tesl.v33i0.1247

Ostrove, J. M., & Long, S. M. (2007). Social class and belonging: Implications for college adjustment. *Review of Higher Education, 30*(4), 363–389. https://doi.org/10.1353/rhe.2007.0028

Papadatou-Pastou, M., Gritzali, M., & Barrable, A. (2018). The learning styles educational neuromyth: Lack of agreement between teachers' judgments, self-assessment, and students' intelligence. *Frontiers of Education, 3*(105). https://doi.org/10.3389/feduc.2018.00105

Parkes, J., Fix, T. K., & Harris, M. B. (2003). What syllabi communicate about assessment in college classrooms. *Journal on Excellence in College Teaching, 14*(1), 61–83. https://pdfs.semanticscholar.org/3be9/bb3dc97f838dcbcf880a0016e7b-f1817efc2.pdf

Parr, P. (1996). *Unspeeded examinations: An equitable and practical method of assessment.* https://files.eric.ed.gov/fulltext/ED397108.pdf

Pennebaker, J. W., Gosling, S. D., & Ferrell, J. D. (2013). Daily online testing in large classes: Boosting college performance while reducing achievement gaps. *PLOS One, 8*(11), e79774–e79774. https://doi.org/10.1371/journal.pone.0079774

Penner, M. R. (2018, June). Building an inclusive classroom. Journal of Undergraduate Neuroscience Education: JUNE, *16*(3), A268–A272. https://www.funjournal.org/wp-content/uploads/2018/09/june-16-268.pdf?x89760

Perry, R., Hall, N. C., & Ruthig, J. C. (2007). Perceived (academic) control and scholastic attainment in higher education. In R. Perry & J. C. Smart (Eds.), *The scholarship of teaching and learning in higher education: An evidence-based perspective* (pp. 477–552). Springer.

POGIL. (2019). *Home page.* https://www.pogil.org/

Porter, C., & & Serra, D. (2020). Gender differences in the choice of major: The importance of female role models. *American Economic Journal: Applied Economics, 12*(3), 226–254. https://doi.org/10.1257/app.20180426

Pratt, S., Harwood, H. B., Cavazos, J. T., & Ditzfeld, C. P. (2017). Should I stay or should I go? Retention of first-generation students. *Journal of College Student Retention Theory and Practice, 21*(1), 105–118. https://doi.org/10.1177/1521025117690868

Raymark, P. H., & Connor-Greene, P. A. (2002). The syllabus quiz. *Teaching of Psychology, 29*(4), 286–288. https://doi.org/10.1207/S15328023TOP2904_05

Reardon, S. F. (2011). The widening of the socioeconomic status achievement gap: New evidence and possible explanations. In G. J. Duncan & R. J. Murnane (Eds.), *Whither opportunity? Rising inequality, schools, and children's life chances* (pp. 91–116). Russell Sage Foundation.

Rogers, E. M. (2003). *Diffusion of innovations* (5th ed.). Free Press.

Rose, D. H., & Strangman, N. (2007). Universal design for learning: Meeting the challenge of individual learning differences through a neurocognitive perspective. *Universal Access in the Information Society, 5*(4), 381–391. https://doi.org/10.1007/s10209-006-0062-8

Rowe, M. B. (1969). Science, silence, and sanctions. *Science and Children, 6*, 11–13. http://static.nsta.org/pdfs/201108BookBeatScienceSilenceAndSanctions.pdf

Rowe, M. B. (1974). Wait-time and rewards as instructional variables, their influence in language, logic and fate control. Part 1: Wait time. *Journal of Research in Science Teaching, 11*(2), 81–94. https://doi.org/10.1002/tea.3660110202

Rowe, M. B. (1978). Wait, wait, wait . . . *School Science and Mathematics, 78*(3), 207–216. https://doi.org/10.1111/j.1949-8594.1978.tb09348.x

Rowe, M. B. (1986). Wait time: Slowing down may be a way of speeding up. *Journal of Teacher Education, 37*(1), 43–50. https://doi.org/10.1177/002248718603700110

Ruey, S. S., Wheijen, C., & Eric Zhi-Feng, L. (2011). Technology enabled active learning (TEAL) in introductory physics: Impact on genders and achievement levels. *Australasian Journal of Educational Technology, 27*(7), 1082–1099. https://doi.org/10.14742/ajet.905

Rychly, L., & Graves, E. (2012). Teacher characteristics for culturally responsive pedagogy. *Multicultural Perspectives, 14*(1), 44–49. https://doi.org/10.1080/15210960.2012.646853

Rydell, R. J., & Boucher, K. L. (2010). Capitalizing on multiple social identities to prevent stereotype threat: The moderating role of self-esteem. *Personality and Social Psychology Bulletin, 36*(2), 239–250. https://doi.org/10.1177/0146167209355062

Safe Zone Project. (2020a). *Homepage*. https://thesafezoneproject.com

Safe Zone Project. (2020b). *Privilege for sale*. https://thesafezoneproject.com/activities/privilege-for-sale/

SAGE. (2020, May 22). *Business cases*. https://sk.sagepub.com/cases

Sambell, K., & McDowell, L. (1998). The construction of the hidden curriculum: Messages and meanings in the assessment of student learning. *Assessment & Evaluation in Higher Education, 23*(4), 391–402. https://doi.org/10.1080/0260293980230406

Santhanam, E., & Hicks, O. (2004). Student perceptions of inclusion in unit/course evaluations. *International Journal of Inclusive Education, 8*(1), 91–102. https://doi.org/10.1080/1360311032000139458

Sarvary, M. A., & Gifford, K. M. (2017). The benefits of a real-time Web-based response system for enhancing engaged learning in classrooms and public science events. *Journal of Undergraduate Neuroscience Education, 15*(2), E13–E16. https://www.ncbi.nlm.nih.gov/pmc/articles/PMC5480850/

Sathy, V., & Hogan, K. A. (2019, July 22). Want to reach all of your students? Here's how to make your teaching more inclusive. *The Chronicle of Higher Education*. https://www.chronicle.com/interactives/20190719_inclusive_teaching

Schoem, D., Modey, C., & St. John, E. P. (2017). *Teaching the whole student: Engaged learning with heart, mind, and spirit*. Stylus.

Sherman, D. K., & Cohen, G. L. (2006). The psychology of self-defense: Self-affirmation theory. *Advances in Experimental Social Psychology, 38*, 183–242. https://doi.org/10.1016/S0065-2601(06)38004-5

Sherry, M., Thomas, P., & Chui, W. H. (2009). International students: A vulnerable student population. *Higher Education, 60*(1), 33–46. https://doi.org/10.1007/s10734-009-9284-z

Singham, M. (2005, August 7). Moving away from the authoritarian classroom. *Change, 37*(3), 50–57. https://doi.org/10.3200/CHNG.37.3.50-57

Skomsvold, P. (2014). *Profile of undergraduate students: 2011–12 (Web tables)*. National Center for Education Statistics. https://nces.ed.gov/pubsearch/pubsinfo.asp?pubid=2015167

Smeding, A., Darnon, C., Souchal, C., Toczek-Capelle, M. C., & Butera, F. (2013). Reducing the socio-economic status achievement gap at university by promoting mastery-oriented assessment. *PLOS One, 8*(8), e71678. https://doi.org/10.1371/journal.pone.0071678

Smit, R. (2012). Towards a clearer understanding of student disadvantage in higher education: Problematising deficit thinking. *Journal of Higher Education Research and Development, 31*(3), 369–380. https://doi.org/10.1080/07294360.2011.634383

Smith, C. (2008). Building effectiveness in teaching through targeted evaluation and response: Connecting evaluation to teaching improvement in higher education. *Assessment & Evaluation in Higher Education, 33*(5), 517–533. https://doi.org/10.1080/02602930701698942

Smith, D., & Malec, M. (1995 July). Learning students' names in sociology classes: Interactive tactics, who uses them, and when. *Teaching Sociology, 23*(3), 280–286. https://www.jstor.org/stable/1319222?seq=1#metadata_info_tab_contents

Smith, D. G., & Wolf-Wendel, L. E. (2005). The challenge of diversity: Involvement or alienation in the academy? *ASHE Higher Education Report, 31*(1), 1–100. https://doi.org/10.1002/aehe.3101

Smith, R. A. (1993). Preventing lost syllabi. *Teaching of Psychology, 20*(2), 113. https://doi.org/10.1207/s15328023top2002_13

Souza, T. (2018, April 30). Responding to microaggressions in the classroom: Taking ACTION. *Faculty Focus.* https://www.facultyfocus.com/articles/effective-classroom-management/responding-to-microaggressions-in-the-classroom/

Spencer, S. J., Steele, C. M., & Quinn, D. M. (1999). Stereotype threat and women's math performance. *Journal of Experimental Social Psychology, 35*(1), 4–28. https://doi.org/10.1006/jesp.1998.1373

Spenner, K. I., Buchmann, C., & Landerman, L. R. (2005). The Black–White achievement gap in the first college year: Evidence from a new longitudinal case study. *Research in Social Stratification and Mobility, 22,* 187–216. https://doi.org/10.1016/S0276-5624(04)22007-8

Steele, C. (2010). *Whistling Vivaldi: How stereotypes can affect us and what we can do.* Norton.

Steele, D. M., & Cohn-Vargas, B. (2013). *Identity safe classrooms: Places to belong and learn.* Corwin.

Stephens, N. M., Hamedani, M. G., & Destin M. (2014). Closing the social-class achievement gap: A difference-education intervention improves first-generation students' academic performance and all students' college transition. *Psychological Science, 25*(4), 943–953. https://doi.org/10.1177/0956797613518349

Stipek, D., & Gralinski, J. H. (1996). Children's beliefs about intelligence and school performance. *Journal of Educational Psychology 88*(3), 397–407. https://doi.org/10.1037/0022-0663.88.3.397

Strassle, C. G., & Verrecchia, P. J. (2019). Toward a more inclusive picture of incivility in the college classroom: Data from different types of institutions and academic majors. *International Journal of Teaching and Learning in Higher Education, 31*(3), 413–423. https://files.eric.ed.gov/fulltext/EJ1244982.pdf

Strayhorn, T. L. (2019). *College students' sense of belonging: A key to educational success for all students* (2nd ed.). Routledge.

Sue, D. W. (2010). *Microaggressions in everyday life: Race, gender, and sexual orientation.* Wiley.

Sue, D. W., Capodilupo, C. M., Torino, G. C., Bucceri, J. M., Holder, A. M., Nadal, K. L., & Esquilin, M. (2007). Racial microaggressions in everyday life: Implications for counseling. *The American Psychologist, 62*(4), 271–286. https://doi.org/10.1037/0003-066X.62.4.271

Summers, M. F., & Hrabowski, F. A., III. (2006). Preparing minority scientists and engineers. *Science, 311*(5769), 1870–1871. https://doi.org/10.1126/science.1125257

Tanner, K. D. (2013). Structure matters: Twenty-one teaching strategies to promote student engagement and cultivate classroom equity. *CBE Life Sciences Education, 12*(3), 322–331. https://doi.org/10.1187/cbe.13-06-0115

Task Force on Re-envisioning the Multicultural Guidelines for the 21st Century. (2017). *Multicultural guidelines: An ecological approach to context, identity, and intersectionality.* http://www.apa.org/about/policy/multicultural-guidelines.pdf

Team-Based Learning Collaborative. (2020, May 22). *Home page.* http://www.team-basedlearning.org/

Theobald, E. J., Hill, M. J., Tran, E., Agrawal, S., Arroyo, E. N., Behling, S., Chambwe, N., Cintrón, D. L., Cooper, J. D., Dunster, G., Grummer, J. A., Hennessey, K., Hsiao, J., Iranon, N., Jones, L., II, Jordt, H., Keller, M., Lacey, M. E., Littlefield, C. E., . . . & Freeman, S. (2020). Active learning narrows achievement gaps for underrepresented students in undergraduate science, technology, engineering, and math. *Proceedings of the National Academy of Sciences, 117*(12), 6476. https://doi.org/10.1073/pnas.1916903117

Thompson, B. (2007). The syllabus as a communication document: Constructing and presenting the syllabus. *Communication Education, 56*(1), 54–71. https://doi.org/10.1080/03634520601011575

Tijmstra, J., & Bolsinova, M. (2018). On the importance of the speed-ability trade-off when dealing with not reached items. *Frontiers in Psychology, 9*(964), 1–14. https://doi.org/10.3389/fpsyg.2018.00964

TILT. (n.d.). *Analog clickers—Color-coded cards as a low-tech tool.* https://uminntilt.com/2014/08/20/color-coded-cards-the-low-tech-clicker/

Tobin, T. J., & Behling, K. (2018). *Reach everyone, teach everyone: Universal design for learning in higher education.* West Virginia University Press.

Townes O'Brien, M., Leiman, T., & Duffy, J. (2014). The power of naming: The multifaceted value of learning students' names. *QUT Law Review, 14*(1), 114–128. https://doi.org/10.5204/qutlr.v14i1.544

University of Buffalo Libraries. (2020, May 22). *National Center for Case Study Teaching in Science.* https://sciencecases.lib.buffalo.edu/

University of California, Davis. (2019). *2019 year of reflective teaching—May 2019.* Center for Educational Effectiveness. https://cee.ucdavis.edu/blog/2019-year-reflective-teaching-may-2019

University of Maryland, Baltimore County. (2020). *Office of Equity & Inclusion.* https://diversity.umbc.edu

University of North Carolina, Chapel Hill. (2019). *New analytics dashboard lets faculty see class demographics.* The Well. https://thewell.unc.edu/2019/03/27/new-analytics-dashboard-lets-faculty-see-class-demographics/

University of Oregon. (2020). *Teaching excellence.* Office of the Provost. https://tep.uoregon.edu/teaching-excellence

Veliyath, R., & Adams, J. S. (2005). Internal consistency in components of international management/international business syllabi: Roadmaps with mixed messages. *Journal of Teaching in International Business, 16*(4), 65–80. https://doi.org/10.1300/J066v16n04_05

Walton, G. M., & Cohen, G. L. (2007). A question of belonging: Race, social fit, and academic achievement. *Journal of Personality and Social Psychology, 92*(1), 82–96. https://doi.org/10.1037/0022-3514.92.1.82

Walton, G. M., & Cohen, G. L. (2011). Outcomes of minority students: A brief social-belonging intervention improves academic and health outcomes. *Science*, *331*(6023), 1447–1451. https://doi.org/10.1126/science.1198364

Walton, G. M., Logel, C., Peach, J. M., Spencer, S. J., & Zanna, M. P. (2015). Two brief interventions to mitigate a "chilly climate" transform women's experience, relationship, and achievement in engineering. *Journal of Educational Psychology*, *107*(2), 468–485. https://doi.org/10.1037/a0037461

Warren, M. J. C. (2016). Teaching with technology: Using digital humanities to engage student learning. *Teaching Theology & Religion*, *19*(3), 309–319. https://doi.org/10.1111/teth.12343

Weimer, M. (2013). *Learner-centered teaching: Five key changes to practice* (2nd ed.). Josey-Bass.

Williams, P., Wray, J., Farrall, H., & Aspland, J. (2014). Fit for purpose: Traditional assessment is failing undergraduates with learning difficulties. Might eAssessment help? *International Journal of Inclusive Education*, *18*(6), 614–625. https://doi.org/10.1080/13603116.2013.802029

Winkelmes, M. A. (2014). *Transparency in learning and teaching in higher education*. https://tilthighered.com/abouttilt

Wlodkowski, R. J., & Ginsberg, M. B. (1995). A framework for culturally responsive teaching. *Educational Leadership*, *53*(1), 17–21. http://www.ascd.org/publications/educational-leadership/sept95/vol53/num01/A-Framework-for-Culturally-Responsive-Teaching.aspx

Wong, G., Derthick, A. O., David, E. J. R., Saw, A., & Okazaki, S. (2014). The what, the why, and the how: A review of racial microaggressions research in psychology. *Race and Social Problems*, *6*(2), 181–200. https://doi.org/10.1007/s12552-013-9107-9

Wood, J. L., & Harris, F. H., III. (2020, May 5). How to respond to racial microaggressions when they occur. *Diverse Issues in Higher Education*. https://diverseeducation.com/article/176397/

Wright, G. B. (2011). Student-centered learning in higher education. *International Journal of Teaching and Learning in Higher Education*, 23, 92–97. https://files.eric.ed.gov/fulltext/EJ938583.pdf

Zhang, Q. (2013). Assessing the effects of instructor enthusiasm on classroom engagement, learning goal orientation, and academic self-efficacy. *Communication Teacher*, *28*(1), 44–56. https://doi.org/10.1080/17404622.2013.839047

Also available from Stylus

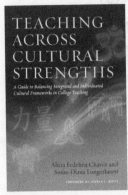

Teaching Across Cultural Strengths

A Guide to Balancing Integrated and Individuated Cultural Frameworks in College Teaching

Alicia Fedelina Chávez and Susan Diana Longerbeam

Foreword by Joseph L. White

"With a focus on student success, especially for this generation with the most diverse students ever to attend college, *Teaching Across Cultural Strengths*, puts the attention just where it belongs: in the magical arena of the classroom where learning is conjured and on the influence of students' and faculty's cultural identities on how and whether we learn. Every faculty member should read this book. Chávez and Longerbeam provide a richly revised understanding of the dynamics of teaching and of the responsibilities of faculty to learn about this new terrain. They need to do so with the same passion and dedication as they do their area of scholarly expertise. Peppered with a steady range of specific examples of how to create more culturally inclusive pedagogies persuasively supported by faculty testimonies of pleasure at how students are more engaged, no one can pretend it can't be done in their courses. The moving quotes from students threaded throughout the book should prick the conscience of those immobilized into only one form of teaching. Faculty need only to listen to students in this book—and in their own classes—to realize the transformative possibilities they can unleash in their classrooms."
—*Caryn McTighe Musil, Senior Scholar, Association of American Colleges and Universities*

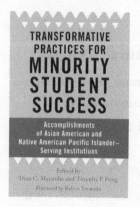

Transformative Practices for Minority Student Success

Accomplishments of Asian American and Native American Pacific Islander–Serving Institutions

Edited by Dina C. Maramba and Timothy P. Fong

Foreword by Robert T. Teranishi

"For far too long the Asian American and Pacific Islander (AAPI) student population has been left out of conversations about student success, forgotten due to the model minority myth. Maramba and Fong have brought to the surface key issues for all in higher education to discuss and learn from. The group of authors they have assembled have both the scholarly background and practice-based knowledge to help the field move forward in its understanding of AAPI students and Asian American and Native American Pacific Islander Serving Institutions." —*Marybeth Gasman, Judy & Howard Berkowitz Professor of Education, University of Pennsylvania*

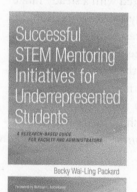

Successful STEM Mentoring Initiatives for Underrepresented Students

A Research-Based Guide for Faculty and Administrators

Becky Wai-Ling Packard

Foreword by Norman L. Fortenberry

"*Successful STEM Mentoring Initiatives for Underrepresented Students* illustrates and elucidates Packard's considerable expertise and scholarship on an enduring and, for some disciplines and education settings, a seemingly intractable set of issues. Rather than 'tinkering around the edges' by addressing only several variables, Packard tackles underrepresentation from the perspectives of both students and of the education system they will encounter. This comprehensive systems approach is refreshing and, in many ways, unique. It offers evidence-based advice to those in higher education who are undertaking the critically important work of increasing representation of historically underserved and unserved students and helps readers understand where and how their roles and actions must be based on efforts that have preceded their own and how their own work will influence others in the system as students pass through it on their ways to STEM careers. It is a refreshing and much-needed approach." —*Jay B. Lavov,* Senior Advisor for Education and Communication, National Academies of Sciences, Engineering, and Medicine

99 Tips for Creating Simple and Sustainable Educational Videos

A Guide for Online Teachers and Flipped Classes

Karen Costa

Foreword by Michelle Pacansky-Brock

"Reading *99 Tips for Creating Simple and Sustainable Educational Videos* is like sitting down with an old friend and learning all of her best strategies for producing video content that will both help and motivate students in their learning. I loved the simplicity and practicality of Costa's suggestions and think that this is the perfect book for instructors who want to dip their toes in the video production waters, but are not sure where to start." —*Kathryn E. Linder,* Executive Director of Program Development - Kansas State University Global Campus

Engaging in the Scholarship of Teaching and Learning

A Guide to the Process, and How to Develop a Project from Start to Finish

Cathy Bishop-Clark and Beth Dietz-Uhler

Foreword by Craig E. Nelson

"Cathy Bishop-Clark and Beth Dietz-Uhler bring to this volume their own contagious passion for the scholarship of teaching and learning—but also an ability to translate their journey into steps that those newer to the work can easily follow. The result is both practical and inspiring." —*Pat Hutchings,* Consulting Scholar, The Carnegie Foundation for the Advancement of Teaching, and Scholar in Residence, Gonzaga University

POGIL

An Introduction to Process Oriented Guided Inquiry Learning for Those Who Wish to Empower Learners

Edited by Shawn R. Simonson

"A timely, comprehensive, and highly informative must-read for anyone interested in implementing active learning in their science, engineering, or mathematics undergraduate classrooms."—***Chris Rasmussen,*** *San Diego State University, Department of Mathematics and Statistics*

Getting Started With Team-Based Learning

Jim Sibley and Pete Ostafichuk with Bill Roberson, Billie Franchini, and Karla Kubitz

Foreword by Larry K. Michaelsen

"The book is full of practical advice, however, which is well-grounded in literature about teaching and learning so that faculty members who are hesitant to transform a course to TBL can still benefit from reading (advice such as how to write effective multiple choice questions and how to facilitate discussions). . . . After reviewing the book, I am motivated to try this model in my teaching." —***David B. Howell,*** *Ferrum College*

Connected Teaching

Relationship, Power, and Mattering in Higher Education

Harriet L. Schwartz

Foreword by Laurent A. Parks Daloz

Afterword by Judith V. Jordan

"Every once in a great while a thinker comes along who upends traditional notions about how things get done. Harriet Schwartz takes on that role in her groundbreaking work *Connected Teaching*. And she does 'break ground': she lets us know from the outset that connected teaching is not about taking the path of least resistance, or being nice, or simply 'talking about' relationship. She also lets us know from the outset that she will be faithful to a fundamental tenet of relational-cultural practice: that a productive relationship is one which all participants have an opportunity to grow.

To that end, Schwartz removes teaching from the traditional hierarchical models of practice and situates in firmly in the more amorphous territory of non-dualism. Throughout this work, she remains true to her basic premise and promise: that teaching is relational stance grounded in both power and vulnerability. While she does not abdicate any of the roles and responsibilities that accrue to her experience and expertise, she allows herself to grow, stretch, and learn in the presence of her students. She offers concrete guidance for navigating collapsing contexts and other challenges wrought by the fast-paced innovations in technology. For example, how does one connect with students who grow up suspicious of any idea that can't be corroborated on Google or who have expectations of 24/7 availability? Likewise, she does not shy away from the tough topics, lived narratives by students and teachers alike whose experience of conflicting social identities and intersectionality can send any carefully crafted teaching plan spiraling off course.

Schwartz is very comfortable in the land of paradox and non-duality. Much as she does in her work with her students, she comes to us as an 'authoritative ally,' imparting her wisdom through bold ideas, grace, humor, and searing questions. In doing so, she charts pathways toward a new relational paradigm, one in which teaching is truly a practice of co-creating a 'we.'"—***Maureen Walker***, *Senior Scholar and Director of Program Development, Jean Baker Miller Training Institute*

Teaching Interculturally

A Framework for Integrating Disciplinary Knowledge and Intercultural Development

Amy Lee

With Robert K. Poch, Mary Katherine O'Brien and Catherine Solheim

Foreword by Peter Felten

"The authors strike an admirable and concise balance between theory and practice. They aim to 'disrupt' current teaching norms with a 'commitment to make intentional, informed decisions that enable our courses to engage and support diversity and inclusion.' In their second chapter, they emphasize three values toward this end: (1) the pursuit of equity and inclusion in classrooms, (2) pedagogical humility while recognizing the developmental nature of expertise, and (3) the importance of reflection and revision. These values are modeled through the rest of the book.

With numerous case studies and bracketed 'Invitations for Reflection,' this slim volume practices a pedagogy of its own and is well-suited for individuals and groups seeking opportunities for practical and meaningful reflection on intercultural pedagogy."—*Reflective Teaching*

"Now more than ever, the college classroom ought to be a place where students from diverse backgrounds engage productively in difficult conversations, yet few faculty are trained to facilitate this challenging work. *Teaching Interculturally* is a thoughtful and practical guide that is grounded in theory but with many concrete examples of classroom challenges, activities, and assignments. This book will be a great asset to faculty communities and to graduate courses on pedagogy."—*Aeron Haynie, Executive Director, Center for Teaching and Learning Associate, and Associate Professor of English, University of New Mexico*

22883 Quicksilver Drive
Sterling, VA 20166-2019   Subscribe to our e-mail alerts: www.Styluspub.com